Basic Radio Journalism

Basic Radio Journalism

Paul Chantler and Peter Stewart

**Focal
Press**

AMSTERDAM BOSTON HEIDELBERG LONDON NEW YORK OXFORD
PARIS SAN DIEGO SAN FRANCISCO SINGAPORE SYDNEY TOKYO

Focal Press
An imprint of Elsevier
Linacre House, Jordan Hill, Oxford OX2 8DP
200 Wheeler Road, Burlington, MA 01803

First published 2003

British Library Cataloguing in Publication Data
Chantler, Paul
   Basic radio journalism
   1.   Radio journalism – Great Britain
   I.   Title   II.   Stewart, Peter
   070.4′0941

Library of Congress Cataloguing in Publication Data
A catalogue record for this book is available from the Library of Congress

ISBN 0 240 51926 4

For information on all Focal Press publications, visit our website at:
www.focalpress.com

Typeset by Newgen Imaging Systems (P) Ltd., Chennai, India
Printed and bound in Italy

Contents

Foreword by Lord Ryder of Wensum, Vice Chairman, BBC   xiii

Preface   xv

Acknowledgements   xix

Chapter 1   The structure of UK radio   1
Overview   1
National radio   1
Local radio   2
BBC local radio   3
Commercial local radio   4
Digital radio   5
Cable and satellite   6
Internet radio   7
Restricted Service Licences   7
Access radio   7
Pirate radio   8

Chapter 2   Working in radio   9
Understanding radio   9
Radio versus newspapers and television; Speed and simplicity;
Making pictures; Person-to-person; Localness
The making of a broadcaster   11
Qualities of a good radio journalist; Starting out
Getting the job   14
Work experience; Local newspapers; Hospital radio;
Student radio; College courses; BBC training schemes;
Traffic and travel broadcasting; Restricted service
stations; Freelancing

v

Contents

Marketing yourself 19
The CV and demo; Persistence
The job interview 22
Preparation; Nerves; Body language; Journalistic tests;
Awkward questions; Thank you!

Chapter 3   News gathering 25
The newsroom structure 25
Head of News or News Editor; Bulletin Editor;
Senior Broadcast Journalist or News Producer;
Broadcast journalist or reporter; One-journalist newsrooms;
Television journalists
National news 28
Radio news agencies; Local intake; Data feeds; Live bulletins;
Television audio; Wire services
Sources of local news 33
The emergency services; News releases; Audio news releases;
Public utilities; Politicians and councillors; Listeners; Colleagues;
Pressure groups; Freelance journalists and agencies; 'Rivals';
Your own station; The Internet
Planning and developing stories 42
The newsroom diary; Newsdesk resource management;
Developing stories; Newsroom contacts; Resisting pressure;
Embargoes
Story treatment 47
Copy; Interviews; Voicers or voice pieces; Cuts, clips and
soundbites; Wraps and packages; Newsroom style guide

Chapter 4   News writing 50
Telling the story 50
For the ear not the eye; Keep it short; Keep it simple;
Keep it happening now; Keep adjectives to a minimum;
Talk to yourself
Language and grammar 54
Writing devices 55
Contractions; Punctuation; Jargon; Journalese;
Clichés; Americanisms; Names; Dates; Numbers; Comparisons
Cues 62
The topline; Going into detail; Into the audio; The audio cut;
Cue layout

Avoiding offence 66

Putting stories in context 67
Attribution; Exaggeration; Cause and effect; Casualty figures;
Organizations; Titles; Descriptions; The truth

Chapter 5   News bulletins 71
The news agenda 71
Your target listener; Socio-economic groups; Relevance;
Quality versus quantity; Place names; The 'life' of a story
Bulletin styles 75
'Infotainment'; Youth stations; Versioned bulletins;
Regional bulletins; The hub; Pre-recorded bulletins;
Multi versions
Bulletin essentials 78
Accuracy; Taste; Balance and fairness; Tone; Comment;
Signposting; Experts; Kickers

Chapter 6   News presentation 82
Reading the news 82
Sound interested; Understand the story; Check and rehearse;
Technically speaking; Breathe in ... and relax; Keep level; Tone;
Microphone technique; Speed; Stress; Quotations; Corrections;
Pronunciation; Listen
Self-op bulletins 92
Getting ready; In the studio; Here is the news ...;
Clock end bulletins; When things go wrong ...
Breaking news stories 97
'We're getting reports that ...'; Going open-ended
Specialized presentation 100
Personality news presenters; The 'zoo'

Chapter 7   Technicalities 103
Audio recording 103
Digital recording
Audio editing 106
Digital editing
Computerized newsrooms 109
The paper-free and tape-free environment
Studios 109
Headphones; Microphones; Playout systems

Contents

Audio and actuality   117
*Sound quality; Sound edits; Dubbing; Levels and equalization;
Location interviews; Studio interviews; Telephone interviews;
Telephone versus quality audio; Studio discipline; Talkback*

Chapter 8   Interviewing   125
Types of interview   125
*Informational interviews; Interpretive interviews;
Emotional interviews*
Interview preparation   127
*Location; 'What did you have for breakfast?';
Watch the language*
Question technique   129
*Eye contact; Listening to answers; Asking one thing at a time;
Leading questions; Cliché questions; Coaching interviewees;
One-word answers; After the interview; Thanks*
Special interviews   134
*Live interviews; Vox pops; News conferences and 'scrums';
Unattended studios; Interviewing other reporters;
Interviewing children; Interviews with criminals;
Interviewing witnesses; Interviewing victims or
their relatives; Interviewing politicians; When interviews
are refused*

Chapter 9   News reporting   140
The radio reporter   140
The briefing; Fixing ahead; Working to deadlines
On location   142
*What to do first; Eyewitness accounts; Dealing with officials;
Dealing with other reporters*
Filing material   144
*Getting on the air; On-the-spot voicers; Q-and-As;
Live reports; 'Car park' voicers*
Audio production   147
Choosing the cut; Wrapping or packaging; Writing cues

Chapter 10   Newsdesk management   150
Running the newsdesk   150
*Getting organized; Labelling audio and scripts; Getting
organized with computers; Taking audio; Deadlines*

Bulletin construction 153
Finding the lead; The rest of the bulletin; Avoiding repetition;
Judging editorial priorities; Follow that story ...!;
Developing the story; Breaking the rules; Flash that snap ...!
Other newsdesk duties 159
The network; Check calls; Headlines and teasers; Allocating
reporters; Giving orders; Priorities; Coping with crisis;
Weather news; Travel news; Stormlines and snowlines;
Bomb threats; News blackouts; Defence advisory notices;
Reporting suicides; Fooling around

Chapter 11   Legalities 171
Libel 172
Libel defences 172
The best defence; The truth; No identification; Consent; Death;
One year; Fair comment; Privilege; Accord and satisfaction
Different kinds of libel 176
Indirect libel; Nameless libel; Unintentional libel;
Criminal libel; Problem areas
Contempt 178
A step-by-step guide to contempt
Court reporting 183
Basic rules; Reporting restrictions; Sexual offences;
Children and young people; Jigsaw identification
Other cases 187
Civil law; Inquests; Official secrets; Injunctions

Chapter 12   Newsroom management 191
Resources 191
Rotas; Budgets; Estimating costs; Cutting costs
Complaints 194
Phoned complaints; Correcting errors; Solicitors; Regulatory
authorities; Privacy
Winning audiences 199
Audience figures; Targeting audiences; Presentation formats;
Promos; Sponsorship

Chapter 13   Small newsrooms 207
Setting up 207
First tasks; Making contacts; Technical requirements;
Filing systems; Calls list

Contents

Going on air   210
Preparing for the first day; Getting exclusives
Recruiting staff   212
Training and coaching

Chapter 14   Programme production   214
The Producer   214
Responsibilities; Qualities
Preparation   215
Programme items; Treatments; Running orders; Pot points
Fixing guests   216
Choosing guests; Approaching potential guests
Studio production   220
*Think ahead; Tech Ops; Discipline; Trails,
teasers and promos*

Chapter 15   Specialized programming   223
The news round-up   223
Content and style; A typical format; Jingles and 'beds'
Features and documentaries   225
Using audio; The essence; Setting up; Editing
Outside broadcasts   228
*Planning; Radio links; ISDN landlines; Telephone links;
Couriers; Standby presenters*
Phone-ins   230
*Selecting subjects; Studio operations; Phone-in presenters;
The delay; Problem phone-ins*
The music–speech mix   233
Qualities of presenter; The right mix; Blending
Elections   235
*General guidelines; Closing of nominations;
Programme packages; Discussion programmes;
Other news items; Election phone-ins;
Opinion polls; Polling day*
The Chancellor's Budget speech   240
Experts; The speech itself
Commentaries   241
Planning; Mood; Style and content; Using silence

Sport 243
Match reports; The sports diary; Daily sports bulletins
Obituaries 245
The obit alarm; Breaking the news; Back to normal

Glossary 249

Index 259

Foreword
by Lord Ryder of Wensum,
Vice Chairman, BBC

Thirty years ago a broadcasting bigwig warned me that radio was a dying medium, a victim of television's popularity and remorseless expansion. Since then, talented youngsters with broadcasting ambitions have tended to swallow the doom merchant's prediction. Seduced by the status of television and the cult of celebrity, they have scrambled to join TV's bottom rungs.

Yet all the evidence points not just to radio's survival, but its success far beyond the expectations of its fiercest proponents.

Radio has overtaken television as the most used medium in the United Kingdom. Over 90 per cent of the population listen to radio every week – that's 44 million people. It contributes to culture – both popular and high. And it is still driven by Lord Reith's objective set out 75 years ago to 'bring the best of everything into the greatest number of homes'.

Radio is not only about national news and national noise. It keeps people in touch by enabling local communities to share experiences and support each other. Local radio becomes more prominent every year. Its broadcasters achieve standards unheard of even a decade ago.

I cannot recall who said that radio is about painting pictures and television is about shooting them. Painting good radio pictures is an art form whether in the hands of Alastair Cooke or Chris Evans, or the late Peter Jones or Terry Wogan. It is journalism of the highest order.

I remain an unreconstructed radio man. Why? Because radio is my friend. I take it everywhere. I get up with it in the morning. I travel with it. I work with it. I relax with it. And, as an insomniac, I sleep with it. My lifelong companion has brought me laughter, tragedy, science, music, talks, sport and news. The range and quality of radio stations in this country must be unmatched in the world. Every second of the day, something exists for everybody. All tastes are catered for, the excellence of the output overwhelms the listener.

It was not always like this. My affection for radio began in the 1950s when chart music was broadcast once a week by the BBC. It took the successes of the commercial, offshore pirate stations of the 1960s to force the BBC into creating Radio One, and the government into licensing commercial wavelengths. By then, men had already landed on the moon. This is how slow we developed radio to suit public needs despite the availability of technology.

We cannot make the same mistake again, otherwise radio journalism will cease to attract good minds as well as zany voices.

Paul Chantler and Peter Stewart have produced an essential book for every aspirant starting out to work in radio. It is a book written with verve and clarity by two professionals with a passion for the business, which every journalist must share to succeed in a competitive industry dominated more and more by digits rather than the valves and crystals of my youth.

Above all, I hope readers of this book will prize individualism. Uniformity kills radio. Dare to be different. Take risks where possible. Treasure the beauty of language. And continue to entertain us in the knowledge that television can never usurp radio's magic, or imperil its place in the hearts of the nation.

Preface

When television became popular in the 1950s, there were predictions that radio would die. Half a century on and radio is actually much more exciting and diverse than ever before.

There is enormous competition for audiences. People are faced with a choice of up to 300 television channels, 1400 newspapers, 8000 magazines and millions of websites – all screaming for attention.

Against this background, the radio audience has held steady, with more than 91 per cent of people in the UK listening to the radio each week. Radio is still an essential part of the daily lives of 35 million people – and news is an important element of many stations.

This means that radio offers a challenging and rewarding career to journalists at all levels, from the well-resourced and established newsrooms of BBC stations with a big commitment to speech radio to the small one-town commercial stations, staffed only by one journalist, broadcasting local news for a few bulletins every morning. It is said more people work in UK radio than TV, so there is ample opportunity.

Basic Radio Journalism is a working manual and handbook for radio journalists, as well as a textbook for broadcast journalism students. We hope that you will find it helpful whether you are seeking your first job or have many years' experience in radio.

The book was originally published in 1992 as *Local Radio Journalism*, with a second edition in 1997. We have extended the scope of the original book to include many alterations, additions and examples, not only to reflect more up-to-date techniques, but also to make the book more comprehensive. However, it is not our intention to cover all aspects of radio journalism. As the title suggests, this new book deals with the basics.

We are grateful to the original co-author of *Local Radio Journalism*, Sim Harris, for his input, some of which we are still using – especially in the sections on newsdesk management, legalities and bulletin presentation. In his place, Peter Stewart brings experience from both commercial and BBC radio.

Over the last decade, there have been many changes to the structure of both BBC and commercial radio in Britain, and these are described in an overview of the industry which also covers the growth in digital, cable and satellite radio. We have rewritten the technical chapter to reflect the fact that digital recording is now used almost exclusively in all UK radio news-rooms. Most references to analogue equipment and procedures have been deleted. The legal section has also been revamped and updated.

There is a greater emphasis in the reporting section on the techniques of production, as well as new advice about reporting live. In our chapter on news bulletins, there are descriptions of the increasingly varied styles of presentation and content. A new section highlights the increasingly impor-tant role of the radio journalist as programme producer.

For the student wanting a break into radio, we have updated and expanded the section on getting a job, with extensive advice on marketing yourself as a radio journalist and dealing with interviews and appointment boards. For the experienced radio journalist, managing a busy newsdesk or run-ning a small newsroom, there are innumerable hints and tips. Our glos-sary, too, has been extensively overhauled with explanations of old and new radio jargon and the different terms used by BBC and commercial stations. Most of the photographs too are new.

The state of radio journalism in the UK is healthy, particularly in the BBC. However, we want to make a plea to commercial radio to treat news out-put more seriously. Sadly, too many commercial stations are regarding news bulletins simply as an interruption to their music output. These sta-tions need instead to embrace and enhance news.

The coverage of local stories on local commercial stations has been par-ticularly affected. News content has become more lifestyle news, more entertainment news, more consumer news, more environment news, more music news, more funny news – almost anything other than 'news' news! Traditional stories about councils, crime and politics are no longer used on some stations. And all of this at a time when local newspapers appear to be increasingly parochial and are selling more copies.

As one senior industry figure puts it, commercial radio news has been given a makeover by the style gurus. Bulletins have become shorter; they are now read at breakneck speed over music backing. And the news presenter has become straight man to wacky DJs.

Commercial radio must remind itself why it did news in the first place – to keep people informed about their locality. Then stations must embrace news as an essential part of their output. As Phil Riley, chief executive of Chrysalis Radio, says: 'Good local beats good national any day.'

There is a clear demand for local news. Andy Griffee, Controller of BBC English Regions, says: 'The vast majority of people in the UK live most of their lives within a 14-mile radius. Indeed, the average distance to "mum's house" is just 12.6 miles.'

However, all local radio journalists have to work hard to deal with the dilemma which says: 'People like local news, but not other people's local news.'

UK radio would be wise to look at what has happened in the USA. Some stations discovered, after shaving their news to nearly nothing in the 1990s, that the audience wanted radio news back. They preferred radio as a source of news and information. When news happened and radio was not there to cover it, stations lost listeners and credibility.

As you will see from what follows, we are the first to promote tools and techniques to make news more relevant and engaging for the audience. News can be accessible and interesting – but it still has to inform. And you should never underestimate the intelligence of your audience.

As Nick Wheeler, Chief Editor of ITN Radio News, once wrote: 'I can't help thinking that if some of the radio news services you hear around the country today were operating in the last war, we would have heard more about Vera Lynn's hairdo than the invasion of Poland. Then they'd still claim they'd covered the story!' Quite.

There are many definitions of news. Two of our favourites are: 'That which is new, interesting and true' by Robert McLeish, esteemed author of *Radio Production* (Focal Press), and 'Subjects I want to know about in a short amount of time' by US consultant Rasa Kaye.

With all the technical and operational changes, it is even more important these days to remember the basic tools and techniques of radio journalism.

There will always be a need for bright young talent in the industry which brings those two most important qualities – enthusiasm and ideas.

However, we must continue to guard against one of the biggest dangers, especially with the increasing use of all this new technology.

Some think of news as that which simply appears on a screen. Never forget that real news is what you go out and find through your own efforts.

Paul Chantler
Peter Stewart

Acknowledgements

We are very grateful to the following people and organizations who have helped in the preparation of the text and illustrations for this book:

Lord Ryder of Wensum, Vice Chairman, BBC; Kelvin MacKenzie, Chairman and Chief Executive, The Wireless Group; Mike Parry, TalkSPORT; Martin Campbell, Head of Programming and Advertising at the Radio Authority; Paul Brown, Commercial Radio Companies Association; Rob van Pooss at UKRD Group; Robert Wallace, Managing Editor at BBC Radio Kent and his staff, notably Dominic King, Rom Cordani and Will Roffey; Margaret Hyde at BBC Essex; Kevin Steel at BBC Training; Dirk Anthony and Steve Orchard, GWR Group; Colin Mason at Choice FM; John Perkins, Nick Wheeler and Jon Godel of Independent Radio News; Andy Ivy at Sky News Radio; Pete Lunn at NewsTalk 106, Dublin; Martin Ball and John Dash at Wave 105, Southampton; Will Jackson at TrafficLink; Sean Marley at Radio City in Liverpool; Jane O'Hara at RAJAR; Penelope James PR; Andrew Edwards of the University of Central Lancashire (for his constructive criticism); Julie Leddy at The Wireless Group; Sim Harris; Mike Vince; Nick Allicker; Rory McLeod; Richard Waghorn; Alix Pryde; Dan O'Day; BBC Radio Publicity; and, of course, the wonderful Beth Howard at Focal Press.

Paul Chantler would particularly like to thank Langley Brown, former News Editor of BBC Radio Medway in the 1970s, who was the personal inspiration for him becoming a radio journalist.

1 The structure of UK radio

OVERVIEW

Almost all radio stations in the UK are owned and operated by either the BBC or commercial companies. The BBC stations are funded publicly through the television licence fee. They provide a wide variety of entertainment and information in both music and speech formats. The commercial stations rely on advertising and sponsorship revenue. Many of these companies are now owned by large groups such as EMAP, GWR and Capital. The commercial stations are, in general, music and entertainment led, but also feature news and information.

There are two main radio transmitting systems in the UK. The most extensive and widely used is the conventional analogue system, which appears on four wavebands, FM and AM (also sometimes called Medium Wave), Long Wave and Short Wave. Analogue radio services are now being joined by digital transmissions, for which listeners need a new radio set.

NATIONAL RADIO

There are five main UK-wide BBC stations and three commercial national services. The BBC stations are: *Radio One* – a pop music station playing chart, dance, urban and alternative music, much of it new or released in the last few years, and including the Newsbeat programme; *Radio Two* – playing hit music from the 1960s to today and featuring well-known presenters such as Terry Wogan and Jonathan Ross; *Radio Three* – playing classical music but also featuring jazz and information about the arts; *Radio Four* – featuring intelligent speech including news, drama, comedy and current affairs, and the home of acclaimed and highly rated programmes such as *Today, The World At One, PM* and *Any Questions?*; and *Radio Five Live* – another speech network featuring live news and sport. There are also BBC radio stations for Scotland, Wales and Northern Ireland.

The three national commercial stations are: *Classic FM* – the UK's first national commercial station, which went on the air in 1992 playing classical music; *Virgin* – playing rock and pop music; and *TalkSPORT* – featuring a variety of sport and news phone-ins, as well as sports commentaries. The latter two stations both broadcast on AM, although Virgin also simulcasts on an FM frequency in London.

In addition, the BBC operates the *World Service*, broadcasting global news and analysis in 43 different languages and funded directly by the government.

LOCAL RADIO

Local radio in the UK started at 12.45 p.m. on 8 November 1967, when the BBC opened Radio Leicester. Before that, there had been regional programmes on national radio but no truly local stations.

The BBC retained its monopoly for six years until the first commercial station, LBC, opened in London in 1973. It was followed a few days later by Capital Radio. Throughout the 1970s and early 1980s, the number of BBC and commercial stations continued to grow throughout the UK.

All local stations were given both an AM and FM frequency, but in the mid-1980s, commercial stations were encouraged to split transmissions, offering different programme services on their two frequencies. Many chose top 40 on FM and gold with more speech and information on AM.

Meanwhile, the BBC grew its local town-based stations into county-wide operations. Thus, Radio Medway became Radio Kent and Radio Brighton became Radio Sussex.

In the late 1980s and early 1990s, both commercial and BBC stations consolidated. Commercial stations, independently owned by local companies, were acquired by the larger groups and some BBC stations combined to cover more than just one English county. When re-licensing, the regulator introduced official Promises of Performance for each station to ensure local content and programming were maintained despite any change in ownership.

In the commercial sector, the battle for audiences became more fierce, with programming and promotional techniques imported from the USA and Australia, where commercial radio was better established. Commercial radio now has about half the total radio audience against all BBC services, national and local. In BBC local radio, more talk and speech has led to stations carving a niche for themselves among a generally older audience.

Despite the greater proliferation of stations, the total number of people listening to radio seems to stay the same. In order to compete with an ever-increasing choice, radio has to become more 'ear-catching' than ever. Localness and local news are essential tools for this task.

BBC LOCAL RADIO

BBC local radio is a speech-based network of stations focusing on local news, current affairs, topical information, community debate, social action and local sport linked by personality presenters with a convivial, friendly style. There are 38 BBC local stations across England serving different and contrasting communities. Some, such as GMR in Manchester and WM in the West Midlands, cover large conurbations while others, such as Radio Cornwall and Radio Lincolnshire, are based in predominantly rural areas.

Each station is on the air for an average 18 hours a day, typically from 6 a.m. to midnight. Many stations join together and become regional in the evenings.

The trend in the 1990s to merge stations for cost reasons has now been reversed. For example, both BBC Radio Oxford and BBC Radio Berkshire have been brought back and BBC Southern Counties produces three different breakfast shows for different parts of its area.

On average, BBC local radio's speech content has increased from about 50 per cent to 75 per cent over the last decade. At breakfast and many afternoon drive times, the stations become all speech. The open line phone-in is an important part of each BBC station's output. It is considered an open gateway for the audience in an era where interactivity will become commonplace.

More than half of all listeners to BBC local radio are over 55. Research shows that as people get older, their sense of local attachment becomes stronger, their roots deepen and their appetite for local radio increases. Because BBC local radio was established in the late 1960s and 1970s, they attract loyal listeners among the older generation.

COMMERCIAL LOCAL RADIO

Commercial radio survives on advertising revenue. In order to attract advertising, a commercial station has to attract a large audience and cater to the largest potential market. Therefore, most commercial stations play different sorts of music supplemented by local news and information.

There are more than 260 local commercial stations in the UK, together with 16 regional stations. Almost all of them broadcast 24 hours a day. The local stations include: big city stations such as Capital FM in London, Clyde FM in Glasgow and Metro FM in Newcastle; medium-sized stations such as Essex FM in Essex, Invicta FM in Kent, The Pulse in Bradford and Trent FM in Nottingham; and smaller stations in rural areas like Moray Firth in Inverness, Lincs FM in Lincolnshire and Stray FM in Harrogate. Some stations join together in a network in the evenings or automate their output using a computer playout system.

Regional stations cover populations ranging in size from one to five million and include stations such as the four Galaxy stations (owned by Chrysalis), three Century stations (owned by Capital), three Real Radio stations (owned by the Guardian Media Group) and others, such as Wave 105 in Southampton and Saga Radio in Birmingham and Nottingham.

There are also small-scale commercial stations serving just one town or city. Because of their size, some have struggled to break even financially. Others have formed alliances to share costs and expertise. Among the most popular are Spire FM in Salisbury, Sun FM in Sunderland and Rutland Radio.

Commercial stations have a variety of formats. Among the most popular are Contemporary Hit Radio (top 40 chart music), Gold (oldies from the

1960s and 1970s), Adult Contemporary (classic hits from the 1970s, 1980s and 1990s) and Dance (R'n'B and urban music). In London, there is a wider range of stations with more diverse formats including Jazz FM (jazz music), XFM (alternative music), Kiss (dance), Magic (easy listening) and Premier (Christian). London has two all-speech local stations in LBC and LBC News.

The commercial radio industry is regulated by OFCOM, a government-appointed body which awards licences, deals with complaints and ensures all stations adhere to their Promises of Performance of official formats – the detailed specification of content and style which form part of their licence.

DIGITAL RADIO

Digital radio, sometimes called DAB or Digital Audio Broadcasting, uses new technology to make radio sound better. It is a more efficient way to broadcast and this means a greater choice of stations as well as improved – almost CD type – sound quality with no interference. There is also space for the transmission of text and data services such as programme schedules and contextual information about programmes. In the future, digital radios will be able to record onto an internal hard disk within a DAB receiver, making it possible for listeners to turn back to something they have missed, such as a news bulletin or weather forecast.

Listeners will have to invest in new DAB capable radio sets to hear digital radio (Figure 1.1). These are more expensive than traditional radios. However, the price is gradually coming down and many more listeners are expected to make the switch to digital. Broadcast digital radio should not be confused with radios which simply have digital displays!

Digital stations are transmitted via multiplexes for specific areas where several services are grouped together and transmitted simultaneously. All the BBC national services are available in digital and the national commercial multiplex (operated by Digital One) carries the three national commercial stations in addition to new national commercial services. There is also an ever-increasing network of local multiplexes.

As well as the services simulcast on both analogue and digital transmitters, there is also a growing number of radio stations available on digital radio only. For the BBC, these include: *1 Xtra* (the home of new black

Figure 1.1
A typical DAB digital radio set

music); *Five Live Sports Extra* (exclusive sports coverage); *BBC 6 Music* (rock and pop music); *BBC Asian Network* (aimed at young British Asians); and *BBC 7* (comedy, drama and children's programmes). For commercial radio, digital-only stations include: *Oneword* (plays, books, comedy and reviews); *Primetime* (music and features for older listeners); and *Core* (club and chart hits).

CABLE AND SATELLITE

There are other types of radio services which can be picked up, but these are not portable or mobile like conventional radio. Cable and satellite services are available through TV sets and have been around for some time. Listening to the radio via digital TV is becoming increasingly popular. Cable stations include volunteer-run community radio services such as CRMK in Milton Keynes and Radio Verulam in St Albans. There is a wide variety of satellite stations, including ethnic stations such as Club Asia and Panjab Radio; football fan stations such as Big Blue for Chelsea and

The Saint for Southampton; stations for gay people such as Purple Radio; and shopping network stations like Homebase FM and Costcutter Radio, which are broadcast in shops and stores.

INTERNET RADIO

Radio over the Internet is growing. There are thousands of radio stations all over the world available to be heard, although sometimes you have to pay to listen. Internet radio is particularly useful for niche interest programming, audio clips on demand and for services not local to where you live. Many UK national, regional and local radio stations 'stream' their output over their website and can therefore be heard all over the world.

RESTRICTED SERVICE LICENCES

Restricted Service Licences or RSLs are low-powered temporary radio services authorized for a period of 28 days. RSLs are for a limited geographical coverage area, such as a town or up to two miles of a city. More than 3500 RSLs have been licensed since 1992.

Numerous groups or individuals run services covering a variety of events or themes such as arts festivals, religious celebrations, school projects, carnivals, charity and sporting events. Many RSLs are used for trial services if a group wants to apply for a permanent commercial radio licence and wishes to demonstrate a level of community support. There are also about 100 long-term RSLs covering hospital and college radio stations.

ACCESS RADIO

Access radio is an experiment which aims to introduce a new tier of small-scale radio stations to be used in innovative, creative, and socially and educationally constructive ways. The stations are non-profit making and many are likely to be funded by local authority grants. There are about 15 stations taking part in the experiment, ranging from Cross Rhythms City Radio for Christians in Stoke-on-Trent to Radio Fiza for the South Asian community in Nottingham.

PIRATE RADIO

There are hundreds of pirate radio stations broadcasting illegally in the UK, usually at weekends in the big cities. Although many play specialist music not heard on other stations, they are breaking the law. Their transmissions interfere with the signals of legal stations and in extreme cases affect emergency service radios and the frequencies used by air traffic controllers at airports. Because of their illegality, it is risky for novice broadcasters to get involved in pirates, as this might have an adverse effect on a career in professional radio.

2 Working in radio

UNDERSTANDING RADIO

The first step to becoming a radio journalist is to understand the strengths of the medium and why it is so potent. You can use these strengths to produce powerful, memorable radio.

Radio versus newspapers and television

Many people think radio is the fastest-moving, most up-to-date, most portable medium available in any location from car to kitchen. They perceive newspaper news as lagging behind radio and television. The downmarket tabloids are seen simply as entertaining and titillating scandal sheets, focusing more on TV and movie stars than real news events. The broadsheet newspapers are perceived as more concerned with detailed analysis and comment.

Despite the advent of 24-hour news channels like CNN, Sky News and BBC News 24, television too is thought of as a complex medium needing a great many people to make it work, with its ability to react fast to a breaking news story sometimes hampered by technicalities. It is no surprise that when a big news story breaks, TV channels revert to 'radio mode' and broadcast telephone interviews with eyewitnesses and reporters while the necessary satellite equipment takes hours to get to the scene for live pictures and good quality sound.

People listen to radio news when they need to know quickly what is going on. They realize that because radio news is so simple and short, it is up to date and has to concentrate simply on reporting the facts.

To quote a rather clever station slogan promoting the virtues of radio news in Dublin: 'You can watch it tonight, you can read it tomorrow, but you can hear it now on NewsTalk 106.'

Speed and simplicity

Radio is probably at its best when it is 'live' or reacting to an event happening 'now'. Because there are relatively few technicalities, a news story can be on the air in seconds and updated as it develops. Radio works best with news stories which require a quick reaction. There is a flexibility which exists in no other media because comparatively few people are involved in the process.

Radio can simply be one person and a telephone. There are no cameras, lights or production assistants. Usually, it is just one broadcaster and a microphone or telephone separating him or her from the listener. You should always strive to make use of radio's greatest assets – speed and simplicity.

Making pictures

Radio is the best medium to stimulate the imagination. By doing what radio does best – getting on the air from a scene quickly and describing the event so the listener can visualize what is happening – you are using the most powerful tools you possess: immediacy and imagery.

The listener is always trying to imagine what he or she hears and what is being described. These pictures are emotional – such as the tearful voice of a mother appealing for information about her missing teenage daughter. Pictures on radio are not limited by the size of the screen; they are any size you wish.

Person-to-person

Radio is a very personal medium. The broadcaster is usually speaking directly to the listener. This is why it is so important to think of the audience as singular. When you talk on the radio, you are not broadcasting to the masses through a gigantic public address system. You are talking to *one* person in the way you would speak if you were holding a conversation over a cup of coffee or pint of beer.

Radio also allows the full emotions of the human voice to be heard, from laughter through anger and pain to compassion. The sound of a voice can convey far more than reported speech. This is because the *way* something is being said is just as important as *what* is being said. ⟩

Localness

The biggest strength of broadcasting news on local radio is that it gives a station its sense of being truly local. Local radio stations aiming for a broad audience ignore news at their peril. In an increasingly competitive marketplace, news is one of the few things which makes a local station sound distinctive and 'close to you'.

News from 'around the corner' is often just as important to a listener as news from around the world – if not more so in many cases. However, there is a danger of becoming too local. Policy judgements have to be made about what is local and what is too parochial or parish pump. Local radio news bulletins are not audio versions of local newspapers, for reasons of space if nothing else. The judgement of how local is local is an important one. For example, a story about a cat up a tree is too parochial for all radio stations. The same story about a firefighter being killed while trying to rescue the cat is not only a good local story, it is almost certainly a national one as well.

THE MAKING OF A BROADCASTER

Working in radio is a very public job. We all have a good chance to hear how it is done whether we prefer Radio One, Classic FM, BBC World Service or the local commercial radio station. But what qualities are News Editors seeking in their staff or freelance journalists?

Qualities of a good radio journalist

There has rarely been a better time to start in radio. More people are employed in radio in the UK than in television. The industry is growing fast and the main problem facing many editors is finding sufficient staff and freelancers who can do the job. Note the words 'who can do the job'. There is no shortage of people who would like to do it. Sadly, not all of them have abilities to match their ambition.

It is essential that you should know what you want to do. The first letters to be rejected by radio stations usually start: 'I would be willing to do anything, including making the tea.' The writers of such letters believe they are increasing their chances of employment by showing versatility. In fact, people who are too dazzled by radio in general are unlikely to be much use in practice.

Apart from journalists, the other major on-air performers are the presenters. The term 'presenter' can cover all kinds of broadcasting, from being a DJ on a fast-moving dance show to reading the shipping forecast on Radio Four. On BBC local radio stations, the presenters of the main programmes at breakfast, lunch and drive time are usually experienced journalists.

A competent radio journalist has to combine the traditional talents of the reporter with the newer skills. Some know a little about a lot. Others, like specialist reporters, know a lot about a little. Traditional talents mean an ability to write clear, easily understood English, a knack of summarizing complicated situations, asking pertinent but pithy questions and – most important of all – a 'nose for news' or knowing what makes a good news story.

In addition, the radio journalist must feel at home with technical equipment and digital editing techniques. This means hard disk editing, recording links and packages, reading self-op live bulletins on air and conducting interviews. If many of these terms mean nothing, do not worry. They are all explained later.

The good radio journalist is flexible, technically competent, capable of working under extreme time pressure, able to prioritize and juggle dealing with a major disaster and a funny story in the same hour. Journalists must also be able to think well on their feet, perhaps recording an interview or writing details of a court case story literally a few seconds before they are due on air.

The quality of imagination in a radio journalist does not mean the quality of making up stories, but having ideas for news stories and their treatments, as well as seeing newsworthy possibilities in unpromising places, like apparently endless council meeting minutes and agendas.

Starting out

There are some journalists in broadcasting who are never heard on the radio. They may be sub-editors working in big national newsrooms like the BBC's General News Service, which serves BBC local radio, or Independent Radio News, which serves many commercial radio stations. Such people are usually highly experienced; their jobs are rarely offered to newcomers.

The novice journalist starting out in radio is more likely to find a job at a local station. That means a smaller station, where everybody has a go at everything. The News Editor may well read the news and report and, during part of the day, the news staff may be reduced to just one person as other journalists may be out on a story or simply off shift. Weekend shifts, if they happen at all, are frequently handled by one person doing everything from presenting bulletins to making hourly check calls and grabbing an interview or two for Monday morning between times.

There is one phrase that should never be heard in small local radio newsrooms: 'that isn't my job'. The versatility of a radio journalist is most fully stretched at a local station. In dozens of small newsrooms, there are no specialists concentrating on just one type of subject like Industry or Politics, there are no sub-editors and there probably is not even a newsroom assistant.

Today's news is most often presented by journalists. The old style news 'reader' still survives on BBC national radio and on the World Service. Under the traditional system, the newsreader provides the voice and the news is written by other people. On local radio, the bulletins are usually presented by the reporting staff, although some big commercial radio groups have experimented with one reader pre-recording separate bulletins for a number of stations, prepared by separate teams of journalists, from a central source called a 'hub', which are then played out simultaneously. This system, though, is the exception to the rule.

There is one more quality not yet mentioned – at least not specifically. It is the most important quality of all in a radio journalist. That quality is *enthusiasm*.

Make no mistake, the job can be hard. It may mean unpredictably long hours, especially when a big story breaks. It may be demanding and stressful, with split-second deadlines to meet every day. It may even be lonely as you keep a newsroom going on a boring Sunday afternoon. It will certainly be unsocial – someone has to work Christmas Day! However, it can also be very enjoyable and rewarding as you get back with the lead story just in time or present a 'hard' bulletin, full of good, breaking news stories. Or it can be creative, when you make a feature out of a tedious story, putting in time and effort to make it sound different.

In other words, the job can be great fun and highly satisfying. It is what you make it.

GETTING THE JOB

There is no traditional way into radio journalism. It is highly competitive and persistence is essential. Although it is desirable to have a high level of education, it is by no means a necessity. Some organizations recruit virtually all graduates; others prefer experience over education.

The best advice if you want to become a radio journalist is to combine the highest level of education with as much practical work experience as possible. For general advice about jobs in broadcasting, check the Radio Academy's website (www.radioacademy.org) or the website of Skillset, the skills agency for the audio-visual industry (www.skillset.org).

Remember also to *listen* to the radio. You can learn lots from simply hearing a variety of different styles of radio news from the national stations like BBC Radio Four and TalkSPORT to your local commercial station. Listen especially to the output of stations for which you hope to work. It is surprising how few budding young journalists do this.

Work experience

Remember the power of offering your services for free! Many newsrooms welcome work experience students as an extra pair of hands and, although you may find yourself doing menial tasks such as filing, it is an invaluable opportunity to look and listen and find out how the great news machine works.

Work experience placements are competitive. Nobody has a right to a placement and there is often a lot of luck involved. Newsrooms have to juggle requests for placements from school pupils and students studying

journalism courses. There is also an increasing number of rules and regulations from the EC about the use of work experience students.

Your best bet is to contact your *local* station well in advance of when you want to do your placement. It is no good expecting a station to offer help with just a fortnight's notice. Many schools and colleges have arrangements with local stations, which can help. If this is not the case, write a short letter to the News Editor of your chosen station – remember to use their correctly spelled name – outlining why you want to work there. An interview may follow.

Local newspapers

Experience of working on a local newspaper is still one of the best ways to get a job in local radio, although the writing and interviewing techniques are different. People from local papers come to radio with a thorough grounding in the rudiments of journalism and, sometimes, invaluable local knowledge and contacts.

They are usually trained in law, public administration and shorthand – all useful skills for the radio journalist. They also have experience in covering all sorts of stories, ranging from flower shows to inquests. Accuracy and balance are second nature to these people. They also tend to know the difference between a police sergeant and a superintendent! Newspapers are also the best way to have developed that essential 'nose' for news.

Hospital radio

In the way that local newspapers provide a grounding in journalism skills, hospital radio stations give a good grounding in practical radio skills. Most hospital stations broadcast on closed circuits to patients in hospitals and hospices, although some stations have been given long-term RSLs to broadcast at low power over the airwaves. There are hundreds of them throughout the UK. It is voluntary work, with a chance to try everything from presentation to outside broadcasts, often learning as you go along, with no formal training. There is also the gratification that you are performing a useful service for patients in hospital. Check the Hospital Broadcasting Association's website for more information (www.hbauk.com).

Hospital stations are funded by a combination of grants, subscriptions and donations. Facilities and the quality of output vary from station to station. One of the best ways to get a job in professional radio is to have a combination of local paper and hospital radio experience. If your local hospital radio station does not have its own local news programme, why not offer to put one together?

Student radio

Many universities and colleges have campus radio stations broadcasting on a closed loop system which can only be picked up in college grounds or on a long-term RSL. Similar to hospital radio in terms of the variable facilities and quality of output, student stations are targeted towards educated young adults who want to hear specific sorts of music, generally dance, urban, alternative and rock music. Student stations have the added advantage of having the resource support which universities can offer. Check the Student Radio Association website (www.studentradio.org.uk).

Some student stations also carry news and essential information about college life. Putting together bulletins of college news and doing interviews for broadcast on student radio is an excellent way of starting a demo tape of your expertise to help get a job in professional radio. Many student stations are developing a growing reputation for innovation, creativity and excellence in both speech- and music-based programmes, and get national recognition through annual awards schemes, the most popular and prestigious of which is organized by Radio One.

College courses

There is now an increasing number of college courses teaching broadcasting skills in general and journalism in particular. Again, there is a lot of competition for places. Courses fall into two main categories – postgraduate courses leading to a diploma or similar qualification, or three-year courses leading to a media studies or journalism degree. The latter combines studying radio with television and other media, but both usually include short attachments with working radio stations.

Some courses run RSL stations as part of their teaching. They will certainly have 'news days', where stories are gathered and prepared in real time.

Prospective students need to take care in choosing the best type of course. Choose a course recognized by the Broadcast Journalism Training Council (BJTC). The Council was established in 1979 to oversee and sustain common vocational standards in the delivery of radio journalism training in colleges. All the main broadcasters are represented by the BJTC. Its website (www.bjtc.org.uk) gives more details and lists accredited courses. However, the BJTC does not provide funding or scholarships.

While many radio courses are practical and vocational, by no means all of them are. Some offer students opportunities to write and present programmes, others encourage students to analyse broadcasting policy, ethics and morals of stories and their coverage, as well as the history of its institutions in a social and cultural context.

There is some sneering in the radio industry as many of the three-year media courses sometimes tend to be more theoretical than practical. However, radio managements should remember that these courses are not simply training courses geared towards the needs of the industry. A media studies graduate learns not only *how* to do it, but also to ask awkward questions about *why* things are done in a certain way and *what other ways* there are of doing things.

The reality is that a media studies graduate or a postgraduate student with a diploma can usually offer a unique combination of skills and abilities, including practical radio and journalism, as well as a theoretical appeciation of news and its place in society.

BBC training schemes

The BBC advertises a number of trainee jobs which are directly linked to operational needs and therefore vary from year to year.

In the past, schemes have been run for local radio reporters but, as needs have changed, it has become necessary to offer training that is bi-media for both radio and television. One of the most recent schemes is the Broadcast Journalism Trainee Scheme. You can get more details from the BBC website (www.bbc.co.uk/jobs/bbctrainees or www.bbc.co.uk/talent).

When considering candidates for traineeships, the BBC puts a high premium on writing and communication, including your clarity of expression and critical skills, as well as evidence of interest and commitment to broadcasting and the community where you live.

Some of the questions the BBC suggests prospective trainees ask themselves before applying to be a broadcast trainee are as follows:

- Are you curious about the world around you?
- Do you worry about what you might miss if you go for half a day without seeing or hearing a news bulletin?
- Do you read local papers as well as the national press?
- Do you listen regularly to a BBC radio station other than one of the national networks?
- Are you a regular Internet surfer?
- Do your colleagues regard you as a team player?
- Do you generate most of the best ideas in your team?
- Can you cope with pressure?
- Do you enjoy public speaking?
- Are you confident about your ability to communicate your ideas?
- Are you trusted by those around you?
- Do you listen to both sides of an argument before making a decision?

If you answer yes to these questions, you are the kind of person the BBC will consider for one of its traineeships.

Traffic and travel broadcasting

Traffic and travel news for radio stations is supplied by a number of organizations which can provide entry-level broadcaster positions. Apart from the BBC's own in-house traffic and travel unit, the two main suppliers are AA Roadwatch and Trafficlink (Figure 2.1).

They employ people to gather and broadcast travel information, and can be an excellent way of obtaining radio experience, as well as learning the skills of marshalling information, writing scripts and broadcasting live.

Restricted service stations

The hundreds of stations broadcasting on RSLs each year provide invaluable experience in all aspects of practical journalism and broadcasting. Again, audio and excerpts from these stations can provide an excellent basis for a radio journalism demo tape.

Figure 2.1
Broadcasting a travel bulletin at Trafficlink in London. Note the computer screen showing pictures from roadside cameras

Freelancing

Because of the competition, it is often difficult to find a staff job after college, local papers, hospital radio or RSL experience. One answer is to offer your services as a freelance radio journalist, working on a day-by-day or weekly basis with a variety of different radio stations. You have to be adaptable, mobile and confident in your own abilities. It is not the option for you if you crave security, but it can be lucrative.

MARKETING YOURSELF

Many jobs are advertised in the pages of newspapers like *The Guardian* and *The Independent*, and magazines like *Broadcast, The Radio Magazine* and *UK Press Gazette*. Many of these publications have websites advertising the jobs as well. There are also specialist radio websites advertising vacancies, such as www.ukradio.com, www.mediauk.com and www.radio2xs.com.

Alternatively, you can seek advice from the BBC Corporate Recruitment department or write speculatively to radio stations throughout the UK. You will be surprised at just how many busy News Editors decide to see someone for an informal chat on the strength of a good letter and demo. Although there may be no immediate vacancies, you will be ahead of the rest if you make a good impression.

The CV and demo

Your marketing pack needs to consist of a neatly presented and well-organized CV, a covering letter (sent to the News Editor with his or her name spelt correctly!) and a demo (Figures 2.2 and 2.3). The demo can either be on cassette tape, CD or Minidisc and should consist of you reading a short news bulletin plus examples of the rest of your work, such as an interesting interview or fascinating feature. It need be no longer than five minutes at most and is usually about three.

Persistence

Target one or two specific News Editors at first, and if you do not succeed at first, be persistent. After about a week or ten days, follow up your mailout with a phone call or e-mail if you have heard nothing.

If you are seeking freelance work, make sure News Editors hear from you regularly and know about your strengths. The idea is to ensure your name is on their list of people to call when they need freelance help. Remember that one job usually leads to others as you spread your own network of contacts.

Whatever you do, keep trying, as persistence is an impressive journalistic skill. It also helps to try and go and see people simply to ask for feedback and advice.

Curriculum Vitae

Name:	John Peters
DoB:	16th August 1977
Address:	2 Blue Mews, Blankstown BL1 2BG
Nationality:	British
Email:	johnpeters@coldmail.com
Telephone:	☎ 020 8123 4567
	☎ 0771 222 2222

Education & Qualifications

2002–2003 **University of Blankshire, Blankstown**
Post Graduate in Broadcast Journalism

1998–2002 **University of London, London**
BA(Hons) Languages & Business Administration Main Subjects included:
German, French, Accounting, International Relations, Marketing.

1996–1998 **Burns High School, Ipswich**
A Levels: French (B), English (B), German (B)

1991–1996 **Burns High School, Ipswich**
6 O Levels

Work Experience

Sept 02–Present **Uni FM – Blankshire University**
I am the News Editor for the University radio station, which involves working
with a team of six reporters, collecting news stories and preparing them for
broadcast.

1998–2002 **UBN Radio – University of London**
I was one of the reporter/presenters of the weekend news programme, and
also contributed to the station's Sunday Morning Glory Breakfast Show from
6–9 a.m. Responsibilities included finding and recording stories, working to
tight deadlines, and as part of a team.

1997–1998 **Witch 666 – Hospital Radio Ipswich**
Dedication collector for the Sunday morning request programme. I learnt how
to talk to strangers and also the basics of recording and interviewing.

Additional Information

Broadcast Equipment:
I am familiar with RadioMan computer playout system and Quick Edit Pro, Dave, Dalet and Brian
editing systems. I have used mini disc and hard disc portable recording machines and can competently drive
a studio desk.

Languages:
English – Mother tongue
German – Fluent written and spoken
French – Fluent written and spoken

Computer:
Experienced user of Microsoft Office products.
Keen user of the internet.
I have a clean and current driving licence.
References available upon request.

Figure 2.2
A typical well-constructed CV

Dear Mr, Mrs, Madam, Mister, Miss, To whom it may concern

My name is Simon Thoms Jnr and I am 19 years old. I am writing to you to get a job. I am a well educated, good looking; very reliable man who knows what he wants and always achieves his targets.

I dropped out of primary school when I was 10 and have been at home ever since. I am very interested in radio because I love listening to it. I therefor think that I would like a career in it with a minimum starting salary of £35k P/A ONO.

Could you please, please provide me with a job because my father is going to retire soon and the responsibility is on my shoulders to support my complete family. So you as a great human being give me a chance.

I assure you that if I am given a chance to serve under your great leadership I will not let you down nor will I leave one stone unturned.

If you want a cv or a tape of me doing some reading — then call me.

Hope to see you soon.

Simon Thoms Jnr.

Figure 2.3
An example of a poorly constructed covering letter

THE JOB INTERVIEW

You will almost certainly have to go through a formal interview before being offered a job or a traineeship. In the BBC, these interviews are known as Appointment Boards.

Preparation

The key to being successful is preparation. For a one-hour interview, you should put in about eight times in effort in preparing. You should research the job description and know a lot about the radio station itself, both from its website and its output. You need to find out whether you will be given any kind of selection test. If so, find out as much as you can about it. You need to know who is interviewing you and what they do. It is also useful, if possible, to talk to somebody who is already doing the job and find out more about the working environment.

Nerves

Most people suffer nerves before an interview, but you should recognize that you need a little bit of adrenaline in order to do your best. You will feel more confident if you have prepared properly and rehearsed some of your answers. Try deep breathing before you go into the interview in order to relax. If you get a dry mouth, try gently biting into the sides of your tongue, causing saliva to flow. Warm drinks are better than cold water, which causes the vocal chords to tighten. If your throat is tight, try yawning with your mouth closed. Breathe through the nose and open up the throat. If you have too much saliva, try putting the tip of your tongue on the ridge above your top teeth and breathe through your mouth. This will dry your mouth without drying your throat.

Body language

Body language is important. Walk in upright and confident, not hunched up. Smile when you walk in and during your interview. Maintain eye contact with your interviewer. Direct most of your eye contact to the person who has asked you the question, but also glance at the others. Sit back in your chair with your hands relaxed in your lap. Without behaving like a windmill, gestures sometimes help you illustrate your points. You should be wearing smart clothes, either formal or smart casual. Nobody will employ a scruffbag.

Journalistic tests

You may be asked to do a voice test and even a written test. There is not much you can do to prepare for the voice test – either your voice will fit with the style of station or not. However, you can do your homework for a written test. It is likely this will comprise questions about the station's broadcast area, maybe asking about recent big stories or the names of local MPs. You may also be asked about current national news stories or even be set a general knowledge quiz. It is also possible you may be asked for some story ideas or how you would deal with certain scenarios – for example, what you would say to an awkward listener on the phone or what stories from those provided you would put into a news bulletin, in which order and why.

Awkward questions

If you know the answer but your mind goes blank, it is usually better to come out and say this. It will buy you time and a sympathetic interviewer will usually try to rephrase the question to help you. If you do not understand the question, it is better to ask for clarification. If the questioning turns to something on which you are weak, give as good an answer as you can. Highlight what you have learned from your experiences and what you have done to improve. If you do not understand the point of a question, ask for clarification. Some interviewers do ask 'trick' questions!

Thank you!

A good tip for after the interview is to send a thank you note. It helps keep your name top-of-mind when the interviewer is making his or her selection.

3 News gathering

THE NEWSROOM STRUCTURE

Newsrooms vary in size depending on the radio station. However, there is usually a similar structure of staff who do specific and necessary tasks. Job titles vary between the BBC and commercial radio.

Head of News or News Editor

This is the most senior journalist in the newsroom, reporting directly to the Programme Director in commercial radio or, in the BBC, to the Managing Editor. They are editorially and managerially in charge. On some stations, the Head of News is involved in the day-to-day running of the newsdesk, including some reporting and presenting. In others, he or she deals more with policy and administration.

Editorial jobs include:

- helping to decide the frequency and times of bulletins;
- setting the overall editorial agenda and news policy;
- being responsible for the detailed content and style of news output;
- deciding the proportion of local to national news;
- making sure stories are fair, accurate and legally safe;
- deciding what stories should be covered and by whom;
- dealing with complaints.

Managerial jobs include:

- recruiting and motivating staff;
- compiling work rotas;

- preparing a budget and working within it;
- booking freelancers;
- arranging payments to agencies;
- attending public relations functions;
- training and coaching junior staff.

Bulletin Editor

This is the duty journalist responsible for hourly supervision of the content and compilation of the bulletins. They will usually read the bulletins themselves and self-op the desk in the news studio or what a BBC station would refer to as the NPA, the News Production Area. Other duties may include:

- intaking stories and audio from reporters either at the station, at district offices, or from a national news supplier;
- checking the latest from the emergency services – 'doing the calls' or checking their websites;
- checking that cues and copy conform to style and editorial policy – acting as a 'bulletin enforcer';
- double-checking the accuracy, fairness and legality of stories;
- looking for follow-up stories and new angles;
- rewriting and freshening stories;
- allocating reporters to stories.

Senior Broadcast Journalist or News Producer

This journalist acts as Bulletin Editor when required, but concentrates mainly on collecting and preparing news stories from interviewing to voicing and audio packaging. The difference between this job and the more junior reporter job described below is that seniors or producers are more often concerned with making policy decisions, generating stories and exploring angles than actually doing the reporting job, although barriers in many newsrooms tend to be blurred (Figure 3.1).

Broadcast journalist or reporter

The broadcast journalists in the BBC or reporters in commercial radio are the 'fire-fighters' of the newsroom. They follow up stories, do interviews

Figure 3.1
The newsroom at BBC Radio Kent in Tunbridge Wells

and report from the scene. Their main job is to collect audio or actuality, write copy and think up new angles. The qualifications for the job include knowing what makes a good story, accuracy, persistence, speed and 'thinking radio' – the best way to cover a story in sound.

With a BBC local station, reporters may be based at a 'district office', of which there are usually several around the transmission area. These may be in, for example, the county town, another large town or somewhere which generates many stories. These offices act as a base from where the reporter can keep in touch with local stories, and ensure they can be first at the scene of a breaking story. A terminal with audio and text editing facilities, linked to an ISDN line, means the reporter can feed stories to the station from the district office. Such facilities may also be installed at a reporter's own home, to reduce costs of buying or renting an office. Other contribution points may be in a local council building, although reporters would rarely work from there, using it only to feed audio.

Some offices also act as a Network Contribution Area, or NCA, from where guests can be interviewed remotely on a quality ISDN line either by the local station or another station in the network (local or national). Some NCAs are based in rooms in the offices of another organization – police headquarters, the county council or a university – and are unstaffed. Doors may be opened remotely from the station itself.

One-journalist newsrooms

Smaller stations operate with one or two journalists combining all these jobs. This is the way many low-cost UK commercial stations work, with one journalist covering the morning shift, another in the afternoon, and possibly a freelancer at the weekend. The main attributes needed are a clear sense of priorities and good time-management skills. Setting up and running a small news operation is described in more detail later.

Television journalists

In regional BBC television centres, TV journalists may assist the local radio station. They produce stories on a central computer system which can be accessed by radio colleagues. In some centres, TV journalists on the scene produce separate reports for local radio. At the BBC newsroom in Tunbridge Wells in Kent, for example, television journalists for South East Today contribute reports for both BBC Radio Kent and Southern Counties Radio.

Additionally, the weather forecasters from the local television news programme are the same ones who present the in-depth weather reports for the radio. And journalists working for television's local Ceefax pages, and those writing the Internet sites for Radio Kent and Southern Counties, will access scripts and audio from both the TV and radio stations to compile their reports.

NATIONAL NEWS

A local radio station would be unconvincing indeed without local news. Equally, its news output must acknowledge there is a wide world beyond 'our patch'. The provision of national and international news for local radio is undertaken by several specialist organizations.

During the day, many local stations mix national and international news from the agency with local news gathered on-site. Over night and at off-peak times, these stations take the live bulletin service offered by some agencies (see 'Live bulletins' section below).

Radio news agencies

Radio news agencies provide national and international stories most of the day as they break. Because radio is a medium of sound, its agencies must provide not only news copy, but also appropriate audio or actuality. The technical implications are that stations must be linked to their national agencies by satellite or landline. News copy is fed directly into a news-room computer system, while audio is fed on a separate channel or line and recorded onto a digital hard disk system.

The BBC's General News Service (GNS)

GNS supplies news stories and actuality to BBC local radio stations by landline. It is based at BBC Television Centre in West London and not available to any other network. GNS provides only copy and actuality for BBC local stations to mix bulletins and there are no live bulletins. The service also arranges guests to be in their studios to talk about national stories, and operates a booking system so journalists at local stations can interview them remotely. You can also book a GNS studio so, for example, a local MP can go there to be interviewed 'down the line' by a local station.

Independent Radio News (IRN)

IRN was formed in 1973 at the start of commercial radio in the UK. The service is taken by satellite by around 260 stations – about 95 per cent of them. It provides a comprehensive service of bulletins in 'kit' form for local mixing, as well as two live bulletin services. IRN also provides 'bespoke' bulletins for some stations which are tailor-made for the specific audiences of those stations. There are also specialist staff providing entertainment, sport, political and financial news and features

Figure 3.2
The main newsdesk at Independent Radio News (IRN) in Grays Inn Road, London

for client stations. Stations do not pay cash directly for the service (apart from for bespoke bulletins); IRN is financed through the Newslink scheme, where national commercials are played out on local stations next to peak time news bulletins. This finances the cost of IRN, which returns a proportion of the profit to the local stations depending on the size of audience delivered. The television news company ITN is contracted by IRN to be the supplier of news and the news operation is based at ITN's London headquarters (Figure 3.2).

Sky News Radio (SNR)

SNR works in a similar way to IRN, using audio from its parent television news services as well as sourcing its own material. Sky News Radio is based at the Sky News Centre in West London, but operates as a stand-alone radio newsroom, providing a 'cue and cuts' service for around 30 local stations to mix with their local news. It broadcasts a generic two-minute top-of-the-hour bulletin of national and international news, and also provides bespoke bulletins. Clients pay directly for the services they require.

UBC

The independent production group UBC Media Group, formerly known as the Unique Broadcasting Company, provides an entertainment and showbiz news service to many commercial radio stations. Stories and interviews are gathered at its headquarters in London and distributed via ISDN landlines, satellites and the Internet, both in bulletin and kit form. UBC also provide a financial news service to some stations.

Digital News Network (DNN)

DNN provides a regionalized rolling news service for certain digital radio stations providing tailor-made packages of both regional news and information to slot into individual channels' programming.

Global Radio News (GRN)

GRN is an independent audio content distributor supplying material filed by journalists and reporters to radio stations worldwide via the Internet. Reporters file using special audio production equipment and GRN provide their reports available for downloading by radio stations on a commercial basis.

News services provided by Trafficlink (previously called Metro Networks) ceased in late 2002.

Local intake

Local newsrooms receive a continuous stream of national and international news stories onto their monitors. At BBC stations, the news text production system is called ENPS (Electronic News Production System), which is used in conjunction with the audio editing system Quick Edit Pro, and the playout system RadioMan. Commercial stations use a variety of computer programs, which means freelance journalists must be skilful at picking up the different systems.

Many computerized newsroom systems automatically sort incoming data into specific lists designated by editors to allow quick scanning of available stories. These may be divided into content (news, sport, finance) or the geographical location of the stories.

Audio feeds are sent out at various regular times each hour; each of the main national news providers (GNS, IRN and SNR) have a regular feed at about 20 minutes to each hour. Of course, a fast-breaking story may mean that audio arrives outside these times. Most Bulletin Editors are familiar with the 'late feed' which arrives just a few minutes before the top-of-the-hour bulletin.

In most digital newsrooms, the audio is automatically 'captured' by a sensing device and stored on the computer hard disk system. It appears in an on-screen menu of audio available for downloading, and can then be edited, stored, moved and called up when needed for playout on air. Some systems are able to 'top and tail' the feed into individual clips, which are ready-to-air. IRN, although still sending feeds in the traditional way, now also lets client stations download audio from an Internet site.

Data feeds

The agencies provide much more in their data feeds than simple cues for audio – whether they be bulletin 'cuts' (or 'clips' at a BBC station) or longer programme 'packages'. A typical hour will also produce some copy stories, at least one summary for headlines, financial news, entertainment news, music charts and perhaps a weather forecast. There will also be a variety of service messages; the feeds are used as a mailbox for the network and may carry all kinds of other information. For example, what time a live feed from a news conference may start, or on GNS, which stations are interviewing a networked guest at which times.

It is part of the Bulletin Editor's job to assess all this information: using it, passing it to someone else or discarding it.

Live bulletins

IRN offers two bulletins 24 hours a day that can be taken direct from London by client stations. IRN180 is a three-minute bulletin which is aimed at speech stations and those targeted towards older listeners. There is a strong emphasis on home and international news with longer audio. The delivery and language is traditional. IRN90 is a 90-second update aimed at stations with a younger demographic. The bulletins cover the top stories of the day and also include lifestyle and entertainment news. The delivery is pitched slightly faster with shorter audio.

Sky News Radio offers a single service of two minutes' duration. As with IRN's live bulletins, some commercial stations use these and 'tag' their local news on the end. Others compile their own bulletins during the day, mixing local news with material sent from the network.

There is no equivalent service at the BBC.

Television audio

Some commercial stations are reaching agreements with local commercial television companies to use TV audio in radio news bulletins. This allows them access to quality audio on big news stories without having to send a reporter to gather it. Access is usually permitted off air, i.e. by the radio station recording the output from the TV news programme. Depending on the agreement, the radio station may have to credit the TV company. Additionally, BBC local stations sometimes use audio gathered by TV colleagues.

Wire services

These are the news agencies which supply national and international news to media outlets. They are known as 'wire' services, as they were origin-ally sent out via telegraphic wires. Now they are distributed via satellite and the Internet. Some newsrooms have direct access to them. Others use the radio news services described above, which compile a lot of their news using the wire services as raw material. The two main wire services arc: *The Press Association (PA)*, which deals with UK domestic stories and only covers foreign stories where there is a domestic angle; and *Reuters*, which is the main source for international and financial news.

SOURCES OF LOCAL NEWS

News arrives in a radio newsroom from many different sources:

- the emergency services;
- news releases;
- public utilities;
- politicians and councils;

- listeners;
- colleagues;
- pressure groups;
- freelance journalists and agencies;
- 'rivals';
- your own station;
- the Internet.

When you have this information, you have to decide the answers to two key questions. First, is it newsworthy? Second, is it reliable? If the answer to both questions is 'yes', you have a story.

'No' to the first question is usually the end of the matter. However, some so-called 'hooks' may not be immediately obvious and you should always be alert to possible links with other stories. Never be afraid to test your decision on colleagues. (This is an obvious drawback to small, one-person newsrooms!)

'No' to the second question will mean further checking. For example, a member of the public reports a serious road accident. You must verify it with the emergency services before using it as a story on air.

The emergency services

The police, fire, ambulance and coastguard services have a unique relationship with the media – both sides need the other. Information from these sources is often the staple diet of dramatic stories featured in local radio news bulletins. As publicly funded organizations, the day-to-day work of the emergency services should be accountable. They often need to use the media to put over preventative messages about crime and safety, as well as appealing for witnesses.

Regular check calls must be made to all the emergency services, usually to a recorded voicebank system (Figure 3.3). Sometimes, the emergency services will call you with tip-offs. Make sure you have met the press officers in each service and ensure that a good relationship continues. If you fall out (maybe a story was given to your rival station), make it your business to resume friendly relations as soon as possible.

Stories from the emergency services are made available to the media via regularly updated voicebank recordings on special phone lines. Some police

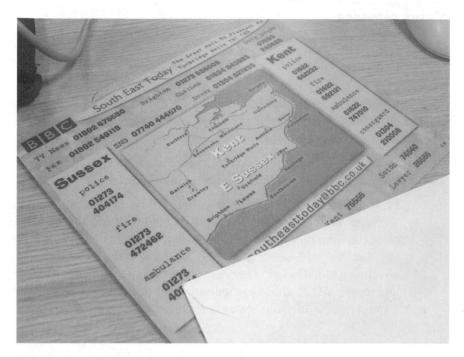

Figure 3.3
BBC Radio Kent's innovative way of marshalling contact numbers – on a mousemat

forces also use the Internet with access through password-protected websites. Some district reporters still have regular meetings at local police stations.

However, press officers are not the only sources of news stories. For example, a good local newsroom will not only make a point of speaking to the press office or listening to the voicebank recording regularly, but will also talk direct to the operational officers on the ground and 'tease' out some of the offbeat stories which occur.

Build relationships with people when the news is good. Then, when a bad story breaks, you already have the contacts – and they owe you a favour! Visit your emergency services' PROs as often as you can. Then, when there is breaking news, they can put a face to a name at an incident. Information is much more forthcoming and you may be put top of the call sheet or given the interview ahead of your rival.

A word of warning: the police do not always observe the laws of libel and contempt as well as they might. Treat all information from them with care and subject it to the same legal tests as you would any other story.

News releases

News releases are an excellent source of basic information but need to be looked at carefully. They are distributed by people who want you to express a story in their terms. In reality, what they want to say may not be a story – for example, shops putting out 'statements' about winter sales. Alternatively, it may be genuine news but one-sided – for example, a release from a political party (Figure 3.4).

In most cases, you will need to contact the source of the release to verify facts, get more information or set up an interview.

Phoning people about their releases can be an education, particularly when public relations (PR) companies are involved. There are good, efficient PR companies who earn the fees they charge their clients by releasing factual, well-researched and well-angled information, and make covering a story easier. There are also incompetent firms who waste time and money all round. Be particularly wary of any PR company sending out a press release to radio stations enclosing photographs (think about it!),

---

NEWS FROM THE BUCKSHEE GROUP

For immediate release   28th October 2002

Buckshee Technologies Ltd, a member of Buckshee International plc, is to transfer the production of hydraulic components from its factory in Newtown to its principal plant in Highworth. This decision follows a review of the company's manufacturing facilities in the light of changes in defence procurement and the continuing need to reduce, wherever possible, operating costs.

The Newtown plant will be closed and the 315 employees will be leaving the company. The company much regrets making the reduction in personnel and will provide job and financial counselling to assist those affected in finding alternative employment.

ends

Note to Editors: Buckshee Technologies Ltd comprises a group of companies supplying the servicing control systems and components for the international aerospace and defence industries.

Enquiries to: Matt Stewart, Head of Media Relations, on 01702 333711

Figure 3.4
Example of a press release giving news of redundancies

referring to your 'readers', inviting you to a photocall, omitting phone numbers or forgetting to include the date of a forthcoming event.

When you do make contact, among the most idiotic responses are: 'Why do you want to talk to anyone? It's all in the press release'; 'We could get someone to talk to you about this towards the end of next week'; and 'You won't actually want to record this, will you?'.

However, if the release comes from an 'amateur' source, you can be more forgiving about errors. Local people like charities, pressure groups and religious organizations do not know the rules like you do.

Audio news releases

Some PR companies send audio clips or full interviews with their news releases as another incentive to get their story on air. These are known as audio news releases or electronic press kits. County councils may send stations an interview with the chief executive, the fire brigade with an officer at the scene of a fire, or a film company an interview with the Hollywood star of a new release. You must decide whether you are going to use interviews with such people who have not been subjected to independent questioning.

You may not be able to get an interview with a fire officer any other way than agreeing to broadcast a piece from the brigade's press office, but should you run an interview with the council's chief executive about job cuts if they have not been rigorously cross-examined? Similarly, should you run an interview with a movie star who is advertising a film they appear in, if you refuse to run something similar from a local store which is also advertising a product?

Public utilities

The organizations which supply our electricity, gas, water, communications and run our trains and buses are all promising sources of news, as what they do will touch the lives of most of your listeners. Treat their news releases with caution as they will usually be 'slanted' towards the most positive angle.

As with the emergency services, ensure you are in touch with the relevant press officers. Make sure you have the names and numbers of local managers too, especially if the main press office is a long way away. Get to know them better by taking up invitations to visit the local sewage works or railway station. It takes some time, but it can be editorially rewarding – and there is usually some lunch laid on as well!

Politicians and councillors

Your local MP will be a constant source of views and comment. Stay in touch with him or her, but remember they have the benefit of a formidable party media machine behind them. MPs usually distribute scores of news releases – some written by their party HQ and merely with a local MP's name on the top – and are almost always available for interview. In such situations, there are no holds barred because they should be expert media performers and able to cope with even the most rigorous questioning.

Local politicians or councillors are slightly different because their expertise varies widely. Some will be more effective than others. Do not overlook their usefulness when you want comments about a controversy. Know the difference between councillors and council officers. Councillors are elected members of the council and officers are salaried staff who make recommendations to members for decision. Both can be useful.

A constant source of local news is the tidal wave of agendas and minutes from councils, health authorities and other public bodies which usually flood into newsrooms. They are frequently tedious – but make sure you go through them, because a good story can lurk deep inside. Many minutes will reflect decisions already taken; agendas will preview recommendations. Remember it is perfectly proper to preview matters for decision by councillors on the day of the meeting. However, if you preview, you must follow up and report what actually happened the next day.

Council press releases will slant the news from their viewpoint, so you must interpret the story for the listener. For example, a release which says 'Blankshire Council has announced the contractor for the Blankstown Bypass as Acme Roads, who will start work in 2006' should be rewritten as 'Work on the Blankstown Bypass will start in three years' time'. The listener has no interest in the name of the company contracted – certainly not as the topline of the story.

Listeners

All kinds of people can phone or wander into a radio station with boring, rambling tales of rows with bosses or problems with noisy neighbours. Sometimes they bring a good story – but, if not, listen patiently and courteously. Even if they have wasted your time, it is good public relations to express sympathy and give them the address of the local Citizens' Advice Bureau. If you do follow up a story, remember not only to check the facts thoroughly, but also that there are two sides to most stories and uncorroborated information should not be accepted at face value. It has been known for troublemakers to make a hobby out of hoaxing the media, with made-up claims. These are often difficult to check and are tempting to run – but be on your guard.

Tip-offs from listeners can be vital to get ahead on big breaking stories. For example, a listener phoning to tell you there is a big fire in his street can provide a good eyewitness account of what is happening. Many radio stations encourage listeners to phone in with tips. However, beware of hoaxers and ensure you get official confirmation of an incident before broadcast. It is a rare occasion where you will put something directly on air without checking.

Reaction to a story can sometimes become a story in itself. Many stations encourage the use of text messages on mobile phones to gauge the reaction to something that's happened, and a station's phone-in may also prove a fruitful source of comment, especially on a quiet news day. However, phone votes should not be used as the basis of a news story as they are not representative of the listening public, only the views of those who chose to call.

Colleagues

It has been said – truly – that everyone working on a radio station should be a 'stringer' for the newsroom. Commercial radio station sales staff are out and about all day selling advertising, so encourage them to call you if they see or hear anything unusual. They are often the first to hear gossip about companies closing or expanding. Other staff, from the Managing Editor to the cleaners, can also come across stories by accident. Make sure they know you will be glad to listen. Colleagues may also be able to put you in touch with an expert on a particular subject or someone they know who lives near to where a news story has just broken.

In BBC radio stations, which are linked with regional television news programmes, journalists should regularly check each other's running orders and diaries for potential stories.

Pressure groups

Pressure groups simply want to put their side of a story as often and as forcefully as possible. Do not let them libel anyone and do your best to balance their story with the other side's point of view.

Freelance journalists and agencies

A good relationship with local news agencies and freelance journalists is usually essential for a local newsroom. It would be impossible for most radio stations to cover legal proceedings in courts without copy supplied by them. Radio journalists do not have the time to sit in court all day nor necessarily the contacts to know which defendant is appearing where and when. Agencies and freelance reporters can also sometimes ferret out a story which has eluded you simply because they have better established contacts or have more time with which to work on a story. However, do not feel hurt and humiliated if a really good story finds its way to the national newspapers from a local agency – the big papers will pay hundreds of times the fee the agency can get from you.

Beware of agencies and freelance reporters who rewrite stories from the local press. Also watch agencies who rewrite news releases. This is easy money for them but a pointless payment for you. Find out why you did not receive the release; perhaps the sender was unaware of your existence.

'Rivals'

There is an attitude on some radio stations that rival stations are not worth listening to. This could be a mistake. It is your job to know what other stations – or TV shows or newspapers – are doing. Use them as a source of tip-offs but never 'lift' a story without checking it thoroughly first. Also, try and find a different angle or someone else to interview to give the story a fresher spin. Alternatively, you may decide *not* to cover a story, purely because another station has covered it first.

Newspapers and magazines can be a great source of stories, and it should be someone's job to scan such publications every day. A BBC district reporter should be able to build contacts without resorting to devouring the local paper each week, although with most newspapers publishing stories each day on their website that is probably unnecessary anyway. Local newspaper letters pages can, incidentally, be a great source of local news on a quiet day – and the editors are thoughtful enough to publish the name and address of the writer!

Some commercial radio station groups have reciprocal deals for news with local newspapers. Taking this one step further, the Kent Messenger Newspaper Group actually owns several stations in the county, and radio journalists have computer access to stories as their newspaper colleagues file them.

It is easy to become distracted with rivalry and going 'one up' on other radio stations. Remember that very few people listen to two news bulletins on different stations at the same time; there is little to be gained by a one-on-one, hour-on-hour battle over individual stories. The best a station can do is garner a general reputation for being 'first for news' or 'number one for news' over a period of time through a combination of effective on-air promotion and positioning.

Your own station

Many stations, especially those in the commercial sector, will often include information about themselves in their bulletins. This may be the winner of a big station competition, ticket details for a forthcoming concert or party, or a story about the station's latest listening figures. Done sparingly, coverage of such events in the bulletins can enhance the credibility of the station; however, some argue that such stories are not news in the real sense of the term and should only be broadcast in pre-recorded trails or presenter links.

The Internet

There is no doubt that the World Wide Web has made the job of a journalist much easier, but it is tempting to fall into the trap of taking all the information you find at face value. One should be aware of which sites are reliable and which ones have a vested interest in pushing a particular line. Some pressure groups may hide behind a reputable-looking website address, while they publish half-truths.

Having said that, radio journalists should make an effort to regularly view the sites of other local media for potential story leads, which will of course, be checked independently.

BBC stations have access to trusted websites via the Corporation's intranet. Many of these are sites or publications for which a subscription has been paid, and can be accessed by all staff. They include newspapers and magazines (domestic and foreign), and reference material such as encyclopaedia sites, or those which find phone numbers for individuals and companies.

PLANNING AND DEVELOPING STORIES

The newsroom is likely to represent the biggest area of 'input' into a radio station. News releases, letters, phone calls, tip-offs, faxes, e-mails and other information all arrives on the newsdesk. It is vital to have suitable systems in place to assess this important information quickly and either action it, pass it on to whoever needs it, or file it away until it is needed.

The newsroom diary

The heart of a local newsroom is its diary. All information about events supplied in advance is written in the diary under the appropriate date. Increasingly, this is an 'electronic' diary as part of a computerized system, otherwise an A4 size hardbound book-style diary is adequate.

It is up to everyone to put entries into the diary as soon as possible. One good system is that supporting papers such as the relevant council agenda, news release or letter are filed in the diary file – with numbers 1 to 31 corresponding to the days of the month. It should be the job of the reporter dealing with overnight stories (i.e. those for next morning) to look through the diary and diary file and process previews of events happening the following day. On the day itself, it is the job of the Duty News Editor to assess what stories need covering given the resources available. In addition, a well-maintained 'futures' file with general cuttings and releases helps to generate ideas, especially on 'slow' news days when little is happening.

Archive files should also be kept. These will contain information about ongoing or recurring stories, such as a murder inquiry and subsequent trial, calls for a bypass or redundancies at a local factory. The files will be added to as the story is revisited, with copies of your own scripts, audio dubbed onto a minidisc, and appropriate newspaper cuttings. Such background information is invaluable when a story develops, especially if the journalist who originally covered the story for the station has moved on. The rules of the archive files are simple: always photocopy printed material rather than use the original, and never edit any part of an archive recording!

It is important that the newsroom is highly organized in its information flow and there is a tray or file allocated to receiving all this vital input from outside. This must be checked and processed regularly and not allowed to amass and overflow, or good stories may be missed completely.

Newsdesk resource management

With the information from the diary at hand, decisions need to be made about how stories can best be covered. In some newsrooms, there are many staff and freelancers ready to be sent out on stories.

A prospects list is compiled every day. This is simply a list of stories to be covered. It is compiled from all the sources of news. Usually, a newsroom conference or prospects meeting is held to decide who does what, with what angle, and for when it is needed (Figure 3.5). In smaller newsrooms, it may simply be a case of deciding which story is worth following up by telephone by the one Duty Reporter. The prospects list usually forms the agenda for the newsroom conference.

The Duty Editor (which can be the Head of News/News Editor or a Producer/Senior Journalist) must always make allowances for the unexpected when planning coverage of the day's news. Reporters may be allocated to cover the opening of a new hospital wing, a Royal visit, a council news conference or a controversial public meeting, but it is important to leave some leeway so that dramatic, unforeseen events can be dealt with, such as a fire, explosion or train crash. For such a reason, reporters on the road should carry a mobile phone with them at all times.

Figure 3.5
The morning editorial conference at BBC Radio Kent

Remember, though, journalists cannot simply be reactive and wait for stories to happen; it is vital to be proactive and chase their own stories through contacts gleaned through working on other stories in the past.

Developing stories

Reporters are allocated to specific stories. Each is briefed and given all the relevant background information from the diary file. It is the job of the Duty Editor to brief the reporter on the possible angles and ways of treating the story. Angles are the various ways a story can be told from different viewpoints. Treating the story means deciding whether the story becomes a copyline, interviews or package (see below). The Duty Editor may also suggest who should be interviewed, and other reporters may also pass on some of their ideas for contacts. It is also important that each reporter is given a deadline so he or she knows exactly what is expected, by what time and in what form. There is no place or time in the newsroom for confusion.

Newsroom contacts

A newsroom needs a system for quickly finding the name and phone number of anyone in the news. The simplest way to organize this is to create a contacts book – a simple A–Z index of people and organizations. Computerized newsrooms usually have an on-screen database version of this available to all; this is usually best as searches can be performed under several criteria at the same time.

It is a good rule that any phone number used by a journalist should be entered in the contacts file. This way a useful and comprehensive list of contacts is available speedily. It is important that the contacts, if written, are listed legibly, that everyone in the newsroom understands the system and what they have to do to find a number or put one in. For example, all police phone numbers – including those of the force press officer – should be listed under 'police' and not under the individuals concerned.

Many newsrooms have succeeded or failed by the quality of their collective contacts. In addition, journalists will inevitably develop their own databases of personal contacts who have been particularly helpful to them or may provide a useful source of stories in future. One good idea, on slow news days when diary stories are hard to find, is to ring round these contacts simply to stay in touch. Get new story ideas from old sources. You will be surprised how often a casual chat with a contact can yield a good story.

One vital piece of advice – never, ever throw away a phone number.

Resisting pressure

There are innumerable outside pressures to which the radio newsroom is subjected.

Political parties regularly put pressure on newsrooms to present an item of news in the way they want, or accuse journalists of bias. For example, Labour supporters accuse newsrooms of Tory bias; Conservatives equally accuse newsrooms of Labour bias. If a speech by a representative of one party is given prominence, the next minute a voice on the phone complains of bias because equal prominence was not given to some speech by a member of another party, regardless of the fact that it had no news value.

Commercial interests working through PR companies try to slip in free advertising disguised as a news item. Usually, such attempts are unsubtle in the extreme and are easily detected. However, you should never be off your guard. In commercial radio, sales staff may ask journalists to cover an item sponsored by a client – or not to run a story which puts their client in a bad light, redundancies for example. You should decide with the Managing Director before such an event takes place, what is expected of you, making the point that the integrity of the whole station may be in jeopardy if it is seen as a mouthpiece for some cause or campaign.

Listeners with personal axes to grind are another source of pressure. They are always ready to complain that we give too much or too little to this, that or the other.

People who want something kept quiet can be another problem. Usually, this is some kind of court case; the argument used is that to broadcast the item would cause suffering, upset or worry to the relatives of the accused person, particularly if he or she turns out to be a person who occupies a position of standing in the community. Relatives of those found guilty of a crime have also been known to call stations demanding the coverage is dropped, in some instances also making threats. You may also get a press officer telling you: 'It's not really a story.'

In all these cases, you must be bound by your sense of responsibility, fairness and independence. Indeed, regulations for both commercial radio and BBC radio insist on balance. You must not bow to pressure.

Embargoes

Some stories are given to a radio station on the understanding that nothing is broadcast before a certain date and time (usually written as 'Embargoed until 00.01 on Saturday 16 August 2003'). This enables a government department or PR company to manage the flow of information and ensure that interviewees are available to comment when the embargo is lifted. The story may be an announcement about a new initiative on crime, an announcement about redundancies at a local factory, or who is receiving the Queen's Birthday Honours. It is an unwritten protocol that embargoes are followed, and the story is not broadcast until the time stipulated. This does not, however, stop reporters from recording interviews in advance – although care should be taken that those who do not know about the story are not unwittingly informed.

It is sometimes possible to persuade a company to lift embargo. They are sometimes put in place for no apparent reason, or until the 'wrong' time. For example, a transport union may be persuaded that an announcement about a strike by the county's bus drivers would be best made at breakfast time, when those affected would be listening, rather than in the middle of the day.

If an embargo is broken by other media, or the originator themselves, you are within your rights to break it too. If your station alone breaks it (whether by design or accident), you may incur the wrath not only of the company that wrote the release, but also those affected by its contents – for example, those being made redundant.

STORY TREATMENT

Copy

The quickest way to cover a story is simply as 'copy' – that is, with no audio of any kind. Copy stories of one sentence or two are used for head-lines; they are also a good way of giving a news bulletin pace and making it sound busy, with several stories following each other quickly. If a story has been running as audio but you are reluctant to drop it entirely, reduce it to copy. However, a bulletin of only copy sounds dull; it is no replacement for fresh, lively audio. This is radio and we want to hear what someone says and how they say it!

Interviews

The traditional way to cover a story for radio is to interview someone. Just who depends partly on you. You could, for example, decide to put a Labour accusation in the cue to a political story and have some interview audio from a Conservative denying it all – or the reverse.

An interview is more often done on the phone for immediacy, on location for a 'quality' package if you have staff and time available, or down an ISDN line.

Voicers or voice pieces

'Voicing' a story is another way of doing it. A 'voicer' or 'voice piece' is less effective than an interview but is sometimes the only way to improve

on straight copy; it is used in many cases when there is too much information to get over in one piece of copy. In court cases, voicers are virtually
standard; only rarely can you obtain audio about a court case – and almost
never while the case is progressing, because any comment could easily
become contempt of court. Voicers are also used when a big story is breaking to put over the basics of a story while audio is gathered (a 'holding
voicer'), or to preview a story – for example, before a news conference, or
before an interview has taken place on air. Preview voicers are a particularly
useful device in setting up a story in the mind of the listener and keeping the
bulletins full of local material on a slow news day. The maximum duration
of voicers varies from station to station; in general, the BBC aim for between
35 and 40 seconds, and commercial radio likes 15–25 seconds at the most –
although some commercial stations have a policy not to use voicers.

Cuts, clips and soundbites

Cuts and clips are the same thing; a cut in commercial radio and a clip in
the BBC are both short pieces of audio, which are also sometimes called
'soundbites'. They could be part of an interview or an excerpt of audio
recorded on location – anything from part of a speech to sounds of a riot.
Good cuts have a proper start and a proper finish; they should not sound
as though they have been taken from something longer. Again, the acceptable duration is slightly longer at BBC stations – up to 30 seconds or so.
Commercial stations like no more than 20 seconds maximum and, in
many cases, considerably less. Many use cuts of no more than ten seconds
to maintain the pace of a bulletin.

Wraps and packages

Once again, the words 'wrap' and 'package' both mean the same and are
usually used in commercial radio and the BBC respectively. The wrap
consists of at least one cut surrounded by a reporter's voice. It can be short –
a 'bulletin wrap' could be a single cut of ten seconds inserted in 20 seconds
of reporter's voice to make 30 seconds. Alternatively, a wrap can run three
minutes or more for use in a news programme. They are an excellent way
of putting both sides of an argument. For example:

> REPORTER: Angry parents lobbying County Hall this morning
> claimed that the increase in school meal prices will mean many

children either starving or living on unhealthy chips. Eileen
Duncan ... whose three children go to St James' Middle School
in Newtown ... says she can't possibly afford more than ten
pounds a week for their lunches alone.

CUT: DUNCAN/22″/Out: '... absolute disgrace.'

REPORTER: But councillors on the education committee are defending
the price rise. Conservative Ravi Singh says the meals are still to
be subsidized.

CUT: SINGH/25″/Out: '... see reason.'

And so on. The combination of scene-setting from the reporter and comment from people affected makes the story come alive. It would, of course,
be even better with the sound of the demonstrators chanting slogans at the
beginning.

Newsroom style guide

You will have noticed that the names of types of audio and durations vary
between the BBC and commercial radio. In fact, there are many more
minor variations depending on the philosophy of individual editors and
the style and format of the station, as well as the needs of the target audience. Almost every station develops its own 'house' style. For this reason,
a style guide is helpful. It should set out the ground rules on durations, cue
layout, audio labelling, writing style and news agenda, together with many
small details that everyone in the news team follows instinctively after a
while. It may also include important but rarely used information – for
example, bad weather or obituary procedures, or what to do if a computer
system fails. The style guide is an excellent point of reference if there is
any uncertainty and makes life much easier for new staff or occasional
freelancers working on shifts.

4 News writing

The business of radio is to communicate. If we fail to communicate, then we fail as radio journalists. Your aim must be intelligibility – *immediate* intelligibility. A carelessly turned phrase, an ambiguity of expression, a complicated sentence and an illogical sequence of events are all fatal to news on radio. There is no room in radio news bulletins for complexity, vagueness or obscurity. You must know what you want to say – and you must say it with directness, simplicity and precision.

Remember that dullness is a sin. No story should be regarded as routine. The way to capture the listener's interest is through your enthusiasm. If you take a jaded and apathetic attitude, it will produce a dull story. There is no reason to reduce every story to a flat recital of facts. Always be on the lookout for the detail that brings a story to life, such as the remark that reveals a personality or a phrase that makes a scene vivid.

If you do not make the news interesting, the listener may 'hear' the stories but they will not sink in.

Any news story can be written in a number of different ways. However, there are some basic tools and techniques which will help the journalist – and the listener.

TELLING THE STORY

Good news writing is the hallmark of good journalism. You can have the best story ever, but if you cannot put it over in a way your listener understands the first time they hear it, then you might as well not bother.

Writing for radio is deceptively simple. It should reflect that you are *telling* the story to someone, not making ministerial-like pronouncements.

You are not 'broadcasting' to the masses, just explainin
what is going on.

For the ear not the eye

You should write in a clear, crisp, concise, compelling and non-stuffy
way. Your words should not be the words of the sensational tabloid newspapers, but you should not be afraid of using informal language when
appropriate. A good story will almost write itself.

Remember, you are writing for the ear not the eye. You should write as
you speak, in colloquial English, with short sentences and one thought per
sentence. Always ask yourself, 'Would I say it that way myself?' or 'Do
my friends talk like this in the pub?' For example, only journalists write:
'Fire-fighters wearing breathing apparatus have been battling a massive
blaze at a retail store.' Real people say: 'There's a big fire at a shop in the
town centre.'

Know what you want to say and say it conversationally in everyday
language, but do not use slang or be slapdash. It takes skill and effort to write
concise, lively copy on what may seem like a complicated or detailed story.

The aim is to write news for radio as natural conversational speech tempered
with order and precision. The result is a style that is crisp, economical,
direct and colloquial. Radio prefers the short word to the long one, the
simple sentence to the complex, the concrete to the abstract, the active voice
to the passive, and the direct statement to the inverted sentence.

Before you write a story from your notes or a news release, ask yourself:
'What is this story *really* about?' and 'What is it about this story that will
really interest my listener?' It is sometimes helpful to read through your
notes or the handout, put it to one side and then try and tell the story on
paper without reference to the original source, apart from to check the
facts. It is no longer a story from a news agency, news release or colleague.
It is now *your* story. And you must tell the story as it appears to you.

Keep it short

Anybody who writes knows it is harder to write shorter. However, shorter
is often more effective.

The topline of your story must be short and snappy. Treat it as your headline. It should hook the listener's attention and make him or her want to turn up the volume. At the same time, the topline should prepare the listener for the tale of a chain of events which are unfamiliar. Remember, your listener may only be half listening, thinking about something else and about to switch off.

Do not make the mistake of trying to tell the whole story in the first line. Many newspapers do this, but it does not work in radio. Give your first line impact. Then lead the listener through the story step by step and thought by thought, with each sentence elaborating on the previous one with a well-ordered narrative. Try writing one short sentence followed by a longer one, as this helps increase the pace.

Put one thought into each sentence and avoid pairs of commas with long sub-clauses in between. By the time you read the end of such a sentence, the listener will have forgotten what the start was all about.

Try not to start with the story's most important words. People do not hear individual words on the radio but pick up groups of words or phrases. Also, try to keep the story fresh by rewriting the first line in two or three different ways for subsequent bulletins.

Be particularly careful about your choice of first word. Listeners often miss the first word as their attention is not fully engaged. It is therefore important not to begin your story with a key word or unfamiliar name. For example, 'Petrol is going to cost more' is a simple direct statement. Unfortunately, some listeners will miss the first word and be left wondering what it is that will cost more. It is usually better to risk being slightly more long-winded and say, 'The price of petrol is going up.'

Keep it simple

All radio news stories benefit from being kept simple. Try to think of word economy when writing. For example, 'A multiple crash on the M25 has left 15 people in hospital' rather than 'Thirteen cars, three lorries and a bus have collided between junctions 7 and 8 on the clockwise carriageway of the M25, leaving more than a dozen injured.'

Childlike simplicity is the essence of good radio writing. When you talk in the pub or over a cup of coffee, you usually talk in perfect radio style. For example, 'Rob's had a car accident again,' 'Carol's starting her new job today' or 'That Robinson boy's been selected for the team.'

Write to make things easier to understand for your listener. For example, 'The council tax in Blankstown may go up again' is far better than 'A meeting of the Blankstown Council finance committee heard last night that expenditure forecasts show an increase which may have to be passed on to householders.'

If you have information which your listener needs to be told, make sure you understand what he or she needs to know and why. For example, 'Blankstown Chamber of Commerce has agreed to provide low-cost public transport to the new retail park in Highfield' actually means 'There'll be cheap buses to the shops in Highfield.'

It is a good rule that if your story starts with someone's name or the name of a group ('Blankstown Council says ...'), then it needs to be rewritten with a more relatable topline.

Keep it happening now

Radio's greatest strength is its immediacy. We are doing news not history. Therefore, the use of the present tense, which gives the impression that something is 'happening now', is often appropriate, especially in the first line of stories.

Make sure you write in the present tense whenever possible. For example, 'Doctors have expressed surprise at the length of hospital waiting lists' becomes 'Doctors say they're surprised at the length of hospital waiting lists.'

Always make the subject of a sentence 'active' rather than 'passive'. For example, 'Paul Hope fired a single shot at the police officer' rather than 'The police officer was hit by a single shot fired by Paul Hope.'

Always think about how you can write about what is happening now. For example, 'A woman's in hospital after ...' or 'A family's waiting at the hospital bedside of ...'. However, beware that you should not give false impressions for the sake of this. Avoid using the word 'yesterday' unless the chronology is crucial.

Keep adjectives to a minimum

Many journalists try to amplify their stories by using too many adjectives. This has the effect of simply annoying the listener. Sometimes adjectives are necessary, but all too often they are over the top. Gimmicks and fancy words simply get in the way of the story. For example, 'crucial relegation clash'. How 'crucial' is it? Will the team get relegated if they lose, or will they just get into trouble at the bottom of the table? Using the word 'crucial' does not make this story any clearer. Make sure any adjectives you use give additional information.

Facts should be treated with the utmost respect. For example, if we do not know that a fire 'ripped' through a building, then we should not say so.

It is perfectly acceptable to add whatever 'colour' is available to a story. But if something did not happen in a certain way, you should not say it did simply to enliven your story. It is far better to have a factually correct story than a stunning couple of paragraphs which are exciting and racy but incorrect.

Talk to yourself

One of the most effective ways to write good radio news stories is to speak to yourself as you write. Sit at your computer and start talking the story to yourself. Say the facts aloud (if other people are around, you might just want to move your lips!). As the words come out in your own personal style, write them down. Then when you do the story on the air, you will be talking to someone instead of reading to them.

LANGUAGE AND GRAMMAR

There are a number of basic language rules designed to create better news writing. The list is not exhaustive and many newsroom style guides have their own favourites. Here are a few dos and don'ts:

- Do use *specific* words (such as 'red' and 'green') rather than general words (such as 'brightly coloured').
- Do use *concrete* words (such as 'rain' or 'fog') rather than abstract words (such as 'bad weather').
- Do use *plain* words (such as 'began', 'said', 'end') rather than pretentious words (such as 'commenced', 'stated', 'terminated').
- Do not overdress the story with *emotive* or *dramatic* words (such as 'astonishing', 'staggering' or 'sensational'). If what you are writing about is any of these things, it will come through without the label.

- Do not use *unnecessary* words such as 'Plans are being drawn *up*' or 'There's more to come *later*'.
- Do not use *unknown quantities* (such as 'very', 'really' and 'quite').
- Do not qualify absolutes. Something is not '*quite* impossible', it is impossible. It is not '*glaringly* obvious' or '*most* essential'.
- Do not use the word 'incident' when you mean murder, shooting, accident or explosion.
- Do not use the word 'just' when it fails to add information, as in 'The council leader's just back from London'. Do you mean in the last few seconds, minutes, hours, days or weeks?

In general, think about the language and phrases you use when you write news. You need to pay attention to the detail and think about the effect of the words you use. For example, a man may have *died* after an accident, he probably was not *killed* after one. It would have been very bad luck if he survived the crash but was shot dead two hours later. He was either *killed in* or *died after* the accident. Also, did the man die *following* an accident? Was he really running behind the car when it crashed?

Grammar needs careful attention also. Beware of the singular and plural trap. For example, the council *has*, not the council *have*. The rule is that if the body you are writing about is a single group, even if it is made up of many individuals, then it is written as singular: 'The council is ...', 'The jury is ...' and so on. However, police are plural and football teams have become that way as well. For example, England *have* won the World Cup, not England *has* won.

There is a school of thought to say that some of the basic grammatical rules of writing English are irrelevant on radio. For example, split infinitives which are grammatically incorrect but sound acceptable (the classic *Star Trek* line 'to *boldly* go' instead of 'to go *boldly*'). Each newsroom will have its own style, but in general you should try to be grammatically correct without compromising the sound of your news writing.

WRITING DEVICES

When you write for the ear, you are simply 'storing' words on paper so that you can tell someone later in the way in which you would speak. Therefore, as we have seen, radio news writing does not always follow the textbook rules of English grammar, as you are trying to recreate how you would have spoken. Therefore, you need to use a number of writing devices to enable you to make sure that a cue or piece of copy sounds as spontaneous and as natural as possible.

Contractions

You are *telling* the story; therefore, what you write should use all the normal contractions used in speech. Contractions make broadcasting sound much more natural and conversational. For example:

It is	becomes	It's
He is	becomes	He's
Do not	becomes	Don't
Should have	becomes	Should've
I am	becomes	I'm

At the start of sentences, it is also better to use a contraction when the third word is 'is'. For example, 'A man's going to make a record attempt …' or 'A hospital's appealing for more life-saving equipment …'.

However, a word of warning about how apostrophes can sometimes confuse news presenters when a last-minute story has not been read in advance. For example, sight-reading this story could cause confusion: 'England's first ever Athletic Academy's opened in Blankshire, and the nation's top talent will be looking to come and train here.'

So, if you are going to hand a script to a newsreader with minutes to spare or live on air, it is probably best to only use apostrophes for possessions, not omissions.

Punctuation

Use punctuation devices to help you recreate in speech what you have written on paper. Full stops are, of course, essential. Do not use commas or dashes, use dots instead … like that! It helps the eye of the newsreader pick up the sense of what you are writing far better. You will also find it easier to write your script and read it on air if you give each sentence a new paragraph.

Do not try to read quotations on the radio, especially when they are long. This confuses the listener, who may lose track of who is actually saying what. Is it the newsreader or the person he is reporting? Turn quotes into reported speech instead. However, there are certain times when it *is* acceptable to read quotes on air.

Jargon

Watch out for jargon when writing news stories. The sources of jargon are usually councils or the emergency services. For example, the police and ambulance services use terms like 'fractured femur' when we would say 'broken thigh'.

There is a whole host of other jargon words to watch out for from the police and fire brigade, such as:

Assistance	(help)
Request	(ask)
Terminate	(end)
Decamped	(ran off)
Released	(cut free or sent home)
Sustained injury	(was hurt)
Absconded	(escaped)

Councils are just as bad. Do not let council officers' jargon creep into your news stories. For example, a new building which, according to council papers, is 'detrimental to the visual amenity' is simply 'spoiling the view'.

Fire-fighters often use breathing apparatus. It keeps them alive. There is no need to say it all the time, although it will often appear on voicebank reports from the fire service.

In road accidents (or what the police would call 'road traffic accidents' or 'RTAs'!), try to guard against attributing blame when describing what has happened. For example, 'A man's died after a car crashed into his motorbike on the M25' becomes 'A man's died after a car was in collision with a motorbike on the M25.'

The phrase 'in collision with' is a useful, though clumsy, way of making sure no blame is attributed, even if you are told the circumstances by official sources. Remember though, that pedestrians are never 'in collision with' a car. To avoid sounding silly, use the phrase 'involved in an accident with'. You obviously do not have to use 'collision' if a vehicle hits an inanimate object because only the driver can be blamed. So 'the car hit the central reservation' is acceptable.

Journalese

A lot of shoddy radio writing is a legacy from newspapers and in particular 'headline English'. This sort of writing was developed by newspaper journalists because it consisted of short words which fitted into the confined space of a headline. These sort of words often do not belong on the radio:

- too often we 'bid' instead of attempt;
- we 'slam' instead of criticize;
- we 'probe' instead of investigate;
- we 'axe' instead of cut;
- things are 'massive' instead of big;
- more things seem to 'plunge' than fall;
- there are 'tots' instead of young children.

Watch out for these words. You can find them most often in the freelance news copy which comes into radio newsrooms written by veteran newspaper people anxious to 'sell' their story by use of hyperbolic language like this. If it is there, rewrite it. It will sound much better.

Clichés

A phrase which has now become a cliché often began life as a useful piece of verbal shorthand. Unfortunately, it has become overused to the point where it means nothing (Figure 4.1). Writing in clichés is a lazy, sloppy way of writing. Make sure you are never guilty of stringing a line of clichés together, even when you are under pressure from a deadline and the temptation is great.

Here are some clichéd words and phrases which detract from the story because they are imprecise, inappropriate or overused. It is not always possible to avoid using them, but do try and your writing will improve in clarity and precision.

row brewing	self-made men
open the floodgates	fabricated lies
up in arms	gifted students
rushed to hospital	notorious gamblers
last ditch	noted authors
pave the way	wealthy recluses
top people	intrepid travellers
eleventh hour	distinguished diplomats
trouble flared	astute lawyers
police quizzed	slick politicians
miracle escape	successful businessmen
limped into port	seething masses
daring raiders	ugly rumours
heartless thieves	true confessions
dawn swoop	tall tales
full-scale murder hunt	high hopes
looming large	badly decomposed
tributes are pouring in	brutal murder or rape
police are stepping up their search for	bears all the hallmarks
	last ditch bid
police are growing increasingly concerned for	eleventh hour bid
	on a knife edge
sifting through the rubble	grim discovery / task
brandishing a gun	hitting back / out
wielding a knife	coming to terms with
thrown his hat into the ring	has been launched

Figure 4.1
A list of well-worn clichés

Some adjectives come to mind as soon as their noun is mentioned, but they say the same thing twice and add little to the sense:

serious danger	all-time record
acute crises	active consideration
mass exodus	high-speed chase
brutal murder	fast getaway

With feature stories particularly (as opposed to hard news stories), use can be made of turns of phrase which fit with the story content. However, be careful that those used are not clichés themselves. It is no longer considered original to say, for example, that increased airline profits mean the airline is 'flying high', or that problems with a train company mean it is 'going off the rails'.

Be careful to avoid topline clichés such as this: 'Detectives are investigating an incident in Blankstown after a man was bundled into a car, driven to London and attacked.' The story here is in the second half of the sentence, not that police are investigating!

Americanisms

There are many techniques we can learn from American radio, but the way Americans have changed the English language is not one of them!

Do watch for the more extreme Americanisms which appear regularly in films and TV drama. Words like 'hospitalized' are familiar on TV but they are not words our listener is likely to use.

Also try to avoid American pronunciation. One of the worst examples is the word 'schedule', which is often heard on air as 'sked-yule' rather than 'shed-yule'. Another is the army rank 'lieutenant', which is some-times pronounced the American way of 'lootenant' instead of the British 'lefftenant'. If we cannot get our own language correct, it says very little for our credibility!

Names

You should aim for a deliberately informal and conversational style. It should not therefore be necessary to use the prefixes 'Mr' and 'Mrs'. For example, Tony Blair or George W. Bush are perfectly acceptable. However, prefixes should be used in subsequent references, i.e. Mr Blair or Mr Bush. The surname should never be used on its own. This happens in America but in Britain it smacks of disrespect and can be interpreted as bias against the particular individual or party.

Prefixes are not necessary for showbiz or sporting personalities, i.e. Brad Pitt, Ronan Keating, David Beckham. The second reference for such people need only be Pitt, Keating, Beckham.

The prefix should also be dropped for criminals such as Harold Shipman and Osama bin Laden, although you must judge whether the use of a prefix later in the story would be unduly respectful.

Use Christian names rather than initials. If you cannot get a Christian name, it sounds better to leave out the name altogether, rather than using an initial which sounds very odd. Some officials, such as police officers and teachers, are often reticent to give their first names. You have to persuade them otherwise. It sounds too formal and will not fit with your news style to introduce someone as 'PC Smith' or 'Head Teacher Mrs Jones'.

Dates

Make sure the dates you use in news writing as relatable as the other information. Avoid making people work out the time-scale for themselves. It is far more relatable to say 'three weeks from today' rather than 'August 27th' or 'next March' rather than 'March 2004', or 'next Tuesday' rather than 'September 24th'.

Numbers

Numbers can be tricky to include in stories, especially when they are large. Only use figures if you must. The listener cannot always take in large sums.

Always write the numbers out in your cue or copy so they are easy to read. Mixing words and figures makes it easier to see instantly what the amount is and how to say it. Writing the words you will say rather than using a sign saves your eye from darting back and forth through the sentence:

400,000	becomes	400 thousand
4600	becomes	4 thousand 6 hundred
£50	becomes	50 pounds
£1.90	becomes	1 pound 90

Never use complex numbers. Always round them up or down:

9.6%	becomes	nearly 10 per cent
£4,898,785	becomes	almost 5 million pounds

If you have a foreign currency, it sounds silly to say a British person 'was fined 9 thousand pounds' by a court in the US. Say instead '12 thousand US dollars' or 'the equivalent of 9 thousand pounds'.

Also, for the sake of sounding conversational, say 'Two and a half million' rather than 'two point five million'.

Comparisons

To avoid using complicated figures, it often helps to use analogies such as 'the pile of rubbish is now as high as a double-decker bus.'

It is often easier for your audience to understand something they are not familiar with if you compare it to something with which they are. The amount of money wasted by a government department, for example, may be compared to 'the national debt of the African state of X'. Radio One's audience of 15- to 24-year-olds were told of an asteroid with the line: 'Space watchers find an asteroid the size of Creamfields heading for earth at 17 miles a second.' The comparison with the size of a recognizable music venue made more of an audience connection, and the 'speed per second' rather than 'per hour' increases the understanding of the story.

CUES

The cue into audio is the link between the reporter, the bulletin presenter and the listener. Ideally, the listener will understand exactly what the reporter is saying through the medium of the presenter. However, this ideal may stand or fall on the quality of the cue. Let us look at a working example of how a cue develops and some of the pitfalls in cue writing.

The topline

A good cue has the story 'up top' but, as we saw earlier, not all in the first line. Cramming too much into the topline confuses the listener. Here is an example of a confusing topline which was actually broadcast:

'The Blankshire case of the murder of a Chinese chef in Blankstown which involves the largest number of defendants ever to appear in one case in the county is to be tried in a ballroom.'

In our working example, here is a crammed topline:

'More than 2 hundred beds are set to close at St John's Hospital in Blankstown in the coming year because the district health authority has been forced to save 1 million pounds to meet government spending targets.'

That is the essence of the story, but you probably had to read it twice to get the sense of it and anyone hearing the words read aloud would certainly lose track somewhere. A better way of writing the cue and topline would be:

> 'More than 2 hundred beds are set to close at a Blankshire hospital because of government spending restrictions.'

> 'The warning has come from the St John's Hospital trust in Blankstown ... which needs to save 1 million pounds by the end of next year.'

By dividing the story into two shorter sentences it becomes much easier to understand first time round – and remember the listener has only one chance to hear it. By contrast, a newspaper story can be read again and again.

It is usual for a local cue to have a general location in the first paragraph followed by the more specific town name in the second paragraph. This is so listeners who are not in the town where the story is happening do not tune-out in the first few seconds. However, you must not fall into the trap of starting each story in a similar way – for example, 'A Blankshire hospital ...', 'A Blankshire school ...', 'A Blankshire MP ...'.

Going into detail

Having started the story with your topline, you need to expand on it. However, be careful of making the cue too long, as the listener may become bored with the story before the audio is played. A good cue provides the context for the audio which follows; it is not intended to tell the whole story unaided.

However, you may add something like:

> 'But the decision is angering some councillors ... who say the trust is already struggling through lack of cash brought about by previous government restrictions.'

This paragraph prepares our listener to hear an angry councillor. But try not to be led astray into exhaustive detail of previous spending cuts, a list of 12 other hospitals in the county affected by economies, or what the BMA said about the government last June. In a long newspaper article, they would all have their place, but you have perhaps one minute or less to tell the whole story – including the audio cut.

Into the audio

A good middle paragraph in a cue sets the stage for the audio cut which follows. We go into the actual audio with an 'in-line' like this:

'Labour's Steve West... who represents Witham ward... says the government is trying to run down the health service at the expense of people in the area.'

You may also want to write the name of the station in order to reinforce station identification:

'Labour's Steve West... who represents Witham ward... has been telling Radio Blankshire the government...'.

The audio cut

The words of Mr West which follow should add something fresh. Avoid, at all costs, a 'double cue'. The above example would be a 'double cue' if his first words were: 'This government is trying to run down the NHS at the expense of people in the area.'

If those *were* his first words, we need a complementary in-line like:

'Labour's Steve West... who represents Witham ward... says these new economies will hit everyone.'

A double cue should be avoided because it tells the listener exactly what he or she is about to hear, so taking all the dramatic impact out of the audio which follows and making it superfluous. Radio news is all about impact.

Cue layout

Every radio station has its own style of cue layout, but any cue should include the following essentials:

- the date;
- the reporter's name or initials;

- a name for the story (known as the 'catchline' or 'slug');
- the cue itself;
- the duration of the audio cut;
- the out cue of the audio cut;
- the total running time of the cue (calculated by reading the cue to your-self, by counting three words to a second) or automatically totalled by the computer;
- any special notes to help the Bulletin Editor.

Cues should be arranged simply and logically. Avoid using capital letters throughout except for strong emphasis and for complicated names and places (Figure 4.2).

Start a new paragraph for each sentence and indent it at the beginning of the line; this helps the cue's 'readability', as the eye finds it easier to pick up indents. It also helps to see how long you have to go before taking a breath when reading!

Keep to the same catchlines or slugs for each story and updates to avoid confusion between stories. Add the letters 'rw' for rewrites, 'ud' for

---

Chantler	28.10.02	pm bulls

EMBARGOED UNTIL 1300

HOSPITAL / West

More than 2 hundred beds are set to close at a Blankshire hospital because of government spending restrictions.

The warning has come from the St John's Hospital trust in Blankstown ... which needs to save one million pounds by the end of next year.

But the decision is angering some councillors ... who say the trust is already struggling through lack of cash brought about by previous government restrictions.

Labour's Steve West ... who represents Witham ward ... says the government is trying to run down the health service at the expense of people in the area ...

CUT: HOSPITAL / West
DUR: 24 secs
OUT: ... harder all the time

(54 secs)

Figure 4.2
A typical cue

updates and 'add' for additional copy. Your cue and audio should have corresponding catchlines so you play the clip with the correct story! Beware of slugs which are too generic and could cause problems ('snow', 'accident') or ones which are too obscure and have little to do with the story.

The bulletin reader should mark each cue sheet with the hour in which it ran. That way it is easier to realize when the story is due for a rewrite, or to be dropped.

AVOIDING OFFENCE

We live in sensitive times. Many of the words and phrases which used to be employed freely are now no longer allowable in normal conversation, never mind news bulletins.

Never use offensive labels. Stick to the facts. If someone is black, then they are black not 'coloured'. You should also say when someone is white or Asian. Race is not the only thing which can cause problems. Sex is another. It is likely to upset many people if you assume that a certain group is all male (or all female). For example:

> Firemen are at the scene ...
> Policemen are warning that ...
> The average nurse says she's not paid enough.

There are a number of alternatives:

> 'policemen' become 'police officers'
> 'firemen' become 'fire-fighters'
> 'ambulancemen' become 'ambulance crews'
> 'housewives' become 'shoppers'
> 'spokesman' becomes 'spokeswoman' if applicable (but never
>   'spokesperson')
> 'chairman' becomes 'chairwoman' if applicable (but never
>   'chair', which is something you sit on!)

However, do not take things to the extreme, where the word is unlikely to be used in everyday speech. You are not a politically correct mouthpiece. For example, a reporter once referred to a group of tough-looking fishermen as 'fisherfolk'!

Sexual matters can be difficult to describe. Obviously insults like 'queer' and 'poof' are unacceptable, but 'gay' has become an acceptable synonym

DISABLED PEOPLE

Language to Avoid	**Useful Language**
The disabled	Disabled people
The blind	Blind people
Deaf and dumb	Deaf people
Mentally handicapped/retarded	People with learning disabilities
Dwarf/midget	Small person
Siamese twins	Conjoined twins
Carer	Personal assistant
A psychotic	Person who is mentally ill
Wheelchair-bound	Wheelchair-user
Handicapped toilet	Accessible toilet
Suffers from …	Has …

Figure 4.3
A list of appropriate language and language to avoid for disabled people

for homosexual. If someone is homosexual, do not look for bland euphemisms. They will not thank you and neither will the listener.

Disabled people do not much care for words like 'crippled' either. Someone who has no legs is a 'disabled person' (better than 'handicapped') and has a 'disability' (Figure 4.3).

One more area where offence can be caused is politics. It is up to politicians to describe their allegiance. If they say they are 'Independent Conservatives' then you must not shorten that to 'Conservative'.

Be careful also of words like 'moderate', 'radical' and 'extremist'. Useful shorthand they may be, but it is not always for us to make these identifications. 'Extremists', for example, can be a term of abuse. Leave the abuse to politicians – report it by all means, but do not join in, even by accident.

Check the meanings *and* impact of words you use. The government *is* technically 'a regime'. But the word is now often used as an insult and is better avoided. If in doubt, look it up. Every newsroom should have a good dictionary. Make it a working tool.

PUTTING STORIES IN CONTEXT

It is important that the listener hears the full story in its original context and is not misled by the way it is written. Remember you only get one chance to put over a point on radio. The listener cannot go back and hear what you said, in the way he or she can re-read a newspaper story.

You have a responsibility which is different from a newspaper journalist. You select exactly what stories you want your listener to hear. In newspapers, there are many stories on a page, all with different styles and sizes of headlines to attract attention. On radio, the listener is presented with a single thread of material with no headlines. Importance is determined by position in the bulletin and there are certain rules which make for more logical writing and, as a result, listening.

Attribution

Never start your story with an unattributed statement or controversial claims. It could sound like fact or even the opinion of the radio station. Especially in controversial matters, make sure the listener knows the source of the opinion being expressed at the beginning of the story.

For example, 'Most managers are mean. That's the finding of a new survey out today' becomes 'A new survey out today claims that most managers are mean.' Each sentence has to be true in itself. For example, it would be wrong to write 'The gap between rich and poor in Britain is growing. That's the claim in a new Labour party report.' Therefore, you should write: 'A new Labour party report claims the gap between rich and poor in Britain is growing.'

It also sounds much more natural and gives the listener a better idea of the authority behind the statement. For example, nobody would ever say in normal speech: 'The price of coffee is going up again, according to the grocer.' Instead you would say: 'The grocer says the price of coffee's going up again.' The same principle applies to radio writing, which is trying to achieve this kind of naturalness in speech.

Exaggeration

It becomes very easy sometimes to exaggerate somebody's case. For example, the most dangerous place on a cue is as an in-line to a cut: 'Mr Greenslade is denying the claim,' when in fact all he is saying is that there is no evidence to support it. The correct in-line in this case would be: 'Mr Greenslade says there's no proof of the claim.'

You should also aim for much more precision when using words commonly used in tabloid newspaper journalism:

- Has the council 'angrily' rejected a claim against it, or just 'strongly'?
- Is a 'massive police hunt' really underway or is it really a 'full-scale police search'?
- Is the party really 'split' or is it only a small group which is out of step?
- Is that 'row' in the Labour group really 'major' or is the case simply being put by a handful of councillors?

Cause and effect

As already explained, you have just one chance to grab your listener's attention and keep it, so stories must be instantly understandable. So explain the *cause* of what happened before the *effect*.

This is especially important with disasters and death tolls. For example, 'A coach has crashed on the M25 in Essex killing 12 people' rather than 'Twelve people have been killed and 20 injured on the M25 in Essex when a coach crashed.'

Remember also to think carefully about what the story actually is. Always ask yourself, 'What is the *real* story here?' For example, police may be appealing for witnesses after a woman died in an accident on the M1, but the real story is the *fact* that the woman died in the accident.

Casualty figures

Always pick low estimates of casualty figures, especially in reporting major accidents or disasters. It does no harm to your authority if the death toll rises, but credibility is damaged when dead people come alive!

Organizations

It is not always necessary to give the full name of an organization, particularly those with long titles. For example, 'train drivers' union' is acceptable for the 'Associated Society of Locomotive Engineers and Firemen' or 'ASLEF'.

Where initials are used – for example, the CBI – the first reference in your story should always be prefaced by a brief description such as 'The employers' organization, the CBI' or 'The journalists' union, the NUJ'.

Titles

It is more logical in radio for a person's title to come before their name. For example, 'The council chairman Steve Murray' rather than the newspaper style of 'Steve Murray, the council chairman'. The role of the person speaking is more important than their actual name.

Descriptions

Think about the value of running a description of someone wanted by police in a crime story. Does it really narrow down the number of people who could be responsible? Take this real example which was broadcast: 'A 63-year-old woman's been seriously assaulted in a street robbery in Blankstown. The attack happened in Dunster Avenue when the woman was punched in the face and her handbag snatched. The only description of the attacker so far is that he is male.'

The truth

The single most important part of local radio journalism is always to tell the truth. At the end of every sentence you write, ask yourself whether what you have just written is strictly accurate. There are frequently untruths in news writing. For example, the use of plural for singular as in 'Tory councillors are demanding ...' when you know of only one councillor.

5 News bulletins

THE NEWS AGENDA

The news bulletin is the showcase of the radio journalist. It is the chance to give the listener a good idea of what is happening in just a few minutes.

Bulletins are governed by a radio station's news agenda: the policy set which determines which stories are covered in what way and in what style.

Your target listener

All newsrooms, commercial and BBC, have different news agendas and it is impossible to generalize. However, the starting point for the news agenda is likely to be the radio station's target audience, determined by the Programme Director. The news bulletins therefore focus on the stories that interest or affect their listener.

Such stories could include, for example:

- the environment (not just the 'green' thing, but what is happening around the area);
- the economy (mortgages, wages, the cost of living);
- crime (how safe is it on the streets? what is being done?);
- health (doctors, hospitals, the NHS);
- education (the state of schools, teaching methods);
- transport and travel (roads and railways);

- sport and leisure (big teams and major pastimes);
- national politics (the personalities and their policies);
- local politics (what is happening of county-wide or national significance).

Some commercial stations have conducted detailed research into what sort of stories their target listeners want to hear. As a result, they have adjusted their news agenda to highlight environmental and health stories.

Other stations are moving away from traditional news values and concentrating almost entirely on 'news you can use', such as consumer stories and health issues. When they do stories about accidents, for example, they focus not on the accident itself but more on the disruption caused. There is also an increasing use of the words 'you', 'yours', 'we' and 'ours' in bulletin writing on some stations to create a sense of empathy.

The majority of UK stations, though, continue to be influenced by the traditional news values of the BBC, with many programmers regarding the local news bulletins as a way of injecting real-life, relatable, local drama into their music output.

Whatever a station's news values, it is all about competing for the listener's attention. The day has long gone when 'listening to the news' was a solemn rite, marked by the family dropping all other activities to gather round the radio set.

It is not that people are less interested in the news. What has happened is that the whole pattern of living has changed. The family circle is now less close, there are frequent interruptions as well as other activities and interests.

Now all radio stations must compete for attention. Radio can no longer 'command' an audience. Radio must *woo* it. That is the challenge.

It is not enough merely to broadcast news. It is your job to make sure that news is listened to *and understood*. To inform, we must interest.

Socio-economic groups

Marketing professionals use this broad classification of the population to help them talk about different types of people. In the main it refers to the job they do, and therefore how much money they earn. For commercial radio, it is obviously important to target the largest group with the most amount of money that can be spent on the products advertised on the station. This is usually the ABC1 combination of categories.

BBC local radio, with its remit of 'extending choice', often targets those who feel left out, the C2DE groups. Although the BBC has to justify its licence fee to the whole population, it also has a duty to serve 'minority groups', and as they have no advertising time to sell, they can afford to have lower listening figures in the process.

- A: Higher managerial or professional person – such as a judge, manager of a large company, top civil servant, head teacher.
- B: Intermediate managerial or professional – solicitor, manager of a smaller company, many mid-range civil servants, school year heads.
- C1: Junior managerial, supervisory, clerical – clerk, office manager, teacher and journalist.
- C2: Skilled manual – machinery operator, lathe worker.
- D: Semi-skilled or unskilled manual worker – rubbish collector.
- E: State pensioner, widow, casual worker and student.

Relevance

The key consideration in whether or not to include an item in a news bulletin is its *relevance*. Each story must earn its place in the bulletin by having an effect on the listener's life as determined by the target focus of the news agenda. This effect can be directly through, say, the listener's council charge being increased, or indirectly by something which triggers the listener's emotions through sympathy or empathy.

When making editorial judgements, you should always ask yourself: What does this *mean* to my listener?

Be careful with world news on local radio. Some stations, especially on the BBC, have a policy of including a high proportion of international news. But others, including many commercial stations, prefer to concentrate on home news. A well-known test at a radio training centre used to give students a news story about rebels blockading a port in Ceylon. What was the relevance of the story to the listener in Britain? Many thought it had little – until they found out it would affect supplies of tea!

Also watch stories which come from council chambers. Many of them are very dull tales of petty political infighting or things which people generally neither care about nor understand. Unless there is a story which really does affect someone outside the councils (such as dustbins being collected, roads being built or schools being shut), think twice about covering it. As a general rule, go with stories which affect *people*. Ditch those which do not. Remember, a story which affects the listener should be written as such – for example, 'Rubbish bins in Blankshire may go unemptied next week because council staff voted ...' instead of 'Blankshire Council refuse collectors have decided to ...'.

It is all about balance and judgement. A radio journalist running a busy newsdesk has to weigh the important against the interesting many times a day.

Quality versus quantity

If a news item needs artificial support to help it stand up, it is not really worth telling. It is an unfortunate fact that many local radio stations throw at their listener a barrage of dull and boring stories simply because they are trying to fill a mythical 'quota' of local news. One commercial radio station group has a policy of always leading with a local story and to have 70 per cent of a bulletin's content as local. Although local stories should carry more weight and appear higher in a bulletin than most national stories, this blanket policy can make for uncomfortable listening. Quality should never suffer for the sake of quantity. The listener soon notices.

Place names

Local radio deals with local stories. Try to emphasize the local angle as high up in your local stories as possible. For example, 'Police are warning women not to walk alone at night after a series of attacks. The call comes after three indecent assaults in Blankstown,' becomes 'Women are being warned not to walk alone at night after three indecent assaults in Blankstown.'

Also try to get as many place names in your bulletins as possible by frequently including lots of short, two-line copy stories from around your area. It quickens the pace of a bulletin and makes your listener feel as though you are covering their town or village, even though you do not always have reporters on the ground. If you find an excuse for giving a list of place names then do it, within reason. A good example of this is when there is a large fire, say in Maidstone, and you can say that 'Crews have been called in from Tonbridge, Tunbridge Wells and Sevenoaks.'

The 'life' of a story

Stories need freshening as much as possible. Rewrite as often as you can. If you are working on a story for the following morning's breakfast bulletins, try to provide a second cut or clip with a different angle in the cue. This helps provide variety in the bulletins, as the two versions will be used in alternate bulletins – for example, one version of the story in the 6 a.m. and 8 a.m. bulletins, the other at 7 a.m. and 9 a.m. Generally, a story will last for no more than three broadcasts. After that, it should be dropped, rewritten completely or moved on. With constantly changing and fast-moving stories, it is easy to freshen each hour and the benefits of doing this – whatever the pressures in the newsroom – are enormous; the listener feels up to date from hour to hour. Certainly, at breakfast time, a listener is more likely to hear two consecutive bulletins than alternate ones, so using two versions of a story helps to keep bulletins fresh.

BULLETIN STYLES

The style of a bulletin is not merely down to the stories chosen by the News Editor. It is also the words chosen in writing the story, how it is read, the duration of the clips, the duration of the bulletin and whether it is presented 'dry' or over a 'music bed'.

'Infotainment'

Infotainment is the term widely used when referring to the populist, often research-led, bulletin style that many commercial stations have adopted. It is argued that more traditional news bulletins are often top-heavy with stories that listeners *should* want to know about, rather than the ones they actually do. News Editors say that this other news agenda fits better with the overall station style as it contains a mixture of 'information and entertainment', often called 'the news you can use'. The stories can be mainly consumer and entertainment news rather than stories specifically from the station's broadcast area. Supporters say in this respect local news means stories which are local to their sphere of interest rather than geographically local.

its way, this policy is no different from that employed by other radio stations, newspapers and television news programmes – providing information in a package that the audience finds most accessible.

Youth stations

Stations such as Kiss in London take the 'infotainment' concept further than most other UK broadcasters. Bulletins are slanted mainly towards music and entertainment news. This kind of broadcast is less about 'the news' but more about 'what's going on in the world'. There may be mention of what might be called a political story in the widest sense of the term, but the angle chosen will be the most relatable and the duration of the story will be short. Radio One is another good example where journalists clearly aim their news: bulletins are short and clearly targeted. The station's excellent *Newsbeat* programme is written, presented and produced in a style that fits with the music around the bulletin.

Versioned bulletins

Several BBC local stations are using their different frequencies to provide more geographically specific bulletins for their listeners. This is, no doubt, in response to newer, smaller commercial radio stations starting, which cover more 'grass roots' stories. With versioned bulletins, it is usual for two bulletins to be prepared, each comprising stories of interest to listeners on a specific frequency – which may be news from towns in that area, as well as county-wide, national and international stories. The bulletins may be read simultaneously by readers in two different studios, or one may be pre-recorded and another read live. It is, of course, imperative that each bulletin is exactly the same duration.

At some of the older commercial radio stations, frequencies are often split between AM and FM rather than geographically. The EMAP Group, for example, has hit music for 18- to 34-year-olds on FM, and music for an older demographic on its network of Magic AM stations. Journalists prepare different bulletins, whose story choice, writing and presentation style reflect that station's target audience. Each localized Magic bulletin, read to a predetermined length, is recorded and then played out centrally alongside similarly recorded bulletins on different frequencies around the country. In the meantime, the journalist is reading a bulletin live to the local FM audience.

Regional bulletins

Often, several BBC stations in one area transmit the same programme in off-peak hours. For example, in the south and south-east of England, BBC Radios Kent, Southern Counties, Oxford, Berkshire and Solent join together between 7 p.m. and 1 a.m. On these occasions the news bulletins comprise stories contributed by the individual stations.

The regional reader is sent stories that are rewritten to suit a regional audience (for example, there may be assumptions made by local journalists which are removed or expanded on to ensure the whole audience understands the story).

The bulletins usually lead with the top national story unless a big breaking story is happening in the region, and that is followed by the top regional story – regardless of which station that is from. After that, the reader will try for a geographic mix – although if one patch has a lot more going on, the bulletin may be heavier on stories from that station. The news presenter must consider how each bulletin will sound in each area and whether each station is adequately covered. It also helps if they have a fairly broad knowledge of the region, so they know the relative values of the stories – and how to pronounce the place names!

The hub

Some British commercial radio station groups are experimenting with this way of working from the United States and Australia. It involves experienced staff at a central newsroom choosing and rewriting national news so it fits with an agreed group style. These are mixed with stories contributed by reporters 'in the field', maybe one or two based at each of the group's stations. Bulletins are recorded by experienced readers based at the central hub, and are played out locally from a computer when needed.

News hubs free staff at the stations to go out and record audio on site, rather than be at the station taking network feeds and presenting bulletins. It also means the bulletins sound more professional as they are presented by experienced readers. Critics, however, point out that job cuts seem inevitable, that field reporters working alone may suffer from a lack of k and motivation, and that readers based many miles away may tle interest or understanding in the stories put in the bulletins.

Pre-recorded bulletins

Critics of versioned bulletins and the news hub system say that news bulletins should never be recorded, as the stories stand the inevitable risk of being out of date.

Supporters argue that a recorded bulletin, sometimes as little as five minutes old, means that listeners get a better read or more clearly targeted bulletin than they otherwise would. To many traditional journalists, recording news bulletins in any way is anathema; news is always live.

Multi versions

A newer technique which has developed in the US and is starting to appear here is the idea of multi version stories, not to be confused with versioned bulletins (see above).

This is simply a way of enhancing and elongating a particular story and 'stripping' it across the same bulletin on each day of the week. You prepare five different angles of one story – say a row about the building of a new airport. These can be voicers, wraps or straightforward interview clips. Then they are presented on air as part of a series over the course of a week in the same news bulletin – for example, the peak bulletin on many stations at 8 a.m. Each part is introduced on air as part of a series – for example, '… and now for the second in our series of special reports about the row over building Blankshire's new airport.' It is important to recap the salient points of the whole series in each cue.

The multi version method gives a story variety. It breaks it up into pieces to keep people listening longer and gets them hooked. If the listener hears only one version of your story, he or she should feel satisfied. However, if listeners hear all the parts, they should feel 'full'.

BULLETIN ESSENTIALS

Accuracy

There is no excuse for sloppy, inaccurate reporting. You must check all the facts and make sure they are correct. If the story comes from the police, make sure you have spoken to the right person – a duty inspector, station sergeant or press officer. If you are making factual statements, make sure you know your facts or check them.

The best advice is *check, check and check again*. If accuracy falls down, so does the radio station's credibility – and with it your own journalistic reputation.

There is an old journalistic maxim which is still as relevant today as it was years ago: 'When in doubt, find out – if still in doubt, leave it out.'

Taste

Be careful not to upset your listener unnecessarily with tasteless gory detail. Some things are gruesome and horrible enough. Remember that your listener may be eating, drinking or playing with the children while listening to the radio. Torsos being cut up or blood-and-guts stories do not go down well with a family at the breakfast table.

Never run a story simply to excite your listener with sex or violence. Naturally, when there are grounds for public concern, stories involving sex and violence have to be covered – for example, a child cruelty case which the social services department should have prevented. However, try to emphasize the reason for legitimate public concern.

When describing a rape, it is sufficient to say 'raped' rather than 'brutally' or 'violently' raped.

When you have to describe acts of violence, you should avoid excitable language. Remember understatement is often more effective and has more impact. For example, 'The man was blasted in the head with a sawn-off shotgun and left lying in a pool of blood' becomes 'A man came up behind him and shot him once in the head.'

Balance and fairness

It is the job of a radio newsroom to reflect all opinions and give people criticized on the air the opportunity to reply. A balance may not necessarily be achieved within one bulletin, but over a period of time. For example, if a protester criticizes the chairman of the education committee about a schools closure on the 8 a.m. news bulletin on Monday morning, it would be appropriate to have the education committee chairman's reply to that on the 8 a.m. news bulletin on Tuesday morning. This allows both sides of the argument to reach the same audience, albeit on consecutive days.

Tone

As well as being clear and concise, a good radio news bulletin should be authoritative and non-patronizing, never insulting the intelligence of your listener. All you need to do is remember these guiding principles and they should automatically be reflected in the tone of your writing.

Comment

Needless to say, you should avoid commenting at all on any story. Your job is to be dispassionate and objective. Remember that your view on a story can sometimes be detected by the tone in which you read it on air. Beware and play it straight.

Signposting

It has to be remembered at all times that people are doing different things when they are listening to the radio – in fact, this is one of the medium's greatest strengths. However, it does also mean that they may not be listening to every part of your bulletin. This is why many formats require the newsreader to use 'signposts' within a bulletin. To ensure the audience knows when the subject matter is changing, they are 'signposted' or 'flagged' within news bulletins with a tag saying 'Health news ...', 'Environment news ...' or 'In showbiz ...'.

Experts

Developing your own panel of experts to add insight to a story is a valuable thing for bulletins. When a big story breaks, say an outbreak of a contagious disease at a local hospital, it is very useful for you to call upon your own local medical expert to interpret and explain. You can build a team of experts in areas such as transport, politics, science, medicine, the law and many other specialities. Take some time to identify the correct people in your area and then arrange for them to be willing to take phone calls from your station. It is particularly important to establish how early in the morning they are able to take phone calls, so they are not bothered at 5 a.m. by a keen young reporter. However, it is useful to be able to call about 7.30 a.m. so a piece can be prepared for your main news bulletin of the day at 8 a.m.

Kickers

These can be funny, showbiz or quirky items which are run for their entertainment or humour value first and information second! Their inclusion not only puts a smile on the face of the listener after a bulletin of more serious content, but also eases the transition back to the music presenter. Some stations have a policy of always ending with a 'kicker' or 'and finally', although you should be careful not to include one if you have to repeat the top story ('the phone number for the murder incident room again …').

If you are going to present a kicker in a situation where the presenter can respond, give them an idea of the story beforehand so they can come up with a quip. There's little worse than a forced funny line, which is not funny. A golden rule about kickers is they can only be used once. Like a joke, the impact is lost on a second telling.

Do not forget to keep your credibility as a newsperson. You can, and should, have a personality as you read the news and be able to present lighter stories as well as the more serious news items. You should be able to laugh along with and contribute to the rest of the programming. But presenters should never laugh *at* you on air, pick you up on a possible inaccuracy, or ask you a question that you may not know the answer to. You are the voice of news for the station. There can be humour certainly, but in time of crisis or a breaking story, the audience must know who they can trust.

6 News presentation

READING THE NEWS

A phrase that is added to many advertisements as a requirement for jobs in radio news is '… and a good microphone voice'. But what is a 'good microphone voice'?

A lot of it is down to interpretation, but it is certainly one which has clarity and credibility and is free from verbal 'ticks'. Those with weak r's or lisps are still uncommon on radio (Jonathan Ross being the celebrated exception!). The balance of male and female voices has levelled – indeed, there are probably more female news presenters than male – although undoubtedly more male *music* presenters. Most listeners are said to dislike shrill voices, which may put some women at a disadvantage, but they also dislike male voices which sound overly young. And although more 'regional' voices are heard on national radio news bulletins (Scots, Irish, Welsh), the likelihood of a strong Brummie, Glaswegian or Geordie accent being heard in the same role seems a while off yet. On local stations, a newsreader with the same local accent as their listeners will be welcomed much more than a local accent from elsewhere – 'received pronunciation' (RP or 'the Queen's English') is still the most accepted newsreading voice.

When commercial radio started in 1973, many stations employed 'news-readers' alongside 'journalists'. The readers were those who had good voices, maybe actors, and their job was simply to read the news. Now most stations have journalists who can read, write *and* report, although news hubs may again employ specific readers to read several bulletins each hour.

As well as the voice, those who read the news must possess other qualities. An ability to convey the information accurately and with the correct tone, emphasis and speed is obviously important – as we shall see. Sight reading is an obvious advantage too. Although most scripts should be read well in advance of going to air (see page 92) breaking news stories require presenters to read straight from a script (which could just be as brief as a few words, usually not even written as a sentence) and make sense of it to the listener. In such circumstances, one must remain unruffled and in control, and the term 'news *anchor*' is a well-deserved one in such a situation.

A good news presenter or newsreader can make even dull stories sound reasonably interesting, but a poor presenter can kill a hot story by reading it incompetently. And that leads to listeners tuning out either mentally or physically. In which case, what would be the point in everyone putting in the hard work of writing and interviewing if the presentation is sub-standard?

The style of newsreading is as important as the stories you choose to run and how they are written. The different ways of presenting the bulletins are merging, and on the whole they can be summed up as 'approachable authority'. But, from the dry and formal presentation of Radio Four to the slick and speedy presentation of Radio One, the bulletins should complement the formats of the programmes around them. Having said that, though, whatever the style, newsreading basics remain the same.

Sound interested

A ground rule for news presentation is that you must actually be interested in the material. That means you must *sound* interested. If you do not care – and let it show – the listener is very unlikely to bother either. If you sound as though you are reading the news, you are doing it wrong. If you sound like you are talking to someone about something interesting, you are doing it correctly.

Understand the story

You must always remember you are telling a story – bringing to life the words printed on a piece of paper. You must understand everything you read. You depend heavily on the reporters who wrote the copy but, because you must understand news to present it, never hesitate to query

83

which is uncertain. If you have to ask about it, the chances are the listener, who cannot ask questions of anyone, will be left ly in the dark.

If it helps you to communicate the ideas, then feel free to express yourself in other ways than purely through the words. You may want to frown when you read a sad or serious story, or smile when you have a kicker to read. A complicated story may benefit in the telling if you gesticulate. Speaking to thousands of people at once is an unnatural thing to do, even more so when you cannot see them, and these techniques are what you would do if you were speaking on a one-to-one basis – which is what radio essentially still is.

Check and rehearse

Unless there is no alternative, avoid reading copy on the air unseen. It is too easy to misread something and realize only as the words are leaving your mouth that you have placed completely the wrong emphasis on the story. Read all your copy out loud in advance if you can. A few minutes spent on rehearsal is never wasted.

By reading through beforehand, you can spot unfamiliar words, foreign place names, super-long sentences, a typographical error, or words which you personally can have trouble with. One of the writers of this book, for example, always changes 'rural' to 'countryside', and always underlines 'county' and 'country' so the wrong one is not said instead.

Other potentially problematic phrases that work well on paper, but can lead to misinterpretation on air, include:

'Chelsea scored two goals, Tottenham one/won'
'He was discovered lying dead by (rather than beside) the telephone box'
'… and has fatal/facial injuries'

Despite years of experience, many readers still have the intro and outro phrases to the bulletin written somewhere in the studio. It has been known, when all has been going smoothly, for the newsreader to use the name of the station they *used* to work for, or even to forget their own name!

Technically speaking

A well-read bulletin can be spoilt by a silly technical mistake. For example, 'I'm sorry about that, we'll try to bring you that report in our next bulletin' or 'I'm sorry, that wasn't the Prime Minister ... it was the secretary of the Farmers' Union.'

These embarrassing and unprofessional slips can usually be avoided. If you 'drive' the bulletin yourself, check the menu of your playout system. Is the audio all cued properly? Is it all in the right order? Have you got all the audio you need at your fingertips? If someone else drives the bulletin, have they got all the audio? Do they understand the order in which the audio must be played? Do they know which story might be dropped if there is an overrun? It may be praiseworthy to 'get out' of a technical error with aplomb, but a thousand times better not to let it happen in the first place.

Breathe in ... and relax

There are a number of good books on voice production and if you have any doubts about your own abilities, read one of them. Be aware, though, that such books are frequently intended for actors, not broadcasters. There is not the same requirement to 'project' your voice on radio because the microphone will amplify it for you. So do not shout. But do sit up straight and breathe properly. This means a couple of deep inhalations before you start. If you try to speak on almost empty lungs, your voice will sound thin and strained, and you will feel uncomfortable.

Never run into a studio and, during the bulletin, remember to keep breathing! That sounds odd, perhaps, but the right place to breathe is at the end of a sentence, not halfway through it. Short sentences are easier for you to write, for listeners to understand – and for you to read! Use audio as a chance to take a couple more deep breaths if you feel nervous. Deep breathing – within reason – has a curiously calming effect. Take the opportunity to breathe just before a cut ends and before you open the microphone. It sounds bad on air to have a new story starting with the reader taking a gulp of air – a sound which is magnified by the way in which the studio output is changed technically for transmission.

Relax. Scrunch your shoulders, stretch and yawn. The latter warms up the throat, particularly important for breakfast newsreaders, whose first words uttered that day may be on air! Do not let that be the case with you – sing in the car on the way in to work. Give your larynx a workout: see how high and low you can go and try some tongue twisters.

In the studio, sips of water taken during audio can help relax a novice reader, as it lubricates your mouth and throat. Avoid drinks made with milk as they can 'clog up' your mouth instead. Also, avoid eating just before going to air: you may have bits stuck in your teeth which feel odd, and you will probably be salivating more than usual, and it's difficult to speak and swallow at the same time!

These tips, and others in this section, will help you become more confident as you broadcast. A nervous voice is usually one which rises in pitch, and that can be a particular problem for female readers as higher voices are regarded by some as lacking clarity and authority.

Keep level

Strange rises and falls in your tone of voice will puzzle and maybe annoy the listener. Do not strain to speak much lower or higher than is comfortable for you. Also, steer midway between a monotone and 'singing' the bulletin, where every story has the same intonation.

You help lead a listener through the story by how you read it: sentences usually rise in the middle and go down towards the end. The trick is to do this *and* avoid speaking *down* to the audience. We are, after all, trying to get a message *across* instead.

If you read the news in a loud voice, you are doing it wrong. If you read the news in a soft voice, you are doing it wrong. If you read the news in the same voice you would use if the other person were sitting in the same room with you, you are probably doing it correctly.

Tone

It is vital to get the tone of your news presentation just right. You need to sound authoritative yet natural and informal. You need to pitch the speed of your reading just right and inject the correct amount of 'light' and 'shade' in your voice. Talking fast and loud does not mean you sound more urgent or dramatic; often it is quite the reverse. As in many things, the key is in finding the correct *balance*. Practice as often as you can – and seek the opinion of others. Get a feel for your voice – how high it can go, how low it can go. Find a natural level for your voice.

Microphone technique

The microphone is a sensitive piece of equipment which will amplify everything it can. That means your voice, your breathing, the squeak of a chair, the rustle of clothing or scripts. So when a microphone is open, move and act with care. This also means clicking your pen or tapping your feet.

Distance from the microphone is important. Too close and the smack of lips and pop of consonants will make the bulletin unpleasant to hear. Too far away and you will be curiously distant, with extra reverberation making listening difficult. Also, if you are too far away, the increase in volume which will be necessary to compensate can make the microphone even more sensitive to unwanted noise.

You need to project your voice to a certain extent when speaking on air – but the balance is between talking normally without mumbling at one extreme and shouting at the other. You have to have gravitas or authority and cut through the rest of the noise that is in the room 'the other end'.

Speed

The usual speed for reading on radio is three words a second. That is the theoretical standard, but in practice (as mentioned many times in this book) your style has to fit with the overall station sound. It is inevitable, then, that a youth-oriented Top 40 station has faster-read bulletins that add excitement and reflect the sounds around – presentation over a punchy music bed giving the impression of even more pace. An adult or easy-listening station will have a more laid-back approach to its newsreading. Think of the world of news presentation difference between Radios One and Four.

In a quick survey for this book, Radio Four averaged 183 words per minute (w.p.m.), but Radio One newsreaders averaged a speed 25 per cent faster – 228 w.p.m. – reflecting the pace of the rest of the programming.

Stress

You can tell the listener which words are important in a story by stressing them. You are the interpreter of news for the listener and if you do not stress the appropriate words, the listener may not be able to follow. You may also lose the listener's attention entirely, or give the impression that you are biased for or against the story you are reading.

Ask yourself what the story is about, what makes it unusual. What is different, new or unexpected. Is there a comparison between two things? Many sentences have an 'axis point' – while this is happening *here*, that is happening *there*. Or a comparison between two or more things (places, people or times, for example). 'The *union leader* says more talks should happen *tonight, before* Tuesday's strikes. But his *deputy* says the deal already offered should go to the vote *first*.'

To see how important stress is, and how easy it is to get wrong, consider this phrase: 'You mean I have to be there at ten tomorrow.' It can be said in eight different ways depending on where you put the emphasis.

By way of another example, read this news voicer:

'The Prime Minister arrived at 10 Downing Street early this morning to start his first day at work. He went in by the front door just after eight o'clock, refusing to respond to reporters, although he did give them a wave and a smile. One of his first tasks will be the formation of a new Cabinet. Last night, there was mounting speculation that he is considering a major reshuffle and, during this morning, the arrival of various party figures at Downing Street have been closely watched. Sources close to the Prime Minister say he is considering new people for the jobs of Chancellor and Foreign Secretary and of course he will have to find a new Transport Secretary. But so far, no names have been announced. This is Jamie Edwards at Downing Street.'

What words would you stress? Underline those that you think are important with a pencil and then compare them to the version below.

Here is the same voicer, with good stress words emphasized. Do not worry if you did not get them all. Try reading the piece out loud, with your stresses, and then read it again with these:

'The *Prime Minister* arrived at 10 Downing Street *early* this morning to start his *first* day at work. He went in by the front door just after eight o'clock, *refusing* to respond to reporters, although he *did* give them a wave and a smile. One of his *first* tasks will be the formation of a new *Cabinet*. Last night, there was *mounting* speculation that he is considering a *major* reshuffle and, during this morning, the *arrivals* of various party figures at Downing Street have been *closely* watched. Sources close to the Prime Minister say he is considering *new* people for the jobs of *Chancellor* and *Foreign* Secretary and of course he will have to find a new Transport Secretary. But *so far, no* names have been announced. This is Jamie Edwards at Downing Street.'

Notice that the stresses are very particular: *Foreign* needs a stress (it is probably the first time that this particular job has been mentioned in the reshuffle), but *Secretary* is a word used for a number of Cabinet posts and does not need such emphasis. Also, there is an implication that everyone already knows that a new Transport Secretary will be needed – so no stress on that phrase.

Making a stress is not simply a matter of speaking more loudly; try pausing slightly before a stress word – let it sink in for the listener.

In a similar way, a particularly unusual event or breaking news story can be read in a similar style – slightly slower and with a modicum more stress. 'Two planes have crashed into the World Trade Centre.' It gives listeners a chance to collect their thoughts before you move on and give more information.

Quotations

Quotations need a special kind of stress. For example, in the sentence 'The Prime Minister accused the Opposition of "cowardice and hypocrisy" over the issue,' a pause on each side of the quotation helps to make it clearer that these were the Prime Minister's actual words.

Corrections

Sometimes you simply get something wrong. It might be your fault because you misread the copy, or someone else's because their mistake was not seen in time. If you know as you say it that something is wrong, an immediate correction is best: '... that should be *forty-two* thousand ...' or 'I'm sorry, that should be *Watford* football club.'

Try not to make too much of a big deal of any correction like this. Simply say it and carry on with the same tone of voice as before. If you sound worried or thrown off your stride, the listener is also likely to take it more seriously too.

Going back to a story later in the bulletin because it was wrong the first time is more noticeable. This is an editorial decision, but if you have made a mistake and it could be serious, as in a court case, there is probably no alternative than to refer back to the story and broadcast the correction. *Do not* repeat the original mistake if you can help it – simply put the correction in context and keep it as simple as possible. For example, 'As you may have heard earlier in the bulletin, a man from Tolworth Cross was jailed for rape at the city's Crown Court today. We'd like to make it clear that his name was *John* Smith.'

Pronunciation

Local place names on local radio stations *must* be pronounced correctly. Getting the name of a place wrong, especially one in your own area, insults your listeners as well as damages the station's credibility and your own. Make sure your station has a phonetic list of the difficult or tricky names.

Never assume that you know how something is said. Check it out and get it right. It is much more embarrassing to be wrong in front of two or three colleagues in the newsroom when you ask for advice, than in front of several thousand listeners on air.

You can be caught out in a number of ways:

- Words that are pronounced one way in one part of the country, but another way somewhere else. If in doubt over whether to say, for example, 'tooth' or 'tuth', go with the 'Queen's English'.
- Sports scores can be tricky. Pity the poor newsreader who said that a tennis match result was '6 minus 4, 6 minus 2'.
- Acronyms are sometimes spelt out and sometimes read as words. There's the 'A-double-E' union but then again there's BECTU (see

elsewhere for advice on this). Some initials and acronyms – BBC, NATO, FBI – are so well known that they do not need explanations, but many are not in this category and should be spelled out, or accompanied by a defining phrase: 'The employers' organization, the CBI', for example. Avoid cluttering a story with acronyms, and don't start a story or a voicer with one: 'NACRO says ...'.

- Local place names. 'Leigh' is pronounced both 'lee' and 'lie'; check which one it is for your area, and there is also Bicester (bister), Towcester (toaster) and Shrewsbury (properly prounced as 'shrows-bree').
- Foreign place names should be read, generally, in their Anglicized form. For example, Paris is not 'par-ee', Sweden is not 'shvay-d'n' and so on. Watch out for the classics Tanzania (tan-zn-ear – not tan-zayn-ia), Bogotá (bogger-tar – not bog-ota) and the favourite Arkansas (arkansor – not ark-ansas).
- If you are writing or reading a story about a car crash, or similar accident, be careful when using the term 'facial injuries'. It is very easy for a listener to mishear the phrase as 'fatal injuries'!

There are several pronunciation dictionaries on the market, one of which is well worth having in the newsroom. Unless you are sure, ask other people about unusual words – another good reason for checking your copy first. Listen, too, when other radio and TV news bulletins are broadcast. The chances are high that network television and radio will get the pronunciation correct because they have so many more resources on which to call if they need to check unusual words. The BBC has a Pronunciation Unit which you can phone for advice, or search through their intranet website.

Foreign names are the worst. As the last resort, if you are not sure, take a deep breath, say the word confidently as well as you can and carry on. If it really is unusual, the listener probably knows no better. But take the first chance you get to check it.

Listen

It is very difficult to know how you sound without listening to a recording. So make an 'aircheck' of your bulletins regularly. Record a bulletin every week or two and listen to it afterwards. It is not ego-tripping; it is sensible and professional monitoring of your performance.

SELF-OP BULLETINS

Traditionally, news on radio was read by one person with someone else performing the technical functions. This is still the case in some network stations, where a team can be involved in getting the bulletin to air. Some local stations still have someone other than the news presenter playing in the audio, opening the microphone and so on, but this person is often the programme presenter who is on duty anyway.

Increasingly, the presenter at a local station presses a button or opens a fader marked 'News' at the appropriate moment and the bulletin presenter takes over entirely. These bulletins are known as 'self-op' (self-operated) bulletins (Figure 6.1).

Getting ready

If you are wise, you will be in the studio several minutes early. That is not because the bulletin might start early (it certainly should not!), but so that you can prepare and be ready to go. The best bulletins are not read, never mind driven, by a breathless presenter who has just been pounding up a flight of stairs to the news studio with only seconds to spare. In some newsrooms, there is a bravado about rushing into the studio at the last moment. It seems some journalists think this makes the news more up to date. Have none of it; the listener will only notice an ill-prepared and poorly presented bulletin. To combat this, some newsrooms have a five- or three-minute 'gate' before a bulletin, where the presenter has to be in the studio to prepare and nothing extra except the most urgent of updates can be added to the bulletin as prepared.

In the studio

Once in the studio, check the audio, the cues and copy. Do you have something missing? Another reason for arriving early is that any discrepancy found at this stage can be put right. If there is talkback to the newsroom, someone else can bring you the missing cue, or load the missing audio in time.

If you are reading off screen, go through both audio and script running orders to ensure they match. An obvious disadvantage of reading off

(a)

(b)

Figure 6.1
(a) Jason Beck reading the news on Wave 105, Southampton. (b) Rosemary Crick presenting a bulletin on BBC Radio Kent

screen is that you cannot alter the script to show pauses or emphasis or reorder stories while reading.

Check that the cues and the audio are in the same order and that your mixing desk is monitoring the correct output. If you are not getting the right programme cue off air, you will not know when to start your bulletin and you may not be able to hear your own audio when you play it. In these days of multifrequency networked local stations with split programming, getting the wrong programme cue is a real possibility. Once again, check in good time. One of the writers of this book was once about to read a bulletin and had opened the microphone blithely humming along with a song, only to discover when he thought the news bulletin was late that he was actually monitoring the wrong station and listeners had heard his rendition of Petula Clark's hit *Downtown*!

Adjust your headphones to the most comfortable volume setting. Remember that some mixing desks monitor 'processed' off air. This means the off-air signal you hear will have gone through an audio processor or compressor to boost the high and low frequencies and make the output more punchy. If you are not used to this, it can be offputting. Some presenters read the bulletin with one headphone on and one off in order to hear the 'natural' sound of their voice while also hearing the audio cuts and the processed sound. Do whatever it is that makes you feel most comfortable.

Here is the news...

In most radio stations the presenter on air will give control to the news studio. This prevents the possibility of a pre-recorded news interview being broadcast on top of the on-air programme! You may be able to tell when control has been given by a light that comes on.

Listen off air and wait for the news jingle to end, which was conventionally at the top of the hour to the second, but is increasingly becoming seen as less important.

Take a couple of deep breaths, then open your microphone while the news jingle – if there is one – is playing, not when it has stopped or faded out completely. Start confidently, with one finger ready to touch the computer playout screen for the first piece of audio.

If your story has audio attached, have your finger hovering over the 'Go' button on the keyboard. Squeeze it gently rather than hit it, as all unnecessary noises should be avoided near the microphone. Close your microphone, move the read script to one side and glance at the next story to familiarize yourself with it, and check that the audio loaded is the correct one. The screen will give you a countdown on the remaining playing time of the current audio clip and you also have the out cue on the bottom of its corresponding cue. A few seconds from the end, take another breath (before you open the mic!) and progress through the bulletin in a similar manner.

Clock end bulletins

Near the end of the bulletin you need to keep a close eye on your studio clock, which should be radio-controlled and accurate to the second. You may have to finish on a 'clock end' – in other words, at exactly five minutes past. It may be that the station will split frequencies at that time and different presenters need an obvious out cue. It may also be that a different bulletin is going out on another transmitter on your station and the single main presenter must be able to pick up off the back of the two bulletins at exactly the same time.

From about four minutes past (in a five-minute bulletin), judge how many seconds you have left in 'real time' and how much time you'll need to read the remaining stories. If you have prepared well, and taken advantage of the on-screen time totalling system, you should be fine, but you need to realize that it may take three or four seconds to read the out cue (which therefore has to be started at four minutes 56 seconds past the hour). The weather can usually be used as a 'buffer': you can extend its duration to fit the time available, but it will sound odd if all you have to say is just 'cold and wet at 7 degrees'. Similarly, a weather bulletin of 45 seconds will also sound out of place! It is therefore good practice to take an extra copy story into the studio with you to read in case of emergency (for example, if an audio piece fails to fire).

At a few seconds to five past, read your out cue and finish dead on time! Go through the unloading procedure on the computer playout system, if necessary, and leave the studio in good order, ready to go on air in case of a breaking story within the next 55 minutes.

When things go wrong...

The number one rule: never swear anywhere near a studio. By keeping to this, the chances of you swearing on air are greatly minimized. It is not just main studios that have microphones and the ability to 'go live' – many production booths where Producers answer phones can also be put to air, so do not let down your guard.

If something technical fails in spite of all your precautions, *keep calm*. This is your bulletin and the listener will take a cue from you. If you seem rattled or nervous, the listener will think something really serious has gone wrong. But do have some insurance. Have some extra copy stories with you that do not have to be used. Then, if you lose some audio, you have some additional material. It is not impossible for a computer system 'crash' to occur during a live bulletin. With the extra copy, you should be able to keep going.

This is why we suggested keeping the top two stories on one side. If you have to end precisely on time, or if a failure has left you ridiculously short, you can always refer back to them for the last 30 seconds or so of the bulletin: '... and finally, the main stories again this hour ...'. This may seem a gesture of desperation, but it actually sounds rather slick and urgent. The listener simply will not realize you are filling for time, especially if you sound confident. Some stations, incidentally, repeat the main story at the end of the bulletin as a matter of policy.

Only if all else fails should you end a bulletin early and then only if you are sure the succeeding programme is ready to take over. Nothing sounds worse than a silence after the bulletin. You are also unfairly giving the listener the impression that it is the next presenter who is in the wrong by not being ready.

If there is a failure, and it must be explained, do so in terms the listener will understand. *Never* say: 'I'm sorry that cut wasn't cued,' but rather: 'I'm sorry we can't bring you that report.' The listener understandably thinks a cut is something made by a knife!

Remember that mistakes which are obvious to you may not be so apparent to the listener. If you read a cue and the audio fails to fire, think before leaping in with an apology. A good audio cue will stand alone, if necessary. Do not apologize for something unless the failure is evident. If you can simply carry on, do so.

If you trip up over a word (and there are times when a newsreader can have several attempts at a particularly difficult word and still get it wrong!), just carry on as though nothing has happened. Only in the most serious of stories, where a mispronunciation would render the story incomprehensible, should you apologize. On most occasions dismiss the fault immediately and move on. It is usually much bigger in your mind than it was on air – although you may subsequently appear on the station's in-house Christmas party 'blooper tape'!

BREAKING NEWS STORIES

As previously mentioned, newsreaders need to be cool under pressure. There are occasions when a story breaks just before or while you are on air and it has to be covered immediately. It may be that a piece of copy is handed to you, or flashes on your terminal, while you are reading another story. You have to be able to continue reading one story out loud, while your eyes 'copy taste' what's just come in. You have to make the decision if and when to use the new information.

It may be that it is an urgent correction or update to the story that is currently being read. If so, you can put the additional item as a 'back anno' after the story: '… and we're just getting information that a man has been arrested in connection with that death.' It may be a change or update to a forthcoming story, in which case you may have to read some of your cue from the paper script and the rest from the terminal. It may be an advisory message: 'the reporter at the county ground isn't ready – don't cross to them until at least 4 minutes 30.' It may be that a particularly keen or conscientious reporter sends through a story that they think you ought to include, but you know has already been covered or have previously decided not to use. Or it could be a breaking story that is so big, it is worth finishing the current story before playing its audio, and reading out the information immediately.

In such circumstances, a news presenter has to tread a difficult line between making the story sound urgent and important – without making it sound overly dramatic and possibly upsetting.

'We're getting reports that…'

You are on air and a message flashes on your studio screen, which you notice out of the corner of your eye. While reading the current story you enter the internal messaging system and cast your eyes over the few words that appear. 'Fire at County Hospital, Blankstown.' As you read one story out loud and the other to yourself, your mind races – from where has this story originated, how serious is the fire, what more do we know? To broadcast just this scant information could be alarmist, and have more *shock* value than *news* value. By the same token it is potentially a huge story and as it is breaking as the bulletin is on air, perhaps it should be covered.

All this flashes through your mind within seconds. You make a decision: it has been sent through from a fellow reporter in the newsroom who undoubtedly has their own reasons. You decide to go with it, and at the end of the current story take a slightly longer pause than you normally would between stories.

'We're just getting reports,' you say slowly and precisely, 'of a fire that's thought to've broken out at the County Hospital in Blankstown.' Your tone of reading has changed almost imperceptibly, but carries slightly more urgency and authority. You call on your own knowledge of the area to ad lib for a few seconds, speaking slowly means you have a few vital milliseconds to gather your thoughts and to help those who are now listening more closely to the radio. 'That hospital of course is only a few years old, and based on the Blankstown Road in the town. When it was opened there was criticism that it was the hospital farthest from a fire station than any other in the county.' That is all you can ad lib at this stage, so decide to 'tread water': repeating the information you *do* know and promoting further coverage of the breaking story. 'So, as I say, this information just coming through to me, that there are reports of a fire at the County Hospital in Blankstown. We're not sure of its severity or whether there's an evacuation in progress, but as soon as we know you'll hear about it on Radio Blankshire.'

You continue with the bulletin, but midway through the next story the studio door opens and a fellow reporter hands you another sheet of paper, and sits themselves down alongside you at another mic and puts on headphones. You can see from a quick glance at the additional sheet that there are questions scribbled on it, and you guess that your colleague has more information on the fire. He confirms this by pointing at you and then himself. You make the judgement call that to interrupt the current story so soon after the 'flash' may sound unprofessional, especially as you only have one other story in the bulletin.

You complete the news that you have prepared and say, 'Now let's recap the story that's broken in the last few minutes: reports are coming in to Radio Blankshire of a fire at the County Hospital in Blankstown. I'm joined in the studio by our reporter Peter Porter, who's got some more information ...' and read the first question on the sheet. As he answers, a calm voice in your headphones which you recognize as being the News Editor says 'Chris Steel from Fire HQ on line 4.'

Not knowing when your colleague's going to finish his answer you wait a moment, ask another question and then press a couple of buttons on your terminal screen to 'patch' line 4 through to the studio desk phone fader. Listening to your reporter all this time, you have an idea that the fire is a potentially big story and when he's finished the current answer you thank him and introduce 'Chris Steel from Blankshire Fire and Rescue joins us on the line now. Chris, what reports are you getting back from your colleagues at the hospital?' You let Chris speak and ask him a couple of supplementary questions. As he answers, you glance at the other questions on your sheet and say to your colleague off air 'any more?' He shakes his head, you recap the story again, using the main additional points that you've gathered, and end the bulletin by reminding listeners to keep tuned for the latest. It's eight minutes past the hour, when a bulletin is usually five minutes. You are buzzing with the excitement of the last few minutes' ad libbing, but know that now the real work is only just starting.

Going open-ended

It is decided that the programme currently on air should be pulled as it is an entertainment show with competitions and music. The News Editor goes to the studio and after the current track ends takes over the show with 'open-ended' coverage of the fire.

She has basic facts known already and is reassured that a reporter is already making their way to the scene. Over the next hour and a half, she interviews a studio-based reporter, the reporter at the scene, and the official from the Fire and Rescue Service. Listeners living nearby telephone the station and are put to air with eyewitness accounts of what they have seen. Even a few hospital visitors call to tell of what happened inside the wards when the alarms went off. Music (and commercials) are dropped, but news bulletins and headlines are kept in place. They act as a round-up of the most important points so far. Travel news is obviously important and kept, and additional bulletins introduced.

Reporters in the newsroom are setting up the guests, and writing a few questions, although they know the News Editor will be able to ad lib questions herself. The bulletin reader clips the live interviews and writes cues for them for inclusion in the bulletins. The Producer of the afternoon drive show is on the phone to unions and patients' groups for comment and reaction for their show.

After an hour and a half, and at a suitable news junction, regular programming returns. It has been decided that, despite the hospital being evacuated, the fire was a small one and contained to a laundry room. There will be full coverage in the evening drive time programme, and the story will be taken on for the morning breakfast show: critics of the hospital's location will be questioned together with hospital administrators. The 'entertainment show' presenter changes his style and drops competitions. Music is checked for unsuitable titles, and dropped as necessary. Extra headlines and travel bulletins are left intact.

SPECIALIZED PRESENTATION

Personality news presenters

Some, mainly commercial, stations have newsreaders who are as much a part of the station as the music presenters. They interact with the DJs and are well known for their style of presentation.

A personality reader is not someone who shouts the news, but one who tells it in a particularly conversational style. They may be particularly engaging with the audience, and have writing tricks and techniques that set them apart from other readers – for example, speaking directly to the listener by using words like 'you' and asking questions. ('When was the last time you got your car MOT'd? Well ... a new type of test is being revved up from today.') There may be more use of puns, rhymes, alliteration or even jokes or comments to make the bulletin a performance or show in its own right. A personality reader is often allowed more of a free rein in their presentation style – as long as they do not break regulations on impartiality. Because they are bold in their presentation style, and probably unique on the station and in the area, they can often be promoted as a reason to listen to the station, along with the other presenters, music or competitions.

The 'zoo'

There has been an increasing trend for news presenters to become active players in the radio 'zoo' formats. This is where the (usually commercial radio breakfast) show has a group of voices heard on air, each with their own contribution to make. The style was born in America and came to the UK on the Steve Wright show on BBC Radio One in the 1970s.

Each person on air has a 'character' that is either presumed for the sake of the show, or real. The characters play different parts of the audience, or represent people the audience will recognize, and are broad brushstroke personalities like those in a sitcom. The on-air staff stick to character in almost everything they say on air – for example, they love moaning, hate foreign food or are always flirting.

A typical line-up could therefore be:

- The main presenter – character: 'the brother'. A young man who loves parties, drinking, sports and gadgets. He is a bit sexist, but will also support his family and children.
- The travel presenter – character: 'the sister'. Also loves parties and drinking. She 'plays the field' with boyfriends but is looking for commitment, is outwardly a ladette but is sensitive at heart and pulls up her 'brother' when he steps over the line with his sexist comments or outrageous ill-thought-through statements.
- The news presenter – character: 'the older brother'. He likes a laugh and goes along with most of what is said, but is more sensible. He can see what may happen and stops things before they get out of hand. Far from a killjoy, he knows the latest bands and films and is 'cool and trendy', but is the university type who knows when to draw the line.

The danger is that the wayward 'brother' could ask the 'older brother' to do or say something out of character. The news person would be justified in telling a funny story at the end of the bulletin, but not in being quizzed about his sex life, for example. The main point is that the news presenter, a.k.a. 'older brother', must *always* know the answer to *everything*. Indeed, this can be a comedy feature in its own right. The trick is to always tell the news person the question before going on air, so they can find out the answer in advance. The news person's character as a 'friendly know it all' is sacrosanct.

How can they be seen as 'the voice of reason' if they have previously recounted the story of the time they were arrested for being drunk? How can they be trusted with a breaking story if, when previously asked a 'simple' question, such as 'what's the warmest it's ever been on this date?', they replied 'I don't know'?

7 Technicalities

AUDIO RECORDING

Radio stations rely on different types of recording systems to store interviews and audio and play out programme material. Old analogue equipment such as cartridge players and open-reel tape recorders has been replaced by digital equipment, where audio is recorded direct onto a computer hard disk, which can then be edited, stored, played out and archived.

Digital recording

Digitized audio signals have now been with us for some time and the basic technique is in daily domestic use with compact discs and minidiscs. With vast amounts of digital storage becoming cheaper, a revolution has taken place in the way radio stations operate.

Digital recording hardware and software in use at radio stations includes the following.

Portable hard disk is the new generation of location recorders. They are reasonably small, rugged and robust portable recorders, such as the Courier machine made by Sonifex, in use at most BBC stations, where audio is captured on a small memory card (called Compact Flash) or a tiny hard disk (Figure 7.1). Recordings can be digitally edited on location if necessary, using a 'graphic scrub wheel', and played back via ISDN or mobile phone. Alternatively, plugging the machine into a computer's USB port, the sound can be transferred for on-screen editing. The advantage is that the file transfers almost immediately, rather than in real time.

(a)

(b)

Figure 7.1
(a) A Sonifex Courier machine as used widely by the BBC. (b) A portable Marantz hard disk recorder as used by IRN.

(c)

Figure 7.1
Continued (c) A domestic Sony minidisc recorder, adapted for radio use

Minidiscs are smaller, recordable compact discs usually capable of hold-ing more than 70 minutes of fully indexible, instantly accessible sound. They are used mainly by commercial radio stations' reporters, and can also be rough-edited 'in the field'. In the studio, they are used for jingles and backing music, but can be used for audio clips and commercials. Indeed, some stations have had their entire music library put on minidisc. Both minidiscs and digital cartridges (see below) have their own digital players, usually with a large rotary control on the front to select the desired track. A digital display shows the title of the track selected and its number. These do, however, use digital compression, so the quality will degrade with successive copies.

Digital cartridges do not use tape at all but record digitally and play back a floppy disk. Usually, a digital 'cart' (or D-cart) carries various items such as clips, jingles or commercials. It does not need to be rewound, so any of its tracks are instantly accessible. Its other major advantage over tape carts is that digital carts never become tangled and rarely jam.

Digital Audio Tape (DAT) was once welcomed as the industry standard, although it has been superseded by more rugged location and studio systems described above. DATs are smaller in size than analogue cassettes and use the same technology as video recorders – a slow-speed tape scanned by a revolving head. The signal is recorded in digital form in which the original electrical variations are represented by a series of pulses or 'bits' of information. Audio in 'bit' form is rather like words typed on a word processor; both can easily be manipulated by a computer. The sound quality remains exactly the same as the original and, unlike analogue tape copies, does not degrade as successive digital copies are made.

Computer hard disk is a studio-based system with a fully interactive massive memory capacity used by many modern radio stations to store all audio from music to jingles, commercials to news clips. Once audio is loaded onto the system as data, any number of individual users can access it simultaneously and independently stop it, start it, edit it or put it on pause, all without any denegration in quality. Because it is computer data, it is also instantly accessible. Hard disk is the best way to make quality material instantly available to a number of users. The BBC standard is RadioMan, commercial radio stations again adopting various other systems, such as RCS, Myriad or Enco DAD.

AUDIO EDITING

Audio often has to be edited before transmission to remove unwanted parts of a recording. In an interview, people tend to cough, pause, make false starts and other mistakes; all these events are annoying for the listener and, if left untouched, would waste valuable time in a news bulletin.

Certainly, no clip should start with redundant words or phrases: 'What I mean to say is ...', 'Err, I think you're right because ...' or with the interviewee taking a breath before they start their answer.

Editing should never be used to change the sense of what someone is saying. It is not acceptable, for example, to splice together a question and answer which did not actually occur together in the original conversation.

Fluffs and unnecessary hesitations can be remedied. But you must be aware of the ethics of editing an interview to make someone sound more fluent. It is no doubt acceptable to edit an elderly lady talking about a flower show, to make her sound fluent. But is it also acceptable to edit the pauses and hesitations from an interview with a car dealer you are questioning over dubious sales practices? Only if it is a loss of concentration is it right to remove it.

Remember to remove any reference to material already edited out. You will confuse the listener if you leave in things like 'As I said before …', and 'I tell you again …'. By the same token, remove any time references if the interview is being prepared in advance. An interview with a football club manager about the weekend match, recorded on Friday morning for playout on Saturday, should not contain a phrase such as 'We're looking forward to tomorrow's match'. Remember, you are the expert: if you have a polite word with the guest and explain when their piece will be broadcast they will usually be more than willing to alter the tense of their answer, or remove it altogether ('We're looking forward to the match').

You should interview in such a way that editing is reduced to a minimum. It takes a lot of time and tends to be more difficult to do, just before the audio is wanted. The tension of an approaching deadline makes a lot of us less nimble-fingered.

Be careful when editing. Done properly, your expertise should not be noticed by the listener because a good edit goes unheard. That is one reason why recordings have been treated with caution for many years as potential legal evidence – they are too easy to change.

Taking care means listening to how your interviewee speaks and making sure you preserve the natural rhythm of that speech by meticulously observing breath pauses. Two breaths cut together sound ridiculous, but it is easily done. If, on the other hand, you remove all breath pauses in a sentence, the statements sound as if they have come from a robot. So, with editing, the golden rule is to *listen twice – cut once*, as you could destroy the original. An advantage of modern digital equipment means you can cut and copy as often as you like without destroying the original.

Digital editing

The most common sort of digital editing is on-screen on a computer. The audio is transferred onto the hard disk of a newsroom or radio station computer system. Using suitable software, you can view the data as a waveform. By using a mouse to point to and highlight the relevant sections of audio, you can cut and reorder the material. You may also be able to zoom into certain parts of the recording to make more exact edits, and of course, you are able to hear what they sound like before you make the 'cut'. The golden rule, though, is to use your ears and not your eyes. On occasions, especially if you zoom in, the waveform does not always match with the sound you hear. On these occasions go with what you know to be correct, rather than what the computer is suggesting (Figure 7.2).

This method can also create fades and other effects, while leaving the original recording intact. This means it is easy to experiment with possible edits until you obtain the desired result.

Even basic systems allow you to insert clips into a track of pre-recorded links to make a package. This can then be mixed with other sounds from the scene of the interview – 'wildtrack' – whose levels can also be altered, faded or cross-mixed with other sound effects.

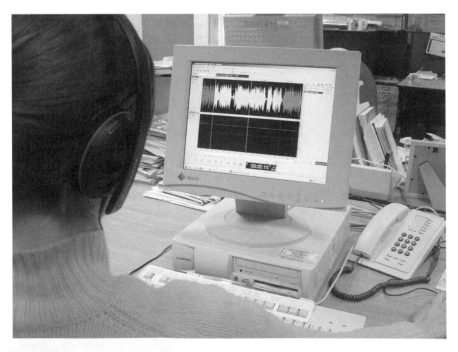

Figure 7.2
On-screen audio editing at BBC Radio Kent

The great advantage is that the original piece of audio remains, and that, together with an 'undo' button, you can always change your mind about an edit.

COMPUTERIZED NEWSROOMS

The paper-free and tape-free environment

Most computer systems take in data from news suppliers (such as GNS, IRN or Sky News Radio) in both copy and audio form. A typical system is that used at BBC stations, ENPS, which files data by category and automatically stores and sorts it into specifically designated lists, allowing quick scanning of stories. You can rewrite copy and edit audio on-screen from a workstation at the same time as data is being filed or updated and other people are also using the same piece of copy or audio. A Bulletin Editor can 'build' a bulletin on-screen, time the total duration and vary the running order up to a tight deadline.

Material can be printed for reading in the traditional way or read off-screen with audio activated either by a mouse or through a touchscreen. After the bulletin, copy and audio can be archived. Items from freelancers are automatically brought to the attention of the radio station's accounts department for payment. Most systems also have the storage capacity to contain a comprehensive and updated list of contacts to which everyone in the newsroom has access.

The ENPS system also allows staff at one station to see running orders and bulletins from other stations, television or radio, anywhere else in the BBC. And that includes foreign offices.

Computerized newsrooms can also take audio and copy data from digital telephone lines called ISDN (Integrated Services Digital Network) circuits capable of sending full-quality stereo signals via dial-up lines throughout the world.

STUDIOS

A radio studio uses a number of sources of sound. These can include:

- microphones;
- digital hard disk;

- CDs;
- phone lines;
- ISDN lines.

A studio mixing desk allows all these sources to be combined into a broadcast signal and sent to the transmitter. Which sources are present depends on the purpose of the studio (Figures 7.3 and 7.4).

Most news studios are operated by the news presenter throughout the bulletin (a 'self-op' studio). They will read the stories, play in audio clips and bring in other outside sources (such as a reporter on an ISDN line from the county cricket ground).

The modern news studio contains at least one microphone, audio playout and recording system, access to incoming sources (such as ISDN or telephone lines) and a small mixing desk to combine these sources on air (Figure 7.5).

Figure 7.3
The on-air studio at BBC Radio Kent

Figure 7.4
The on-air studio at Wave 105 in Southampton

Figure 7.5
'Mic and cans' at BBC Radio Kent

Such a studio can be used not only for live bulletins, but also for recording interviews (either from a telephone line, ISDN or in the studio), dubbing interviews onto the hard disk from a portable recorder, recording packages and editing. A second microphone also makes a live voicer possible, using a reporter in the studio with the bulletin presenter.

Many news studios – especially in commercial radio – now include an audio processor to help boost the 'punchiness' of the sound, not only from the microphones, but also other sound sources to make the output sound more consistent. A directional microphone, however, is much more critical from which to keep the right distance – too far away and you will sound weak and distant, too close and you will 'pop' the microphone and sound muffled.

Some studios – intended for programmes as well as bulletins – are arranged around a round table with microphone leads fed through a centre hole. The presenters sit on one side of the table with a line of sight to the production team, while guests have their backs to the control room next door. This is sometimes helpful when a guest is boring and the presenter needs a visual indication that the interview should be wound up!

The news studio, booth, or NPA at a BBC station, often has direct line of sight with the main on-air studio. Failing this, a CCTV camera is in operation between the two, mainly so the presenter can be sure the newsreader is there before they introduce the bulletin! Either way, a talkback system is always in operation, allowing off-air communication between the two sound-proofed studios while audio is being broadcast (Figure 7.6).

Headphones

Headphones (or 'cans') are necessary for three reasons. Firstly, so that the presenter can hear the sound of what is actually being sent to the transmitter. Without headphones our ears hear sound differently; they compensate for a slight echo in a room, for example, and don't recognize if someone's not speaking directly into a microphone. On location, a reporter may wear headphones to check on recording levels and the mix of sound from an interviewee over background sound.

Another reason is so the presenter in the studio can hear sources that are being mixed through the desk, when they have their microphone open. Sound heard through a studio speaker would be picked up by the mic and cause a 'howl round' screech if the microphone channel were not muted.

Figure 7.6
An on-air phone and talkback system in the control room at BBC Radio Kent

But muting speakers, without using headphones, would mean the presenter would not be able to hear the output.

The third use of headphones is so a presenter can be given instructions, without them also being heard by a guest. A producer may, for example, want to tell them that there are no more callers to take to air, or to pass on the latest information on a fire as a presenter ad libs.

At many stations, built-in level limiters are used to protect the wearers' hearing being damaged by long-term exposure to high sound levels. Protection of the ears must be taken seriously; after all, they are the tools of our trade!

Microphones

Different microphones are for different occasions. They have different heads which pick up sound from different directions. Be advised that some microphones are 'condenser' or 'capacitor' types – they need an electric current from a battery to work, so remember to check that one is installed and the mic is turned on!

Bidirectional mics are sensitive to sound in a 'figure of eight' pattern. They are usually fitted in studios where they are not moved. Ensure that you speak into one of the sides of the mic, so your voice is picked up – sometimes they are knocked and your voice will sound thin and literally 'off-mike'. (There is usually a label which indicates which is the front or back, rather than the side.) They are useful if your guest is directly opposite you, as both voices can be picked up in equal quality.

The cardioid microphone will record noise from within a heart-shaped area, i.e. from the front and a little from each side, as its name might suggest. These are also called unidirectional mics.

Omnidirectional mics pick up sounds from all round, so they can sometimes record unwanted noise. They are, for example, not necessary in a face-to-face location interview, where you want two voices and only some background noise. They are good effect mics, where you do want to pick up general ambience.

Lip mics are usually used by commentators, or to do some television voice-over work. They are held very close to the mouth and only pick up noise directly in front of them and so are good in noisy places such as a football stadium (Figure 7.7).

If you or your interviewee speaks too closely to a microphone, a 'popping' sound known as a 'plosive' is heard when letters such as 'p' or 'b' are used. This is because of the sudden rush of air emitted from the mouth on such occasions. You can avoid this by holding the microphone to one side of your guest's mouth when they are speaking, or by using a pop-shield. This is a foam covering which goes over the top of the microphone and which dissipates the air rush. Reporters' microphones often have 'mic flags' advertising the name of their station, so if they were ever involved in a televised 'media scrum' or news conference, the station's logo would be seen. Now, some stations are taking to getting this printed on the pop-shield instead, as that part of the mic is more difficult for TV camera crews to cut from the bottom of the picture!

Playout systems

Most computerized playout systems work in basically the same way. For the purposes of this book we will describe the RadioMan system, as this

Figure 7.7
Using a lip microphone to cancel out background noise

is the one which is used by all of the BBC stations – commercial stations use any of half a dozen other products.

RadioMan makes an audio log of everything that goes out on air. This is saved in files whose names correspond with the different programmes, so it is easy to find and then clip an interview that has just been transmitted. This is usually the job of the Bulletin Editor or newsreader. By loading up the waveform of the programme into Quick Edit Pro, they can find, name and save a clip. The cue to that clip can then be written, using the same slug, and entering the clip details (name, duration, in and out words) in the red box provided.

At the same time, a bulletin running order can be put together in another part of the RadioMan system. Folders for each bulletin are created by a one-button process at the start of each day, so all the editor has to do is locate the folder for the next hour and drag across, from previous hours, text that they want to use. Alternatively, they can create another story file on the screen, write the story and save it in that, or any other hours', running order. Each running order is split in half horizontally by a single

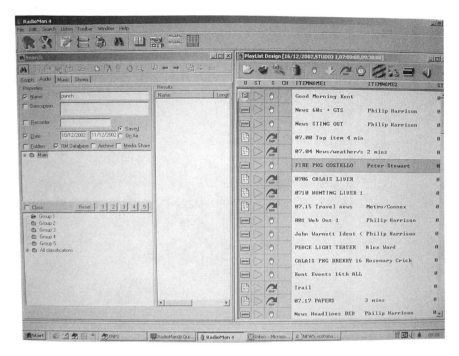

Figure 7.8
The RadioMan production screen showing a programme running order of audio ready to be played

black line. Everything 'above the line' is what is intended for the next broadcast, and the system will add up the durations of the text and audio to give a running time at the bottom of that block of stories. 'Below the line' is where you can save 'holding stories': alternative cues or copy lines that you will use in subsequent bulletins.

It is convention with this system to write a story name in capitals if audio is attached, and in lower case if it is a copy line. That way, just before 'the gate', the reader can quickly see what clips need to be loaded onto the playout part of the system. Despite this being a computerized newsroom, it is at this stage that a pen and paper are needed to note down the names of the cuts, as the audio loading page cannot be seen on a split screen!

Enter the name of the clip into the search facility, specifying criteria such as the date the clip was saved or what file it is in. Pick the correct cut of the alternatives provided (you may have two clips and a package all with the same slug) and drag and drop that into the audio running order. Repeat the process to build your stack of virtual audio clips. Scripts are printed

Dubbing

Dubbing means transferring a piece of audio from one recorder to another (and comes from the word 'double'). This may be, for example, from a portable hard disk machine to a computer hard disk for editing in a digital newsroom.

Levels and equalization

The importance of good audio volume levels cannot be underestimated. It is silly to have spent time and effort preparing a story only to have it unheard by the listener because the volume is either too low or too high and distorted.

Levels must be monitored at all stages of the broadcasting process – when the initial interview is recorded, when it is being dubbed, when it is being packaged and as it is broadcast. If the levels are too low for any length of time, a processor attached to the station's transmitter will try and boost it, resulting in a great deal of hiss.

Levels are measured in the studio by using a peak programme meter (PPM). Different stations have different rules about the level to which audio peaks, but generally you should aim at just over PPM 5 for the loudest sound. Telephone recordings contain a narrower band of frequencies, so the PPM level for phone audio should be slightly higher, to a maximum of PPM 6. The effective volume is then the same. Meters on the desk often flash red if the sound level is too high (Figure 7.9).

Equalization controls (EQ) on a studio mixing desk can be either a help or a hazard. They are glorified tone controls similar to, but more sophisticated than, the bass or treble controls on a domestic stereo system. You can use them, for instance, to remove high frequencies such as tape hiss or the low frequencies of an air-conditioning system. They are also used to adjust the tonal qualities of voices. However, you should be careful you know what you are doing; you may end up producing a muffled piece of audio which suffers from the same problem as low or high levels, i.e. the listener cannot hear it properly.

ocation interviews

Many are the times reporters have left the radio station with their recording machine, without first checking that there's a microphone attached! These and taken to the news studio, where it is wise to double-check the order of the audio before going to air. A similar process is completed to create an audio running order for a programme (Figure 7.8).

AUDIO AND ACTUALITY

The 'live' recording of a real event or person is usually called 'audio' in commercial radio and 'actuality' in the BBC. It makes a bulletin sparkle and you should try to use it wherever it is justified.

Audio can be anything from a 17-second cut of the Prime Minister speaking in the Commons to a location interview with the fire chief in charge at a train crash.

Remember, though, that audio should add to a story. Think carefully about what it says and how it will fit into the overall story. Do not use audio just for the sake of it or simply to prove you were there.

Sound quality

Be careful about the technical quality of audio. If it is not good enoug simply do not use it. Try not to feel compelled to use an inferior qual piece of audio just because of the effort which has gone into getting Remember that if *you* have trouble picking out what is being said w you are preparing the audio for transmission in a studio, by the tin reaches a portable radio, it will make no sense at all.

Audio should be intelligible in itself and capable of being underst the first hearing. If your listener has to spend two or three seconds to guess what is being said, you have failed. It is far better for the s reach the listener as copy or a voicer rather than use inferior qualit which cannot be understood.

Sound edits

Listen carefully to your selected piece of audio and make sure e is essential. Edit out really bad 'ers', 'ums' and stumbles, but not to make the audio seem too unnatural and pay particular a making sure edits do not disrupt background noise. Make sure are 'clean', with the correct breath pauses.

Figure 7.9
PPM meters on a mixing desk at BBC Essex. From left to right: prefade, desk output and station output (*Source*: Ingrid Bardua)

are much more robust than they were years ago, and can take some pretty rough handling, but loose connections do occur and it is advisable to check yours works (and that the connection is compatible with your machine) before you leave on a story.

On location, check again that the equipment works! Many reporters wear headphones during the recording so they can hear the sounds being recorded. The tradition is to ask the interviewee their name and title, which means you can set the levels on your machine and you have a recorded log of their details. Listen back to ensure that the recording is there and that it is not distorted. Outside recordings rarely are, but inside buildings, corridors and offices, the microphone picks up all sorts of echoes. If this happens, you may want to move to a place with more of a 'dead' sound, somewhere with carpets and curtains. If this is not possible, the trick is to stand with the interviewee in a corner of the room and work with the microphone much closer to each of your mouths. But, remember to turn down your record level! For the same reasons of echo, avoid interviewing someone across a desk, as the sound will bounce off its surface.

Stand up with them (and probably stand up *to* them as well!) and you will get a much sharper interview in sound quality and content.

However, you should remember that part of the reason for going out on a location interview is to get location sounds, and there's little point if the interview sounds as though it was recorded in your station studio.

Hold the microphone, together with a loop of the lead, over the connection at the base of the mic. That way there is less chance of a crackle or rattle if there does happen to be a loose wire in the socket. Stand close to your interviewee, close enough that you do not have to keep moving the microphone when asking your questions, but not so close that you make them feel uncomfortable by invading their 'body space' (Figure 7.10).

One of the tricks to learn is to look interested in what they are saying, rather than sounding interested as they say it. If you or they make a mistake in a recording, you can probably edit it out, but you won't want a news clip of one of their answers to be broadcast with you being heard in

Figure 7.10
Wave 105 reporter Toby Bennett interviewing an eyewitness on the scene of an incident using a Sony minidisc recorder

the background ('yes, I see …'!). To this end, maintain eye contact (glancing occasionally at the levels on your recorder, checking also that it is running), nod and smile. If you feel their answer is becoming too long or wandering from the point, you can raise your eyebrows or open your mouth as if to interrupt. This will usually bring the interviewee to the end of their sentence.

At the end of your interview, ask your guest if there is anything else they want to add, before checking again that a recording has been made. Listen back to the last ten seconds or so, but resist the temptation to let the interviewee hear the whole piece. They may want to start changing some of the answers and this is not practical because of reasons both of time and independence.

You may want to move around while recording – for example, if you want your interviewee to show you around a new hospital that has just been opened, or if you want to interview them as they climb into a car. On these occasions make sure the microphone isn't knocked and the connections remain as stable as possible.

Studio interviews

When interviewing a guest in the studio it is relatively easy to monitor sound levels, as there is no extraneous noise. Before going on air, advise the guest how far to sit from the microphone (about 25–30 cm), ask them not to bang the desk (either on top or underneath – as the sound will be picked up through the base of the microphone), and to turn away if about to cough or sneeze. The guest will not need to wear headphones (indeed, the sound of their own voice heard through them may be a distraction), unless they need to hear telephone calls from listeners.

Guests are usually seated with their backs to the control room so only the presenter can see any hand signals from a producer (for example, giving a 'wind-up' sign).

Telephone interviews

The best tool in the newsroom is the phone. You can reach almost anyone in the world by phone. Most people will drop what they are doing, no matter what it is, to come to the phone. With the proliferation of mobiles, it is even easier.

The first thing to note is that recording anyone surreptitiously is against both BBC Producer Guidelines and commercial radio regulations. You must tell an interviewee that you have started recording and that you may use the interview on air. If you are recording a 'wind-up' conversation, you must tell the victim afterwards that they have been recorded, and get their permission before transmission. Other occasions where a recording may be made without the interviewee's knowledge (for example, to expose bad practice) will have to be cleared by a senior member of staff before it goes ahead.

When you are recording a telephone interview, you must be careful to monitor the levels because of the slight distortion caused by the equipment. It is surprising how many people do not use their telephone correctly – either speaking too closely into the mouthpiece (which causes 'pops' and a muffled sound), or by holding the mouthpiece under their chin (which causes a quiet and hissy sound). Do not be afraid to ask them to move their mouthpiece if you would otherwise be left with material that cannot be broadcast.

Remember to dip the telephone fader when you ask a question, and to dip yours when they reply. Otherwise, the sound of your voices will be slightly 'coloured' by the phone line.

Telephone versus quality audio

There are two theories about the merits of telephone versus quality audio in newsrooms. It has been generally accepted that face-to-face quality audio is better than audio recorded over the phone. Remember, it sounds far better to interview with background noise giving atmosphere, such as a busy office, a factory floor or a traffic-clogged street. This gives the impression of being 'busy'. Except where the background noise is excessive, it is hardly ever necessary to 'find a quiet corner' somewhere and record an interview. This will sound simply as if it had been recorded in a studio, which reduces the point of getting audio in the first place.

Phone audio has traditionally been thought of as a lazy and cheap way of doing interviews, avoiding the time and cost of travelling to a location.

This is not necessarily the case and there has emerged a clear editorial justification for doing interviews like this.

Research shows that the listener does not mind phone cuts at all. In fact, he or she thinks the story is actually more 'immediate' if it is done on the phone. It sounds to them as if you have reacted fast to a story rather than done something which has required planning, travelling and a lot of time.

So phone audio not only makes use of radio's greatest strength – its immediacy – but also makes good economic sense for small stations with few staff and limited resources.

Studio discipline

When you are around a radio station for any length of time, it is easy to forget the rules that are there for a purpose. This is a working on-air environment and must be treated with professionalism.

The first rule of studio discipline is silence. The red light means the studio microphones are live (there may also be another light to indicate which studio is broadcasting). If someone is in a studio, and the red light is not on, be aware that the microphone may be opened at any moment. A good indication of this is if the presenter is wearing headphones.

If you have reason to go into an on-air studio, ask permission of a producer first (if there is one); alternatively, wait to be indicated to by the presenter and, once in the studio, only speak when you're told it is alright for you to do so.

Guests should only be in the presentation area by prior appointment. If they are booked for an interview they may wait in a control room or 'green room', in which case they should speak in hushed tones so as not to distract the producer or phone operator. Guests on a studio tour should be cleared with the presenter or producer well in advance, and again before entering the production area.

Talkback

Finally, a few words about talkback. If using this intercom system to talk to the presenter from another part of the building, keep your message short, say who you are and where you are talking to them from (so the presenter knows which button to press to reply). Each talkback system should be used in conjunction with an off-air feed (which may be as simple as a radio). Use it to ensure that the person to whom you want to speak is not broadcasting at the time. Used properly for passing on information on a breaking story to a presenter, the talkback system is an invaluable tool. Used improperly – for example, by a reporter asking an unimportant question when the presenter is trying to interview the local MP – it can be the reason for an angry exchange of words.

8 Interviewing

TYPES OF INTERVIEW

The purpose of an interview is to gather usable audio to illustrate your story. This audio may be live or recorded. If it is recorded – which is more likely – the end result could be 15 seconds or several minutes. The cut itself could be used for a news bulletin, a package or a documentary. In spite of these varied uses, the principles of good interviewing are the same. But before you start, you should have a good idea of the type of interview you are about to do and its purpose. You will probably be guided in this by the brief given to you by the News Editor. Remember the reason for getting audio through an interview is to have someone else like an expert, official or eyewitness say something that the newsreader cannot – comment.

Informational interviews

This is primarily to reveal facts or opinions. For example: 'How many ambulances are off the road because of a maintenance problem?'; 'Which way do you as an MP intend to vote in tonight's crucial Commons vote?'; 'Why weren't the main roads in the county gritted before last night's frost?'

Note some of the words used. The crucial words to use when asking questions are: *who, what, where, why, when* and *how*. Questions starting with these words elicit answers other than just 'yes' or 'no', therefore making them much more useful on radio. They are known as 'open' questions. 'Closed' questions such as 'Do you think the county's roads were sufficiently gritted last night?' can lead an interviewee simply to say 'yes'. The interview intended to reveal information is most likely to achieve its objective if the questions are short and direct but 'open'.

There are exceptions. In some cases a direct 'closed' question can achieve a dramatic effect: 'So, after three deaths in as many years, are you going to resign?'

Interpretive interviews

The interpretive interview is quite different. The subject of the interview needs to interpret some facts which are already known. The *fact* is that interest rates are rising again; the financial expert can be asked what *effect* this will have on mortgage rates. You should still, though, ask questions using the word 'what'. In this case, you are no longer dealing with an existing situation; the expert is being asked to look into the future and sketch the probabilities, usually based on knowledge of what has happened in similar circumstances before.

Emotional interviews

The emotional interview is by far the most tricky type. Good reporting covers all shades and colours of human emotional experiences. There is the happiness of the sporting record breaker; the anxiety of a mother whose child is missing; the anger of a man who has been attacked and robbed. In an emotional interview, a certain amount of silence is more telling than any words, as the subject pauses to gather his or her thoughts, perhaps in the midst of mental turmoil.

Journalists are sometimes criticized for exploiting the emotions of others who may be in trouble or despair. In reality, no one can be compelled to talk if they do not wish to, and it has been said that people suffering in some way can find relief in recounting their feelings. After a big train or motorway crash, there is rarely a shortage of survivors who are anxious to tell their stories. It is often suggested by journalists that the act of describing a narrow escape seems to reduce the shock. However, that is not to condone the actions of a small minority of reporters – sometimes from newspapers – who undeniably overstep the bounds of decency in their efforts to get the big 'tear-jerker'. Journalists do not have the licence to cause extra misery to people who are already suffering enough.

INTERVIEW PREPARATION

If you are to ask sensible questions, you must know something about the subject. That is not to say that you need to be an expert yourself, but a few minutes of research is important beforehand.

However, you may well get pushed into an interview without any chance to prepare whatsoever. In that case, use your interviewee as a research resource. Let us say you are about to interview a union representative who is calling for a strike. You know little more than his name, his employer's name and the union he represents. If you ask for an outright briefing before the interview, he may respect your honesty or he may feel contempt for your lack of knowledge, however unavoidable it may have been. So start the recording and ask a wide-ranging question: 'Why do you think that a strike is now inevitable?' It is difficult to answer that question without giving a clue to the last offer from the employer! Now that you know the last pay offer was an extra 4 per cent, you can go on to ask what would be acceptable and so on. The interview has begun.

Location

You may carry out an interview almost anywhere. Most are recorded, but even live interviews can be conducted in many places outside the traditional studio. When you go out on location, make the most of opportunities which may exist to include location sound when these are relevant. Some well-meaning interviewees will offer you a 'quiet room'. They are rarely of any use unless they are a purpose-built studio. In particular, many rooms in offices and factories can be full of gloss-painted walls and hard metal objects. The resulting recording will sound as if it was made in a swimming bath, full of harsh echo.

The 'quiet' room, even if it is reasonably well furnished and acoustically tolerable, still has one overwhelming defect – it is deadly boring. The point of going out on location is to paint an audio picture for the listener. Our colours are sound and our brush is a microphone, but the principles are the same. So question the airport manager with the sounds of jets taxiing on the Tarmac in the background; interview the union representative near the production line; talk to the teacher with children in the playground (if the school bell rings, carry on – it all adds hue to the audio picture!).

If all else fails, simply conduct the interview outside. The combination of birdsong, distant traffic, footsteps, the rustle of trees and similar sounds combine in what is sometimes known as 'atmosphere' or 'atmos' for short. Indeed, there are sound effects CDs consisting of nothing else, which are intended to create a counterfeit exterior background for commercials and plays recorded in studios. Atmos is a curious phenomenon – we simply do not notice it in reality, but it jumps out of the radio! Background atmosphere is definitely better than the 'deadness' of an empty room.

You need to be aware of the dangers of background sound. Do not let it be too loud or your interview will be drowned. Your interviewee may also be distracted and feel obliged to shout. Do realize that some background sounds, like roadworks, will make seamless editing almost impossible. The noise will change abruptly with every cut. Do not be tempted to add sounds from effects CDs which are not there! That is not objective reporting. It is acceptable, though, to record some extra background sound after an interview – say 30 seconds of general background without any speech. Known as 'wildtrack', this clean sound can help if an edit is unavoidable, as it can be dubbed into the main recording to cover a splice. It is also useful as a background to your links when putting a wrap or package together.

'What did you have for breakfast?'

This question has gone into the lore of radio reporting. Newcomers – and some old hands – think it helps to ask the interviewee about the first meal of the day in order to get some recording level and get the conversation going. It is all rather artificial and is better avoided – especially after one famous politician answered: 'An interviewer'!

It is much more practical to ask an interviewee for his name and job title. You can take some level on that and your recording is immediately tagged with crucial information.

A chat before the interview is fine – assuming you have the time. It is perfectly acceptable for the interviewee to ask what, in general, the piece will be about, if that is not already obvious. You can do a little more discreet research at the same time. But never allow an interviewee to insist on a list of questions in advance. You cannot let yourself be tied in this way because, by agreeing to ask certain things, you are also agreeing not to raise other matters which may become more interesting as the interview progresses. One experienced reporter says how, if asked for a list of questions in advance, he replies: 'Only if I can have a list of your answers!'

Never have an in-depth discussion with the interviewee beforehand. Often, you will get your best material when the recorder is switched off. They are also likely to say '...as I said before...', which the listener would not have heard.

Watch the language

Of course, everyone should use words acceptable for broadcasting. But there is another kind of language – the language of the body. The interviewee may inadvertently reveal a lot about his mental state by his posture. Folded arms may be a sign of defensiveness; wringing hands, crossed legs and tapping fingers may reveal various states of tension. Tapping fingers, by the way, must be stopped with a courteous request. Otherwise, the recording will probably be spoilt by a most peculiar thumping sound. Be careful also about the way you hold the microphone. Do not move your fingers too much or this will be picked up and also remove rings which might scratch against the outer casing of the microphone. It is also easy to shove the microphone under someone's nose, which is highly distracting. Try to tuck it neatly under the interviewee's chin (Figure 8.1).

QUESTION TECHNIQUE

Doing an interview is a tricky business – and much more so for radio people than those who work in print. That is because not only do we have to get the information, we also have to get good audio.

You encourage an interviewee to talk by asking questions. That is your job. But do not be tempted into dominating the conversation – the listener wants to hear the voice of the interviewee rather than that of the interviewer.

Develop a real interest in your interviewee. Make them feel important and show interest and curiosity about their ideas and opinions. Have a chat or a conversation with them. Try not to 'interview'. Rarely 'grill'. Come up

Figure 8.1
When interviewing on location, make sure to tuck the microphone just under the interviewee's chin to allow eye contact and loop the lead to give some slack should it be accidentally pulled away

with questions that keep the flow going. Do not keep jumping from one subject to another.

Eye contact

Encourage your subject with eye contact; it is friendly up to a point, but glance elsewhere now and then, otherwise it becomes aggressive. Use nods of the head to show that you are listening and understanding. Do *not* say 'yes' or 'I see' and other audible means of encouragement we use in conversation. Your words will be a real nuisance when the interview is played back.

If you need to check your audio recorder – to confirm the level or make sure the recorder is still running – then do so, but look back at your subject quickly. The interviewee will be disconcerted if you gaze elsewhere for long. He or she will think you are bored!

Listening to answers

This is another good argument against prearranged questions. You *must* listen to what your subject is saying:

> SUBJECT: 'So a man of my height, just over six feet six, does have a real problem finding clothes that fit.'
> REPORTER (not listening): 'So how tall are you then?'

Do not simply stick to your prearranged list of questions. Listen and use your natural curiosity, otherwise you might miss the real story.

Asking one thing at a time

Make an effort *not* to ramble:

> REPORTER: 'Would you say, then, that bus drivers have had enough, that is, that they are saying they aren't paid enough so that they might take action – er, actually go on strike?'

Do not ask multiple questions:

> REPORTER: 'Is it true that treating the roads cost the county more than thirty thousand pounds last winter and that you had to use salt as well as grit and that it didn't work well in places?'

Do not start quoting alternatives – then stop in mid-sentence:

> REPORTER: 'Are you recommending to victims that they go to the police or the council or the Citizens' Advice Bureau or ...?'

Try not to interrupt, unless your subject is never going to stop until you intervene. Interruptions often sound untidy, and they are very difficult to edit sensibly into a short cut.

If you are in any doubt about suitable questions, remember the basics: *who*, *what*, *where*, *why*, *when* and *how*. For example: 'What's happened?'; 'Where's the accident?'; 'Who's involved?'; 'How many people have been injured?'; 'Why did the coach overturn?'; 'When will the road be clear?' There is no particular order of priority. It depends on the circumstances. However, this kind of direct questioning will get you information quickly. Then you ask any necessary supplementary questions.

This classic question is a good example of keeping things short:

> 'Obviously, err Reverend, you don't like the idea of erm these prep schools being used as fashionable schools for middle class parents, but erm do you really think that erm it matters if they believe, the parents themselves, in a Christian education as such, I mean would you be happy if they particularly wanted and believed that a Christian or the Anglican sort of education was right for their kids, would you like the church schools to remain in that case, as long as you were convinced of their sincerity, rather than the fact that they were doing it simply because it was a fashionable middle class thing to do?'

The answer was: 'That's a very good question. I don't know'!

Leading questions

These questions encourage a certain answer and they are useful up to a point for creating the opportunity for an interviewee to say something which may make a good cut. Do not overdo these questions, as you are in danger of putting words into your subject's mouth. Beware also that they are necessarily 'closed' type questions which could lead simply to a 'yes' or 'no' answer: 'So would you say that mothers must take extra care?'; 'You must be very angry about the decision?'

Cliché questions

Think about your question technique. Each question you ask should serve a specific purpose. Do not fall into 'knee-jerk' interviewing habits:

> REPORTER (to sobbing woman): 'How do you feel?'

Coaching interviewees

Sometimes you have to coach your interviewees to get the best out of them, especially if they are nervous and not used to being on the radio. Take this real example when a reporter is trying to get an elderly cyclist to say one full sentence that can be used in a clip:

'What's the most miles you've done in a year?'
'Err ...'
'Let me tell you it was two years ago you did 6000 ...'
'That's quite correct and I was going to break the record'
'You tell me. Say, "Two years ago I did 6864 ..."'
'That's quite correct'
'So *you* say it, "Two years ago I did ..."'
'Yes, I did, and the last year ...'
'You did what?'
'I was going to break the record, till I had a bad illness'
'So how many miles is the record?'
'*That* was the record'
'What was?'
'The 6000 ... err ... what was it now?'
'6864'
'That's right, yes'

One-word answers

Sometimes your interviewee is determined to give one-word answers. This means you have to think on your feet. This is a transcript of a real interview. Try and think what questions the reporter could have asked to get fuller replies:

'And by the time the police had come presumably the gunman had gone?'
'Gone'
'Can you give me any idea of how much money was in the safe?'
'No'
'Would you care to make an estimate?'
'No I wouldn't'

'Was anything else other than money taken?'

'No'

After the interview

Do not go on longer than is reasonably necessary. Remember that you have got to listen to it all back afterwards. If you want a 30-second cut, 15 minutes is too much to record. Five should be plenty and ten more than ample. If you are after a clip and you hear what you want during the recording, wind up as soon as you can. There is no point in going on in the hope of something better. It is not a good idea to let the interviewee hear the interview back. It takes up too much time and may take away your independence.

Thanks

Remember to thank your subject. It is good public relations, as well as common courtesy, and you might need to talk to them again in the future. Some radio stations take this even further by sending a short standard thank you letter or e-mail after an interview. If you can, give your interviewee an idea of when the piece is likely to go out. Do not promise anything as you cannot guarantee the broadcast time. They may encourage friends, colleagues and family to listen.

SPECIAL INTERVIEWS

Live interviews

Live interviews are difficult, especially when the big story breaks and you need to interview live into the news bulletin. You may have just 60 seconds allocated to the story. Get going quickly. Ask basic questions and keep them very short, otherwise you may waste the whole interview on one answer. Concentrate on information. Interruptions may now be unavoidable.

Vox pops

Vox pops – literally the Latin *vox populi* or the voice of the people – are useful for lightweight subjects such as how people celebrate St Valentine's Day, or a more heavyweight breaking story of really universal interest like a rise in income tax.

A good vox pop consists of short statements from members of the public, chosen at random in a street, neatly edited together in a stream of comments. Try to vary your subjects between young and old, male and female. The cue should make it absolutely clear what the question was. Out in the street, stick to that one question and do not be drawn into a long interview with one person. Names of interviewees are not necessary for once – and neither is it necessary to name the reporter. Here is a sample cue, adapted from a real story, about a Royal birth: 'Princess Sharon's new baby girl is to be called Tracey Jane Frances Victoria. The choice breaks with tradition as there's never been a member of the Royal Family called Tracey before. We went out on the streets of Southend to see what people think about Princess Tracey ...'

If there is a clear majority of opinion on a controversial subject, your vox pop should echo that slant. If most people do not like the idea of a princess called Tracey, then most of your clips should express the general opposition. Choose a humorous clip to end, if the subject allows.

Remember that not everyone likes being approached at random by a radio reporter. Keep smiling, keep your recorder running, stay courteous and do not pester people who do not want to know. If you are a nuisance, you will bring the name of your radio station into disrepute and you could be 'moved on' by police.

Go somewhere appropriate to the story. If it is about the price of beer going up, interview people in a pub. Be careful not to trespass on private property – for example, shopping centres.

One good trick is to approach people who cannot move on – at a bus stop, for example. Many people naturally dislike approaching members of the public for vox pops. You have to steel yourself. Chat them up, say they are doing you a great favour and you only want a moment of their time. Approach people who are in groups. If one responds, the others will also.

News conferences and 'scrums'

These can be free-for-alls. Some are relatively well organized in a hall or conference room – even a church. Others are impromptu affairs on a doorstep, which start when a VIP emerges from a meeting. Do not be afraid to be at the front of the scrum. You and your microphone have just as much right as any other reporter – especially if the microphone has a flag with your station name and logo. Television crews may not appreciate having your microphone in their shot – that is their tough luck. On the other hand, do not deliberately block their view with the back of your head.

If the VIP is going to say something once and disappear, you need the story just as much as anyone else, so be firm with any of your professional colleagues who try to elbow you out of the centre of the story because you are 'only radio'. Sadly, there are a few reporters who may try this, claiming they are more important. Do not be intimidated. In this game, everyone is equal.

At more organized news conferences, do not hesitate to request one-on-one interview facilities as soon as you arrive. The organizers may be genuinely ignorant of radio's needs and suppose that questions shouted from the body of the hall will be adequate, as they can be for newspaper journalists. It is acceptable to 'share' or 'pool' recorded interviews on these occasions, if necessary. All radio reporters record at the same time and each one should get in a question or two. Do not worry if the result is a mixture of questioning voices, including reports from 'the opposition'. Consult your editor, naturally, but as a general rule, such interviews are dramatic and deserve a good piece of airtime.

If the TV people say they need an interview first, say you will have recorded yours for radio by the time they have finished setting up their lights and microphones!

Unattended studios

These are common in local radio and are frequently situated in civic centres and other public buildings in towns distant from the radio station. The unattended studio (sometimes called a 'remote' studio) is linked to the main station by landline or ISDN line, which gives good quality speech reproduction.

The radio station often asks an interviewee to go to the studio, let themselves in and turn on the equipment so they can be interviewed 'down the line'. There is always a microphone, a phone and usually some form of simple mixer. There should be clear, understandable instructions about what needs to be switched on and what phone number should be called, so that the interviewee can alert the newsroom to his or her arrival.

The interview itself is conducted using the quality line to carry the subject's voice to the radio station. Questions are usually asked via the phone. If the questions are recorded simultaneously at the radio station end by the reporter through his own microphone, the result is a full 'quality' interview, even though the two parties may be miles apart.

Interviewing other reporters

Some stations, particularly BBC local stations linked with a regional television station, may have access to a special correspondent with specialist knowledge in Home Affairs, Health or the Environment. When talking to an 'in-house' expert, only ask them information of which they can be sure. They can certainly give their judgement on a situation, based on their experience and understanding gathered from speaking with those involved. But you should never ask them to speculate on something of which they cannot be sure, or which would put their impartiality in jeopardy.

Interviewing children

Before you interview children you need to ask the permission of a parent, guardian or head teacher if appropriate. Then, if permission is granted, you should be particularly careful in your interviewing technique. No inducement, financial or otherwise, should be offered as a condition for the child saying what they may believe you want them to say. Similarly, you should be careful you do not ask leading questions, or prompt them into saying certain things. Be aware that younger children may, unconsciously, find it hard to distinguish between fantasy and reality. Older children may also lie – but on purpose.

Interviews with children on sensitive subjects – crime, family troubles, drugs and so on – should always be arranged through a third party, representatives of which should be present during the interview.

Interviews with criminals

Legally you should be very careful, and take further advice if you want to go ahead with such a recording. If you record someone who has left the country but is still wanted here, you should note that what you broadcast may prejudice a trial. Any interview with someone wanted by police in this country may in itself be a criminal offence – as you may know where they are and be legally obliged to tell police.

In short, such interviews are rarely allowed, and even when they are care should be taken that their crime is not glamorized or information given which could lead to copycat actions. Certainly, no payment should be made.

Permission for any interview with a prisoner has to go through the authorities and is unlikely to be granted. If a prisoner calls you from a prison phone it is not illegal to broadcast it, although you would be well advised not to put it out live. You should also be aware of the possible impact such a broadcast may have on those affected by the original crime.

Interviewing witnesses

If recordings are made before a trial, you should be aware that you may influence the trial itself and therefore be in contempt of court. Your questioning may also cloud the memory or judgement of a witness – and you should therefore wait until they have appeared. Even then, keep a copy of the full raw unedited piece in case there is any later criticism. You should never ask a witness about their individual court appearance.

Interviewing victims or their relatives

It should go without saying that those traumatized by a recent loss should not be cajoled or encouraged to be interviewed if they do not want to be. A tip is to approach those concerned through someone else, a neighbour, clergyman or friend. Sometimes those who are grieving do want to be interviewed in order to talk about their loss, or their anger at what has happened. In such circumstances, it is a good idea to introduce your piece with an explanation that this is the case, so you are not seen as being intrusive. You must also be careful that you do not broadcast something that may pre-empt a court case.

Interviewing politicians

These expert media manipulators may try and put certain conditions on an appearance: they may want to know what the questions are in advance, or only appear if it is a live programme and so on. It is up to you as an independent broadcaster to ensure that you remain impartial both in your questioning of the subject and in your agreement or otherwise to their 'terms'. Beware they are expert interviewees and many have been taught techniques of how not to answer questions!

When interviews are refused

As a broadcaster you do not have the right to force people into an interview situation. Anyone can decline the opportunity to speak, even if you believe it may put him or her in a bad light. It is, however, your duty to explain on air if a certain view is not represented – though not every refusal is worthy of such a comment. This technique is sometimes known as 'empty chairing'. Check with a senior colleague before you use phrases such as 'not available for interview' or 'refused to comment'. Be aware there is a difference between these two statements and they should be used fairly.

News reporting

THE RADIO REPORTER

The traditional image of the reporter is of a scruffy figure in a trenchcoat, foot in the door, notebook in hand, demanding 'What have you got to hide?' or 'The public has a right to know.' If such reporters exist, there is no place for them in radio. Radio reporters do not threaten or browbeat; they do not resort to deceit or bribes. They also look smart as they never know where they might be sent. The Prime Minister will not want to be interviewed by a scruffbag!

The job of the reporter is to get the information or audio, get it right and get it on the radio – fast. Radio reporters know where to go to get the information, and who to talk to. They have an instinctive 'nose for news', ask lots of questions, are boundlessly enthusiastic and never give up until they have what they want.

A reporter also needs a touch of scepticism or suspicion. He or she accepts little at face value and sometimes realizes that, lurking behind a chance remark, a single fact, a few obscure sentences, an official silence, there may be more to be revealed.

Nowadays, it is usually the BBC and the larger commercial stations who employ full-time reporters. In medium-sized and smaller commercial stations, reporters are expected to combine their skills with news presenting, bulletin editing and writing. Reporting is only one aspect of the job. But, of all the journalist's skills, it is probably the most essential.

The briefing

All good reporters do their homework before going out on a story. It is useless for a reporter to be following up a story without knowing background information. You should keep fully informed and check cuttings and previous stories, if available. To a certain extent, the newsdesk will be able to brief you when assigning you to a story. This may take the form of a complete file of previous stories, or may simply be a name, address or phone number. Whatever, it is essential to think laterally and gather as much information as possible, within the time-scale, before actually going out on the road.

Remember, driving time is good thinking time (within the bounds of road safety!). While you are driving to the story, think about what you want to achieve, what is expected of you and how you are going to tackle the subject. For a moment, go back to basics, and ask yourself: 'What is this story *really* about?' Then, 'How would everyone else do it?' and 'How can I do it so it sounds different?'

Fixing ahead

There are two different sorts of reporting jobs. The first is a diary assignment – a function, event or interview notified to the newsdesk in advance, usually by a news release or phone call. For this, you need to arm yourself with the relevant background papers, read them and then, the most important thing of all, *think*.

You will usually be told (though sometimes it is up to you to decide) how much material is required and in what form. For example, a launch of a new counselling service for people suffering from depression may produce a 35-second bulletin wrap, a cut or clip alternative and a four-minute package for a programme.

You will also be told when the various pieces are required. You could be sent out at 2 p.m. and told something is needed for the 4 p.m. news. Or, if it is not immediately important, the piece would simply be an 'overnight' for the next morning.

On this sort of job, most of the information about where and when to turn up is made available in advance. Sometimes a phone call is needed if you have particular interview or audio needs.

The other sort of job is the instant reaction callout. A bomb has exploded, a fire has started or a police officer has been shot. There is little time to think or plan ahead. You simply get to the scene as quickly as possible and tell the story. If it is a big story requiring live coverage, your newsdesk will need not only to despatch you with the radio car but, in addition, arrange permission for access and parking.

Working to deadlines

It is important that you as the reporter know what your newsdesk needs and when it needs it. The deadline is vital. It is no use having a brilliant clip of audio of a stunning eyewitness account of an event if it misses the bulletin. Know what is needed before you leave the newsroom. Ironically, you will find that you work better having a deadline and being put under pressure.

In a major incident, it is important to stay in touch with the newsdesk as much as possible so that you can be told of changes in deadlines and requirements. News is all about what is happening *now*. Your deadline could be five minutes before a bulletin or it could be while the bulletin is on the air as you do a live insert from a mobile phone or radio car. Whatever it is, make sure you stick to the deadline and file something – anything – by that time.

ON LOCATION

The big story has broken, you have been briefed, told of your deadlines, researched any background, grabbed photocopies of previous stories, remembered to take a mobile phone (and switch it on!), remembered to grab your portable audio recorder (with microphone, recharged batteries and disk!) and you are on your way through the traffic to the story, all the time thinking about what to do, how to do it and how to get the story on the air. You will be listening to your station's output, or that of your rivals, to glean as much up-to-date information being put out as possible.

What to do first

On arrival at the scene of the fire, explosion, shooting or whatever, you have first to assess the situation. Find out if the event is still happening or has finished. Make contact with the emergency services. Try to grab an interview with the police officer or fire chief in charge straightaway. If it is a dramatic event which is still continuing, phone the newsdesk immediately. File a 'holding' voicer from the scene, describing what you can see. After you have done this, ask your newsdesk to contact the emergency services and find out who is in charge and enlist their co-operation.

Remember the power and the glory of a story often lies in its sound. Record and use that natural sound. Turn on your portable recorder and start recording background noise or 'wildtrack' for later use in wraps and packages. Record at least a couple of minutes. If there are explosions, sirens or shots, keep the recorder rolling. Later, use the sound of the event underneath your report to give the listener the feeling of being on the scene.

Describe what is happening as you can see it and hear it. It does not matter if this appears to sound like rubbish at first; just keep recording and talking without making a judgement and you may be surprised at the results of your commentary and what you will eventually be able to use.

Eyewitness accounts

Usually at these incidents there are bystanders watching what is going on. Try to find an eyewitness to the incident you are reporting. Keep the recorder rolling. Make sure you identify yourself, but get them talking in front of a microphone. Most people are only too happy to describe what they saw and what they did and thought. You only need a few seconds of the most dramatic account. Ask questions. Do not forget, at the end, to get their name and record it on your portable.

Dealing with officials

The emergency services have a job to do. Theirs is the most important job, not yours. In many cases, they are in the business of saving lives. Let them get on with it. Try not to get in the way. However, watch out for the fire-fighters who are resting or police officers who are waiting and watching, and try to get instant reactions and descriptions from them. Of course, this will not always work and you will sometimes be told in no uncertain terms to go away.

eral, deal with the senior officers. If there is a press officer on the (which usually happens in major incidents), make sure he or she knows who you are and what you need. They will usually organize an on-the-spot briefing from a senior officer. Make sure you know where and when this is being held and if there are plans for regular updates.

Always keep in touch with the newsdesk via your mobile phone and tell them what is happening. Keep filing your eyewitness accounts and from-the-scene voicers.

Dealing with other reporters

It is up to you whether or not you associate with the scores of other television, radio and newspaper reporters who will turn up at a dramatic event. Usually, it is best to work in a group and help each other out, although always be on the lookout for the exclusive eyewitness that the others have failed to spot.

It helps to pool information, especially official information, to make sure everyone is broadcasting the same facts. Facts are sacred and not exclusive, but views, comment and interpretation can be up to you.

FILING MATERIAL

Once you have arrived at the scene of a dramatic news story, it is important to get something on the air as soon as possible.

Getting on the air

Of course, the telephone is the best way of getting a story on the radio quickly. The most flexible phone to use in these circumstances is a mobile.

By far the best way of getting on the air with quality audio, though, is by using a radio car with a UHF transmitter. Radio car facilities vary from station to station but, in essence, they are simply a way of connecting a microphone and recorder to a mini mixer and sending the signal back to base via a big aerial. The aerial is raised by a small electrical pump, but it is vital to ensure that there are no overhead obstructions such as power or telephone cables before pressing the 'up' button. Once the link is established, the studio can receive audio and voicers in quality and either

Figure 9.1
Journalist Tim Gillett broadcasting live from the BBC Essex radio van. Note the telescopic transmitting aerial in the centre of the vehicle (*Source*: Ingrid Bardua)

broadcast them live or record them for editing and later transmission. Most BBC local stations are now equipped with larger radio vans with enhanced facilities for self-contained outside broadcasts of speech programmes (Figure 9.1).

On-the-spot voicers

If something dramatic is happening, try to ad lib your report. This will convey the drama of the event. If you have time, script your piece or work from notes. Some radio stations now equip their reporters with laptop computers, which help in these circumstances. If you cannot type your words, make sure your handwriting is clear. Many reporters have come to an embarrassing silence midway through a report because they cannot read their own scrawl! Try to sound dramatic, but do not go over the top and 'ham it up' too much. Do not shout, but sound forceful. End with a standard out cue or SOC – for example, 'Jamie McKeller, BBC News, Blankstown' or whatever your own station style requires.

Q-and-As

Usually, your piece will be pre-recorded. Sometimes it is better and more dramatic to do a live piece into a bulletin or programme. Make sure you can hear the off-air cue properly down the phone. Be sure to know when you will be needed and for how long. Try to get in a position where background noise can be heard. Again, remember the rules about working from a script if possible.

Question-and-answer pieces (also known as 'Q-and-As' or 'two-ways') happen when a presenter questions a reporter from the scene. If you are a reporter, make sure you are fully informed and up to date about what is happening. Try not to waffle just for the sake of it. Give the facts and do not speculate. Be responsible in what you say. Remember that in a siege, for example, a gunman could possibly have a radio tuned to your station and be listening as you describe the position of the police firearms team. If this is the case, you will not be able to tell your listener the whole story. But you are there to report what is happening, not to influence it.

Q-and-As should be planned where possible, but if you are asked something about which you do not know the answer, be honest and say so. There is another phrase you will hear used: 'head-to-head' is a straight interview between a reporter and a guest.

Live reports

Unless you are very gifted, live reporting on the scene of a fire, flood, hijack or train crash will lead to a string of clichés. The words will be colourless and unexciting. Yet you will have to give perhaps continuous coverage for several minutes on what is going on, as well as conveying some idea of the sights, sounds and smells.

Think of the scene like the start of a Hitchcock movie. Very often, the Master of Suspense moved the camera in from a town, to a street, to a house, to a window, to a person. In a similar way, you can bring action to life by slowly zooming in on the action:

- The scene – the overall situation, where it is, why it has happened.
- The mob – the general players, the crowd, the numbers and the mood.
- The players – the main characters in the story, who they are.
- The action – what is actually happening right now.

Much of this can be done before you arrive. Use staff at the station to find out many of the basics for you. Then when you arrive you will be able to size up the situation, and speak with eyewitnesses, those affected and the officials.

Another trick is not to give out too much information too soon. If you know that the cross to you will last two or three minutes, stagger your information so you have enough to fill that time.

'Car park' voicers

In certain circumstances, it can help to enliven a script or story by recording it outside, maybe in your station's car park on a portable recorder rather than in a studio. It is an effective production technique which creates an impression of being on the spot. The outside effects of passing traffic and birds will help 'lift' the mainly studio-based bulletin. However, do *not* claim in your standard out cue that you *are* on location. One day you will be caught out!

AUDIO PRODUCTION

Once you have arrived back in the newsroom, having filed all your phone or radio car pieces from site, you begin the daunting task of trying to put all the material together. On big stories, you will be required to assemble at least one short bulletin piece and a longer programme package from what could be as much as 45 minutes' worth of pre-recorded material, such as interviews and background sound.

You are crafting a piece, like an artist. Radio is theatre of the mind and you have to be creative when using words and sounds.

Choosing the cut

Remember the different ways of getting something on the air. You are probably, first of all, looking for an audio cut – a 20- or 25-second piece from an interview. Secondly, you are listening for an alternative cut and, thirdly, you need to wrap everything together. Do not forget the immense value of listening to everything you have recorded, in order to begin the selection process, on the way back to the newsroom from the scene while you are in a car or taxi. It saves valuable editing time if you can walk into the newsroom with a clear idea of what you are able to deliver and start dubbing and editing work straightaway. With experience, you will be able to identify possible cuts as you interview. Some recorders allow you to mark the recording as it is made, so cuts are easier to find when you return. At the very least, make a note of the counter on the machine.

Choose the most dramatic quotes from the audio you have gathered. Use the audio to get across descriptions, opinion or interpretations. Concentrate on the facts in the cue. Do not edit so tightly that the audio sounds unnatural, and make the cuts long enough to register with the listener. A cut of just three seconds is easily missed, although these may be useful for a tease or promo cut.

Choose a cut that has a proper start and ends decently – in other words, a self-contained statement. Do not choose a cut which starts 'But … ' or 'Well … ' (if you can help it). Try as far as possible to exclude your own voice. As you become more practised, you will develop an 'ear' for a cut, as soon as your interviewee says it. Always spend time 'cleaning' the audio. If the interviewee stumbles too much, the whole point is lost.

Wrapping or packaging

To construct your wrap or package, you will first of all need to listen to all your audio and make notes about what bits you want to use. Choose the cuts you want, then the wildtrack or background sounds. There are several different ways of putting a package together depending on the computer audio playout system you use. In general, put the cuts in separate computer files. Label them carefully so they can easily be identified. Write your script, then go to the production studio and record the whole wrap in one go. You can tighten up the audio if necessary later on.

Be sure to know exactly what is wanted from you. By this, you should know whether it is for a bulletin or programme and how long it is supposed to be. Try to make as much use of audio and background sounds as you can. After all, sound is what radio is all about. Once again, this is a creative process. Show off your sound. Audio can make the difference between an excellent piece and an average one. For example, the story everyone does twice a year about the clocks going back can be enhanced by putting the sound of clocks, chimes and cuckoos from a local clock-shop or jewellers under the report to make it come alive.

The more the listener feels he or she is at the scene, the better. And do not forget the value of using music as background or as a 'stager' at the start of your wrap; after all, music is the staple diet of many stations and it is a powerful way to connect to a listener. However, as with words and phrases, avoid musical clichés. You will not be the first to use Abba's *Money Money Money* under a piece on lottery handouts or Rod Stewart's *Sailing* under a piece about boats.

Writing cues

Do not include anything in your pre-recorded wrap or package which is likely to be out of date by the time it is broadcast, otherwise this will ensure you have the headache of a last-minute editing job. Make sure there is space for this information to be included in the cue.

It is particularly important, when material is coming in to a Bulletin or Programme Editor at breakneck speed, to make sure all the technical information about duration and out cue is included and marked clearly on both the cue itself and the computer file stored for playout. In particular, ensure that your piece is correctly timed.

When writing up the story, remember all the rules of good radio writing – and stay accurate. Use 'emergency landing' if that is what you are told. Do not use that phrase instead of, say, 'unscheduled landing', which usually happens if someone on board a plane is unwell.

10 Newsdesk management

The newsdesk is the centre of the news operation. Information arrives in a varying flow, depending on the time of day. Peak times tend to be the early morning up to the 8 a.m. bulletins (which on the vast majority of stations attract the biggest audience of the day as people get ready for work), in the hour up to 1 p.m. and once more in the early evening 'drive' time from 4 p.m. A big, breaking story can quickly generate numerous audio clips and a mountain of copy.

RUNNING THE NEWDESK

Getting organized

An untidy newsdesk can be a nightmare. The best stories can be mislaid at the last, crucial moment in a pile of disorganized copy.

So run a newsdesk as you would a military operation. In newsrooms still using paper, plastic office trays are good to contain copy. One tray is for current bulletin material. Another tray should contain stories from earlier in the same day which have been used and superseded. Do not let old copy stray too far – something in it could be needed to update a running story ('...just how many jobs are there at that company? We were quoting that figure this morning...') and the contents of the 'used' tray will form the overnight 'clip up' – the daily file of stories kept for reference.

If there is room, further trays can hold the cues for the national audio, if you use it, and also freelance copy. And still more trays can be used to take the cues for stories which have been written for later in the week. This may seem like too many trays, but they keep the paperwork together. Used and unused scripts will otherwise find their way across desks, behind PCs and onto the floor. Stories will be missed and facts go unchecked.

It is good practice to think several days ahead to stories that you know are going to happen (such as an announcement, launch or visit), and to write and record them in advance. You can also schedule 'holding' stories (those which are not time-specific) to certain days. This saves the end of the week scramble to find enough material to fill weekend bulletins, which can otherwise sound like a list of 'what's ons'.

A white board on the newsroom wall, divided into the days of the week and then again into breakfast, lunch and afternoon news periods, helps all staff focus on when stories can run. That is not to say that breaking news or time-sensitive stories should be left to another day, but that you make the best use of your time, staff and resources. For example, if a reporter is driving to an interview, can they do another one in the same town while they are there? If you are speaking on the phone to a local MP about a current issue, can you also record an interview with them about a Private Member's Bill they are raising in the House next week? If you can, schedule the additional stories as appropriate.

On an hour-by-hour basis, assemble the next bulletin in skeleton form as soon as you come out from reading the previous news. You can then add to it during the hour. It has been known for a Bulletin Editor to chase audio on a late breaking story – only to realize that what they have is the only audio available.

This whole process is made much easier by the use of computers. Very often, editors are able to drag and drop scripts from one bulletin line-up on-screen to another. Other 'holding' stories, updates or copy versions are then added as necessary.

Labelling audio and scripts

These can be labelled in whatever way suits you best, but it can be useful to have a recognized house style. Indeed, the BBC's ENPS system has an in-built command, which makes you input such information in a certain way.

Clips from the BBC's GNS have catchlines or 'slugs'; IRN audio cuts are numbered. Labelling audio properly, and in the same way as their corresponding cues, saves valuable seconds and ensures the correct audio is married to the correct script.

A label should show the catchline of the story – preferably just one word – as well as the name of the person speaking (or name of the reporter for a voicer), the duration and out cue (the last two or three words, so that the news presenter knows when it ends and can continue smoothly). For example:

COMMONS/Blair act
23″ OUT: … they were in power

STRIKE/Chantler voicer
28″ OUT: … early next week

There are various conventions for audio labelling. Different stations have their own habits, but generally 'fx' means a sound effect:

OUT … (laughter fx)

If a word or phrase is said more than once, the repetition is shown as follows:

OUT … their problem (×2)

The (×2) means that the news presenter will wait to hear that phrase twice before carrying on.

Another abbreviation is 'act' for actuality – meaning a clip of an event, interview or speech, but not a reporter's voice ('VP' – 'voice piece'; or 'vcr' – 'voicer').

Getting organized with computers

Needless to say, it is usually easier to organize a computerized newsroom than a traditional one, simply because many of the functions of organization, such as archiving and sorting, can be established and triggered automatically.

There is a growing number of different software systems being designed and used for newsrooms; however, most share a common way of handling cues and cuts.

There will be a template for writing cues and copy. All you have to do is fill in the blanks for the catchline and the body of the script. It will probably be automatically dated and timed for you as you write. After preparing the story, you file it ready for broadcast. If you are the Bulletin Editor, you can call up a list of stories ready for use, read and correct them if necessary, and reorder them either for printing or for cueing on the playout machine in the news studio ready for you to read on air from the screen. After use, the stories can be archived under date and time.

Taking audio

The news supplier will 'feed' audio at regular intervals, although news does not operate to a schedule and a cut can easily turn up outside these times. This means you should keep a constant ear on the supplier's output.

Always check the audio stored before playout. You may want to 'tidy' up a piece of audio using the waveform digital editor.

A newsroom is a busy and noisy place. You almost have to divide your brain into compartments to cope with keeping an ear over all the different sound sources from the audio feeds, colleagues, TVs, phones and output monitors.

Deadlines

Be ruthless about deadlines. Put into effect a 'gate', so that three or five minutes before a bulletin, you can 'close' it to new material and go into the studio. If you are on your own in the newsroom, do not worry about that updated audio which arrives two minutes to the hour. You might miss the start of a bulletin for the sake of one update, which would be a disaster. *The bulletin matters most.* In the end, the listener is probably only listening to one radio station and he or she does not know what stories you have failed to carry. But the listener will notice if the bulletin sounds odd and breathless or is not there at all!

BULLETIN CONSTRUCTION

Finding the lead

Having a tidy and well-organized newsdesk means that you can see what stories are available and you can then move on to the next step – putting the bulletin together.

The first decision is to choose the lead story. The lead will be the most important story – the one which, in your judgement, will be the most likely to grab the listener's attention. Some leads choose themselves – the Prime Minister resigning, or hundreds of people dying in a plane crash, or the Russians just landing a man on Mars!

But there are other days when there is no obvious top story. In this case, choose the best three or four, those that 'sound like leads', and cycle them in different bulletins. There is no rule that says the top two stories in the 10 a.m. bulletin should not be reversed for the 11 a.m. However, the first words of the bulletin should be fresh. This may mean rewriting a story with a new cue, so go ahead and do it. What does sound bad is the 'lead' story which turned up in exactly the same form as the second story in the previous bulletin.

If you are looking for leads, pay close attention to the most recent TV news or bulletins on other radio stations, or even (especially in the early morning) what the newspapers are doing. There are limits to this; the tabloids may lead with a vicar-and-blonde-in-a-sex-romp story, which is probably unsuitable for your station. If all the nationals agree on a lead (which is not that common), then they are probably correct. Remember, though, that they wrote their stories several hours ago – look for an angle which will update the news for the breakfast audience.

One more point: if your bulletins are 'mixes' of national and local stories, do not be afraid to lead with local news when you can. A strike involving 200 people in a local factory may be more important in your area than a bigger industrial dispute elsewhere. Some stations lead with local stories as a matter of policy, but critics of this say rigid rules about local versus national can result in distorted bulletin priorities. At the same time, the USP ('unique selling point') of a local station is its localness; people are tuning to you for local news. Maybe a national story has a local implication or there's someone local who can give their opinion about it. This may be a local representative of the headteachers' union talking about A-level results, or the local green group on an environmental summit.

Do not be afraid to ask the opinion of your colleagues, about what they consider to be the most interesting story. Do not follow what they say blindly, but listen to their reasons as they may help you formulate your own.

The rest of the bulletin

Stories in the rest of the bulletin are often easier to put in order once your lead is established. There is no shame in simply running copy stories. In fact, many stations insist on a high 'copy story count', as this improves the pace of a bulletin and can give listeners a better overview of what is happening. For local stations it also means there is increased opportunity for more local place names to be mentioned.

If there is a major story which dominates most of the bulletin with several cuts of audio and voicers, acknowledge the others by saying ' ... in other news ...', then do a couple of lines on each.

Try to avoid using the same introductory phrases again and again. Even though there is nothing wrong with it, a constant stream of lines like 'Peter Porter reports ...' is unimaginative and can have a soporific effect on the listener. Use phrases such as 'Here's a report from ... ', 'Dan Robson has more on this ... ', 'Richard Morgan explains why ... ', 'Steve Gaisford outlines the problems involved ...' and so on. When there is a reporter in court, say so: 'Trevor Thomas was in court.' However, beware of clumsy phrasing: 'In court was our reporter Trevor Thomas'!

In the intro to each cut, ensure the listener is prepared for any distracting background noises. A line in the cue which says 'Rob Barnsley spoke to the councillor in a busy canteen' will prevent the listener being overtly distracted by the clinking of crockery and will enable concentration on what is actually being said.

Each story should be self-contained. As far as possible within the constraints of brevity, your listener should not need to know what was reported yesterday to understand what is being said today.

Remember that stories about the same general subject should be linked (' ... and still on the subject of house prices ... '). This is called creating an 'umbrella' of stories by topic, theme or thread. It works well if, in a mixed bulletin, you can follow a national piece with a local angle on the same story. Try to end with what is called a 'kicker' – something light, curious or genuinely funny (note the word 'genuinely'!) – as this makes for an easier transition into general programming from the news, but do not fret if there is nothing like that around. Try recapping the lead story again if your station does not forbid it: ' ... and the main story again this hour ... '.

This recapping has a pleasantly urgent ring to it, and also helps the listener who tuned in just after the start.

Avoiding repetition

Repetition is one of the biggest complaints from listeners about radio news. The problem that newsrooms often have is lack of staff and lack of time. In a one- or two-person newsroom, it is inevitable that copy can sometimes run for several hours. Many journalists believe that an entirely fresh audience tunes in every hour, but this is not the case. Although there is a rolling audience, 'real people' (unlike news junkies such as ourselves) do not listen to the radio in hour-long bursts. Some stations even call their bulletins 'updates' when they are just a bundle of repeated stories. Listeners quickly tune out when they realize that the stories are merely repeats.

Obviously, the ideal situation is for copy to be used only once. Radio's strength is freshness and immediacy, so we should rewrite with new details or a fresh angle.

- Highlight an impression of immediacy with time-sensitive phrases like ' ... and we've just heard ... ' – but remember to change that for the next bulletin!
- A reporter filing from the scene can send three or four versions for use later in the day. The same phrasing in a report can grate if used in successive bulletins.
- Interviews can be cut into several stories with different angles (it is faster than chasing and producing a new story).
- Write two versions of each story. That way you can alternate the versions and give an impression of movement.
- Computers make it simple to change the topline of a story or alter a phrase in the middle. It is the easy option, but it is better than nothing if you are short of time.

Judging editorial priorities

When choosing any of your stories, think of the Four Is: what *importance* does it have to the listener? What is its *impact* on their lives? What is its *interest*? And what is its *immediacy*?

In other words, are they stories that listeners *need* to know, even if they will not be directly affected – for example, the change of government in the United States.

Are the stories relevant to the way they lead their lives, affecting their health, families or how much money they have in their pocket?

What about the interest a listener will show in the stories? Is it likely to cause an emotion: make them laugh or cry, be angry, or thankful? Will they be amazed at the story's content: the largest, smallest of something or be intrigued by its quirkiness?

And is the story new, or linked to a recent theme? News of a fire that has just come into the newsroom may lead your bulletin one hour, but may be out and therefore dropped down the running order in subsequent bulletins. Or if the story is topical it may warrant a higher place in the bulletin than if it were not. For example, a story of a child being bitten by a dog may deserve to go higher if it is the third or fourth such incident in recent months.

Sport usually goes at the end of a bulletin unless the event is of wide significance ('England have just won the World Cup!'), or has news value ('Wembley Stadium is going to be rebuilt ...' or 'Dozens of football supporters have been arrested after ...'). On these occasions, such stories may lead a new bulletin, but ensure you liaise with your colleagues presenting the sports news that may follow you!

These judgements are confused further when you consider the local radio newsroom. It is the station's mission to cover events in the county, city or towns which they cover. Local stories are weighted so they go higher up a bulletin – however, the basic Four Is still count as a good checklist.

The running order of a news bulletin can be likened to chatting up someone in a pub. For some it is a natural skill, but for most it is something which has to be learned through experience, learning from mistakes and feedback, and watching and learning from others. In a similar vein, there are many ways to approach someone in a bar, just as no two news bulletins edited by two different people would be the same.

Follow that story...!

Once you have carried a good story, do not let it lie down and die too quickly. Nothing sounds odder than a lead which unaccountably disappears from the next bulletin entirely. Move a story slowly down in successive bulletins before dropping it and keep your story fresh with rewrites. A story which had good audio can be run as copy only later in the day. Should a good new angle develop, your story might well move up again. A story further down the bulletin can be dropped for an hour or two and then brought back. Watch, too, your balance of local, national and international news. A good mixed bulletin should contain all three, but in varying amounts depending on what is going on.

Often, you are able to extend the life of a story by letting it start as a voicer, running an interview with someone affected by the story ('setting it up'), and then with someone else criticizing it ('knocking it down'). This is particularly worth bearing in mind if, late one afternoon, you realize you are short of stories ('the overnights') to leave for the breakfast team the next morning. You must, though, be careful of running a story, and reaction to it, long after it was newsworthy.

Developing the story

With the life of a breaking story, a fire for example, you may be dropping the story down the bulletin throughout the day and then have a different angle later that is strong enough for a lead:

Day One
Breakfast, lead audio – The fire has broken out. Where is it? When did it start? What is on fire? How many fire-fighters?
Mid Morning, second or third story – Investigations are underway, crews are damping down, the extent of the damage being assessed, the owner of the property speaks about his or her loss.
Afternoon, lead audio – Breaking news. A body has been discovered in the building. Rough description of the person. Interview with police. Could it be murder?
Evening news round-up – Pulling together all the audio and angles of the day.
Day Two
Breakfast, mid-bulletin copy – Enquiries continue. Who was the dead person? Post-mortem results due today.

Breaking the rules

You may want to consider breaking the 'rules' sometimes, to use sound more creatively. That way, your stories and bulletins may have more impact.

- Start your bulletin with audio, either before your main intro or immediately after it. This is best done with breaking news, and also with strong audio.
- Begin a bulletin with a live report from a reporter 'at the scene', who does their own introduction. 'It's eight o'clock. This is Matt Stewart live at the scene of a major blaze in Blankstown, where the UK's largest tyre factory's still alight after 24 hours ... .'
- Use a clip of audio at the start of a bulletin as a 'headline sequence' to tease what's coming up.
- Use audio of an interviewee, or another reporter, to tease an upcoming story. 'This is Matt Stewart – join me in the bulletin live at five, for the latest on the Blankstown tyre factory fire.'

Flash that snap ... !

A really good, dramatic and happening now story may not wait for the next scheduled new bulletin. A 'snap' usually becomes a 'newsflash' on air. Keep snaps short, only run them when news is really 'hot', and try not to break a story within a few minutes of the bulletin unless it is top priority. A decision on whether to snap should be taken by the editor, but it is the Bulletin Editor's responsibility to be on the alert for breaking stories and refer them upwards if necessary.

OTHER NEWSDESK DUTIES

The network

It is your local station's job to contribute to the network when a good story breaks locally. Where stations carry the national bulletin live, there is often a clash of interests.

A local story given to the network too quickly may turn up in the national bulletin and eclipse the local news which follows. This is a difficult situation, and one argument in favour of mixed bulletins. Some stations with a really good local story often mix their bulletins 'on demand', so that local listeners do not hear an excellent local story broken by a national newsreader.

In a very competitive radio market, where several 'rival' local stations overlap each other's areas and they all take the same national news supply, it is even more of a tricky decision to decide what, if anything, to give to the network. This is because the network gives instant access to your hard-won audio to your opposition. Be careful. Matters such as this need policy decisions by editors in consultation with station management and often depend on the politics of the marketplace. As commercial radio station groups merge, arranging themselves geographically and setting up news hubs, this is unlikely to be an issue.

Check calls

You may be working in a very small newsroom, but one vital job which cannot be neglected, if you are to keep the flow of news coming, is regular check calls to the emergency services. The police, fire and ambulance control rooms (and coastguards in some areas) expect calls from the media, but since not everyone in these services is equally willing to pass on information (some police officers especially remember the days when they were instructed 'don't tell the press anything'), it is wise to cross-check with all the services. In addition, the police may be called to a fire but they may not think it worth mentioning unless someone dies or it looks as though arson could be the cause. The fire service control, on the other hand, is more likely to give details of any call-out, serious or not.

There has been much coverage in the past of whether the emergency services, notably the police, release all the information they have. This may be because they are concerned about a perceived fear of crime, or that constant reporting may contradict lower crime figures. Some forces, even their press officers, sometimes seem more than a little reluctant to pass on potential stories, or only do so if asked about particular cases. Fire and ambulance staff, however, rarely have similar problems. It is therefore essential to maintain good relations with press officers.

An up-to-date 'calls list' is an essential. All the emergency services have specialist officers for the media and, as we mentioned earlier, there are the media voice-mail phone lines – and sometimes Internet sites – available to newspaper and television as well as radio journalists. Listen to them as often as possible, preferably once an hour at peak times and before major bulletins. If you have to speak to a press officer, it almost goes without saying that being polite and friendly will usually illicit more information than being accusatory that details of a story had been kept from you. Out of hours, a call may be routed to a control room or duty inspector rather than a press officer. Remember that these staff are not obliged to take your call, and they may be involved in a current emergency as they speak with you.

Headlines and teasers

Depending on your station's policy, you will need to write headlines for putting on air at half past the hour or at other headline break times. These headlines are usually no more than two sentences on each story and are completely self-contained, i.e. they must encapsulate the whole story. It is rarely possible simply to use the top two lines of the main cue. Write fresh headlines for each story, which are new words, but *not a new angle*. It is a good idea to make it a rule for each reporter filing a story to write a headline which can be stored and used if required.

Many stations also like their music presenters to promote and 'tease' the news bulletins. This is an excellent habit to cultivate and is well worth the extra effort to put something together which can be used. For this, you need to supply a taster of what is coming up in the form of, say, the top local story and the top national story. Again, write these fresh from the original story.

Remember the difference between 'headlines', 'teasers' and 'coming up' promos. A headline tells the whole story in shortened form: 'Robbie Williams has decided to quit Britain for good. The singer says he's fed up with the taxes ... and the weather.'

A teaser does just that, teases the listener into wanting more information about a story: 'We'll tell you why Robbie Williams and the British weather just don't get on.'

A promo is somewhere in between, saying what has happened but also promoting the full coverage to come: 'We've got an exclusive interview with Robbie Williams on why he's leaving Britain to live in the States.'

Allocating reporters

If you are lucky, you may have one or more reporters available to follow up running stories. They are an expensive resource, so use them with care. Ask yourself whether it is more effective to send someone out on a single story which may take most of the morning or give them several stories to chase from the newsroom, relying on phone or down-the-line interviews. The correct answer could be either option; it all depends on the merits of individual stories, how many staff you have available, and the demands of bulletins and programmes.

Giving orders

The Newsdesk Producer, sometimes called the Bulletin Editor, has a relatively senior job. It follows that reporters will be taking direction. Producers, therefore, should remember that people respond better to requests rather than demands. It is the Producer's job to make the story clear to the reporter as far as possible. If you, as Producer, have a particular angle in view, do not expect the reporter to read your mind.

However, a good reporter, even if well briefed, will still be on the watch for other angles and may come back with something quite unexpected. It may not have been the way you saw the story initally, but do not be too quick to criticize. After all, the reporter on the spot should be better placed to judge a story. If that judgement really was in error, follow it up calmly later on, having made the best of what you were given at the time. Nothing is worse than a big row about what should have been (but now cannot be) done before you have to present a bulletin!

Priorities

Sometimes a quiet news day can explode with action and drama, with several apparently good stories breaking almost simultaneously. If that happens, stand back, keep calm and consider what to do first. Do not over-react and leap at the first thing to hand, because first may not be best. You must weigh up each potential story. Generally, pursue the easier ones first. You may get two or three finished in a short time. Then concentrate on the more difficult and time-consuming possibilities. It is a mistake to let everything else drop for the sake of one attractive but elusive story. You could end up with nothing.

Coping with crisis

Occasionally, the pace goes on warming up until it is too hot for comfort. If a spectacular story breaks, you do have to let other things go, albeit reluctantly. Consider that if County Hall is on fire with 2000 council staff evacuated and the town centre sealed off, you will not have time in your bulletins for much else anyway.

Do not hesitate to call for help within the radio station itself. People who are not journalists are nevertheless excellent at staffing the phones when, say, a foot of snow brings your area to a standstill. Staff from the Managing Director's office or the sales office are often intrigued at a chance to 'have a go' at news, even if it is under strict supervision.

Allocate your real journalists with care, pursue the major angles first and always think in terms of the next bulletin – preferably the next two or three. Do not overlook what is going out live – get a recorder running on the output if the story has spilt over into general programming.

On air in a crisis when reporting a disaster, one of the major concerns is to prevent distress. You have a responsibility to ensure that no listener is needlessly alarmed. At the beginning of a disaster story, you should try to give all the details of time and place, which will help isolate the circumstances of the accident. For example, in the case of a collision between two trains, you should say where it happened, the routes of the trains and their starting point departure times. When reporting accidents to public transport vehicles in large towns or cities, you should try and locate them as precisely – and as early in the story – as possible. The name of the hospital to which casualties have been taken is also helpful, together with any emergency phone number released by the police for casualty enquiries.

Weather news

The philosophy of giving people the news that interests them can be used in weather reports too. When people wake up in the morning, one of their main interests is the weather. They want to know what to wear and whether to take a coat; if they should put the heating on, or how the tomatoes in their greenhouse have coped overnight; if they should leave for work a little earlier because of ice or snow on the road.

> 'Bright and sunny now but a 50 per cent rain risk factor, top temperatures of 16 Celsius, 61 degrees Fahrenheit, lows tonight of 8 Celsius, 46 Fahrenheit, tomorrow 18 Celsius, 64 Fahrenheit. Right now it's 12 and 53.'

This certainly gives the facts, but the chances are seconds after you have finished saying it, the listener has thought: '*What's* the weather going to do?'

Give the weather in simple terms, in a way that is easily understood and remembered. Tell the weather rather than recite it. Make it relatable.

- 'Dress for rain and 15 degrees today.'
  Make it relatable further still by saying your listeners may 'need a raincoat/an umbrella rather than a parasol/it'll be wet for that big United match this afternoon/don't bother getting your barbecue out.'
- 'Today's weather will be 5 degrees hotter than yesterday's.'
  The listener has already experienced the previous day's weather, so they have got a comparison. Therefore, they know whether to dress with more or fewer clothes.
- 'The weather is getting better today, mostly sunny and 19 degrees.'
  Again, they have a relatability check.

Travel news

Radio gets its largest audience at the breakfast and tea-time rush hours, and most of those listeners are driving. So, travel information is of great use in these programmes.

Most stations will get their information from a supplier such as Trafficlink or the AA. They get it from phoning the police, councils and utilities to find out what is happening in their areas. They also use the Internet 'jam cams', police cameras or encourage listeners to call in. (In effect, the listeners are keeping themselves informed.)

But the authorities very often want to play down delays. Police sometimes much prefer to have hundreds of cars in a queue and know where they are, than have them cutting down unfamiliar roads in a hurry and causing another accident which would put a further drain on resources.

Added to that, listener reports may exaggerate a problem (what is their interpretation of a 'serious problem'/do they use the route often enough to know what's abnormal?) or be bogus altogether.

When a major problem does occur, the most useful traffic reports will suggest alternative routes. Armed with this knowledge, drivers can decide whether or not to strike out or sit it out.

Do not advise people to stay clear of town centres because of hold-ups. Shopkeepers (your advertisers and listeners) will be furious that you are driving away business. Just talk about the hold-up itself.

Present the travel news from the general to the specific: 'On the M99, northbound at Blankstown, there's a broken down lorry in lane 1.'

Stormlines and snowlines

Stations regularly gain audience in the winter months with the arrival of unsettled weather and you can help by making the content of your bulletins even more relatable to your listeners at this time of year.

It is a time when radio scores points massively over local newspapers and TV stations. People cannot get out to buy the papers (which cannot possibly have up-to-date information anyway). And TV can only skim the surface of what is going on regionally. You can be truly local radio, offering your listeners an invaluable service in these times. Very often, new listeners will sample the station to find out the latest situation on road closures and school closures; do not miss an opportunity to 'convert' them – say the name of the station regularly.

Because of their information provision, stormlines or snowlines are often run by the news teams. Information comes into the station via fax, e-mail and phone calls, then processed and given out on air. The public should use the usual phone-in number to give information on cancelled events, and there should also be a dedicated number for the press offices of emergency services, councils and headteachers with more important information such as school closures.

You must check, well in advance of the onset of autumn, that your contact details for schools, council emergency planning officers, utilities, hospitals and so on are up to date. Call those concerned and introduce yourself. Check on how they will distribute any information and that they have your correct contact details. Headteachers should call your ex-directory number, quoting their DFE number and a recognized 'code word' for security purposes. This stops pupils or parents trying to 'close' a school themselves! Take the opportunity to remind the headteacher that any necessary information will be broadcast on your station, and ask them to tell the pupils your station name and frequency – perhaps in a letter to parents, again well before the need may arise.

Back at the station, in the event of snow or storm, a call-down system for alerting staff should come into operation. This is often called a 'cascade', 'pyramid' or, more appropriately, 'snowball' system, where each departmental manager calls one or two members of their staff, who then call two or three others. This is a time when the station must pull together to provide an invaluable community service. There is no room for those who say 'it's not my job' – everyone from the Managing Director/Editor to receptionist or sales person should be aware that they may be required at the station to take information on the phones, run messages to the studio or make cups of tea.

In advance of winter, prepare plenty of stationery and ban anyone from using it. If you are 'snowed in' there will not be a chance for you to nip to the suppliers for more printer paper, or notepads on which to take details of cancelled events! Know what system you will use to handle the flow of information. Will you print sheets of information for the presenters to read, or send it directly to a screen in the studio? If you have an AM and an FM station, think if you want to broadcast all the information on one, and keep regular programmes on the other (obviously cross-promoting the choice of listening). How will you break up the flow of information so it is most easily followed by the listener? An alphabetical list of schools, a geographical split, or just as they come to hand? Will you have the ability to post all the information on your website? If yours is a commercial station, is there a sponsorship opportunity for this service? Strongly dissuade people from calling the station to *get* information. Say on air, and if they call, that all the details you have will be broadcast and that they should keep listening. It will be a logistical nightmare to offer a personal information service to each and every listener, and would dispense with the point of you running a radio station! It also discourages people from listening to the radio – something that we certainly do not want to happen.

Another point well worth making here is how to deal with people who are offering to give help to their neighbours or the elderly. Do not deal with these people directly, but ask them to contact volunteer agencies and charities instead (The Red Cross, WRVS and so on – make sure you have their numbers to hand!). The station must not be in a position where some kind of perceived 'authority' has been given for a stranger to enter the home of a vulnerable person.

As far as news coverage goes, you will be reporting on the weather situation in some depth – the bulletins can be a focal point for a complete information round-up. Include the travel situation, the number of schools, businesses and events closed, a detailed weather report and so on. Many 'human interest' stories may also come out of the situation: the woman who gives birth in a police car on the way to hospital, the child who falls through an iced-over pond, the farmer or power workers who battle through the elements to feed their animals or repair electricity cables.

But you can also have a brainstorming session in advance of winter to come up with more 'holding' story ideas:

- AA/RAC or local/regional car start company on the number of call-outs to flat batteries, frozen locks.
- Local or regional builder or glazier to interview after a night of storms, to talk about roofs blown off.
- A friendly approachable tree surgeon, to talk about blown-down trees.
- Sales reports on shovels, toboggans and snowblowers.
- Travel agents on sales of holidays to the sun.
- What is the coldest place in the area? A local meteorologist (probably from the local paper or TV station) may be able to help you locate the highest place that you can keep an eye on.
- What is the coldest place to work in the area (an ice-cream factory, hospital morgue)? How do staff there cope in the cold months?
- Preparations at the local hospital for broken legs (or worse), blood supplies, labour wards.
- The supply of salt and sand. Where is it? How much is stored? How many vehicles does the council have? How soon can they be on the roads?
- How do your local traditional summer activities cope? The gardens, the beach or the theme park?
- The local electricity or gas company. How much does consumption rise by?

Do you want an additional reporter (as well as the one provided by an outside source like AA Roadwatch or Trafficlink) out on the road? Travel news will be in high demand. Give them a mobile and a minidisc and get them to drive down major roads in the area, pulling over from time to time to give live reports into news and shows. They could interview stranded motorists, tow truckers and so on. But they must be careful not to be stranded and become a story themselves.

Are you running an ROT so you can cut and clip callers that the presenter takes to air, and turn round for the news? They will undoubtedly have people phoning from across the area with on-the-spot weather and road reports and tales of woe. Coach the presenter to take the numbers of the best callers so you can phone them back and do a news interview.

Bomb threats

In these increasingly sensitive times, it is possible that even a small station may receive a bomb warning, or a threat of one. Despite the chances that the call is from a terrorist rather than a hoaxer being small, stations should treat all such calls as legitimate until proven otherwise.

All those who are 'front-line' staff should be briefed on what to do in the event of a threat – that's journalists, receptionists, studio producers and on-air staff. A form, which can be downloaded from the Home Office website (www.homeoffice.gov.uk/oicd/bombs/pdf), should be provided, read and understood. It asks those who take the call to identify the sex, age, accent and so on of the caller, together with the exact words spoken. It also prompts you to listen to any sounds in the background of the call, and even to dial 1471 to help identify its source. Needless to say, the police should be contacted immediately with such information.

In the newsroom you will have to balance the public's right to know about disruption caused by roads or buildings being closed, with the 'oxygen of publicity' being given to any terrorist threat. There is also the argument that to publicize the reason behind what has happened may encourage hoaxers. Hoax calls are usually not reported, unless they had a large and obvious knock-on effect – for example, traffic flow. It is usual in such situations to say any disruption is due to 'an incident' or 'security alert'.

News blackouts

News blackouts are usually co-ordinated by the police, who may tell the media about, for example, a kidnap, blackmail or threat, in return for secrecy. It may be that lives are at risk, or negotiations are at a difficult stage, and any publicity may be detrimental to the outcome. The fact that police are open to journalists and tell them about such an operation means that the story is not uncovered and reported, unknowingly putting lives in jeopardy. If you are advised of such a blackout and voluntary agreement, tell your senior station management at once. On-air staff and journalists should be advised that any 'unusual' news stories, tip-offs or calls should be referred to a senior member of staff before it is broadcast. Obviously, you must keep the details of a news blackout to as few people as possible, but guard against the risk of a story going out by mistake. It could be something as innocuous as a caller to a phone-in competition who reveals details of police activity, so all on-air staff should be vigilant.

In return for the news blackout, it is usual for police officers to speak to the media once it is lifted, and give on-the-record interviews and background information – as much, that is, as is then legally possible.

Defence advisory notices

This system, previously called D-Notices, advise what kind of information may damage national security if broadcast. The lists themselves are in the public domain (www.dnotice.org.uk) and cover:

- Military operations, plans and capabilities.
- Nuclear and non-nuclear weapons and equipment.
- Ciphers and secure communications.
- Sensitive installations and home addresses.
- United Kingdom security and intelligence services and special forces.

Guidance should be sought from senior station staff, the police or Home Office, if you come across information in these categories.

Reporting suicides

Usually, radio stations do not cover suicide stories. That is because they intrude on the private grief of a family that is already distraught over the death of a loved one. There is also some evidence to show that inappropriate reporting of such events can lead to copycat suicides.

However, in some cases, a suicide becomes a news story that should be done – for example, the death of Conservative MP Stephen Milligan, who was found dead on a kitchen table wearing women's stockings with a plastic bag over his head. Or the death of rock singer Michael Hutchence in an Australian hotel room after a drugs overdose and, even more so, the subsequent suicide of his lover Paula Yates.

A simple guide is to report a suicide if it is in a public place where other people were at risk – for example, someone jumping off a motorway bridge – or if the victim is well known.

Fooling around

Stations invariably try and play a practical joke on their listeners on 1st April. To give the gag extra credibility, station management often wants the joke to be repeated in the news bulletin. What you end up doing is down to your individual station, but it is worth bearing in mind that, by giving the gag credibility, you could be in danger of losing exactly that for forthcoming bulletins for the rest of the year.

If you are going to take part in the hoax, do it well. The story should be written and presented in a similar style to that of the rest of the bulletin and an interviewee should sound authentic (although it is pretty difficult to get someone to sound natural under 'spoof' circumstances).

The tradition of news being involved in April Fools Day is well documented. In 1957, the respected broadcaster Richard Dimbleby presented part of TV's *Panorama* programme on spaghetti harvesting!

Alternatively, it may be you that's caught out by someone else's hoax! Be extra vigilant, and triple-check everything that comes into the station on that day. If you fall victim to a prank (perhaps by another media outlet), then it is certain that your credibility will be blown. Just because another media outlet has used the story, it does not mean that it is OK. Maybe they have been duped!

11 Legalities

Journalists do not have special rights under the law, except for a few occasions when a journalist has a legal right of access which is denied to the public – for example, at a youth court. In addition, some journalists have tested their traditionally proclaimed right to protect their sources, but not always with success. Generally, the journalist has the same rights and responsibilities as any citizen.

It is vital for all radio journalists to have a working knowledge of certain key areas of the law. Because there is room here for only a brief summary, as the law is ever-changing and because there are different laws and processes in Scotland, Northern Ireland, the Channel Islands and the Isle of Man, you would be well advised to read more detail in a specialist legal book. *McNae's Essential Law for Journalists* by Tom Welsh and Walter Greenwood (Butterworths Law) and *Scots Law For Journalists* by Bruce and Bonnington, Alistair McKain (W. Green & Son) are particularly recommended.

Staying within the law demands a knowledge of the legal process and of the constraints which the law imposes. The two main areas which concern journalists are *libel* and *contempt*. These are both incorporated in the 1998 Human Rights Act, which guarantees people a range of civil and political rights. For example, Article 10 is the right to freedom of expression, and Article 6 guarantees the right to a fair trial.

The laws of libel and contempt are complex and change from time to time. There are also a number of exceptions to the general rules. If in doubt, take legal advice or consult a specialist book on the subject – before the broadcast!

It is worth noting that BBC stations have 24-hours-a-day access to a duty lawyer who can help with legal issues, but nothing is better than knowing legal basics yourself – at least enough to know when you should ask for further advice.

LIBEL

The law says everyone has a right to a 'good name' throughout their lives, unless and until there is undeniable evidence to the contrary by, for example, being convicted of a crime.

You should not broadcast anything which would 'reduce a person in the eyes of right-thinking people, expose a person to hatred, ridicule or contempt, cause him or her to be shunned or avoided, or tend to injure him or her in his office, trade or profession.'

Anything published which damages someone's reputation is potentially *defamatory*. Defamation is divided into slander (spoken) and libel (published). All broadcast defamation is defined as libel because broadcast speech is more wide-ranging than normal speech and, because it is on the radio, is effectively published.

The other difference between slander and libel is that someone must normally suffer injury – for example, by losing their job – as a result of slander in order to win damages. There are a few exceptions to this general rule, but slander will rarely, if ever, trouble the radio journalist. So far as libel is concerned, mere proof of defamation is enough to win the case. The actual amount awarded, of course, can vary from trivial to extortionate, although judges now give guidelines on the amount.

To be upheld, libel can only be committed against a clearly identifiable individual or group. It is not possible to defame the dead. Beware, though, because a group of people can be libelled without individual names being used. For example, 'Tory councillors in Blankshire are lining their own pockets as all the council's contracts go to their friends.' This is a plain accusation of a corrupt practice. Any Conservative councillor in Blankshire could claim libel damages.

LIBEL DEFENCES

The best defence

The best defence to libel is not to commit it in the first place. Remember that the comments of interviewees are not just their responsibility. You take on some of the blame by broadcasting them. Be on your guard for what people say.

The truth

The next best complete defence is that what has been said is true. In law, truth is properly called 'justification' ('veritas' in Scotland). Truth has to be proved to the satisfaction of a jury – libel is one of the few civil cases to have a jury, although a judge will initially decide whether the statement is *capable* of having a defamatory meaning. However, there are some cases on record where someone has won damages even though the statements were accurate. This is because a listener could have drawn a defamatory conclusion from the way the facts were presented. The conclusions drawn by a reasonable person can certainly change if some facts are left out, for example.

No identification

If nobody has been named outright or can be identified from 'clues' given in the report, then it is likely that no libel has been committed.

Consent

This is obviously difficult to prove, but you must do so if this is your defence. If you have evidence that the person libelled knew of and agreed to the broadcast, then you will escape a court case.

Death

The dead cannot be libelled and their family cannot continue with a case that has started if the person who believes themselves libelled dies midway through the hearing. However, the family could sue if they believe they are affected by what was had been alleged. So, if you say that 'Councillor Colin Caterwall took backhanders to give council contracts to certain businesses' and Mr Caterwall dies midway through the court case, his family could still seek compensation for the linked allegation that they knew and benefited from the deals.

One year

Somebody who believes that they have been libelled has one year (previously, and still, three years in Scotland) to bring a case. In radio there is only a need to keep recordings of transmissions for 42 days, but of course a recording or transcript may have been made without your knowledge. A thorough journalist will therefore keep their notebooks, or related papers about a complicated story from which action may be sought, for one year. If, within three years, a new transmission is made of the allegations (for example, in an end-of-year news review), the clock starts ticking again.

Fair comment

It is possible to defend a libel action by pleading 'fair comment'. This means the views expressed were honestly held and made in good faith without malice. A defence has to show that the remarks were based on demonstrable facts not misinformation.

Criticism is an essential part of the political and democratic process, and is not necessarily libellous even if it descends to abuse, although you need to be alert. For example: 'Tory policies in Blankshire are hard-hearted and selfish. The poorest people in the community will once again be the losers while the rich will get richer. It's the same old miserable story of Damn You, Jack, I'm All Right.'

In the context of a reasonable debate, this is not a libellous statement. It is considered fair comment on a matter of public interest and it is legally acceptable for people to express honest opinions and beliefs.

Despite there being no legal liability, you should give the Conservative group in Blankshire a chance to put their point of view in the interest of balance.

In general then, local and central governments cannot sue for defamation, as it would affect freedom of speech.

Be aware that some other words are potentially libellous and you should be careful how they are used and in what context. One of these is the word 'cruel'. Allegations of cruelty should be made only after very careful consideration. Also, make good use of the words 'claim' and 'allege' in any story likely to prove controversial and critical of someone.

Every case is different and public opinion changes over time. The jury which considers a libel case is made up of the 'right-thinking people' used to determine if a statement is defamatory. So, in the past it may have been defamatory to call some 'homosexual' or a 'communist' when they were not; nowadays the case may not be so clear-cut.

Privilege

Another defence is that the libellous words reported were covered by 'privilege'. There are two sorts of privilege. *Absolute privilege* is enjoyed by anyone speaking in a court, such as a judge or lawyers, or by MPs in Parliament. *Qualified privilege* is attached to reports of these proceedings, although there are certain conditions. These conditions are that the report is fair, accurate, without malice and broadcast *contemporaneously* – that is, as soon as possible.

This means that accusations reported may well be malicious and untrue. But, if uttered in an open court or in the Commons and accurately reported as soon as possible, the allegations are protected by privilege and that is an end to the matter.

A defence of qualified privilege is also available to reports of other public proceedings, such as council meetings, official tribunals and other meetings to do with matters of public concern. The same defence may be used in relation to a fair and accurate report of a public notice or statement issued officially by the police, a government department or local authority.

So, you can report that the MP for Blankstown North has called his colleague, the member for Blankstown South, 'a rogue and a pervert', if that was what was said in The House. But you cannot get him to say it on the phone to you later and broadcast that with absolute privilege. To broadcast such an allegation could leave you with a libel case.

Accord and satisfaction

Accord and satisfaction would apply as a libel defence if an apology had already been broadcast and the plaintiff had agreed that it was acceptable redress.

DIFFERENT KINDS OF LIBEL

Indirect libel

Libel can occur by innuendo or suggestion, as well as outright statement. For example, if a presenter made regular 'jokes' about a local headteacher which alone did not amount to libel, added together the teacher may have a case.

Nameless libel

If anyone can establish that someone could take the offending words to apply to them, then they can sue. This is the case even if you do not name the person concerned but they can be identified. Additionally, if someone else *not* intended recognizes themselves in what you say – or someone else believes it is that person – they could also sue. That is why it is much safer to talk in broad terms: 'All estate agents are liars and cheats' is permissible, as no single agent has been identified. But if you make the same comment about 'all estate agents in Blankstown High Street' you would be in trouble, unless you can prove that what you alleged was true for each and every one of those businesses.

Unintentional libel

Unintentional defamation can result from an innocent confusion of names. It is one reason why the name of a defendant in a court report is rarely enough by itself – an indication of the address, age and perhaps occupation makes confusion with someone else less likely.

Criminal libel

Criminal libel is a much more serious sort of defamation. This charge can result from obscenity, sedition or blasphemy. A criminal libel action can also stem from a normal civil libel case, if a court decides that the defamation is so serious that it could lead to a breach of the peace.

It is therefore possible to libel criminally a dead person, if a court decides that the surviving relatives were likely to be provoked into a breach of the peace as a result. The penalties for criminal libel include a prison sentence. If there is any suggestion of such a charge, seek legal advice at once.

Problem areas

If you interview a child (see Chapter 8), it will be natural to ask them the following series of questions: What school do you go to? Who is your favourite teacher? Who is the worst teacher? Why? However, the answer to that final question could land you in trouble, if the child says something which 'injures a person in their office, trade or profession'.

Registered trademarks can sometimes be used out of context, leading to a risk of legal action. If your phone-in programme takes callers who talk about their 'Hoover', or an 'Outward Bound' course, they may not actually mean products or activities from those companies. They should use 'vacuum cleaner' or 'activity course' instead.

Phone-in programmes can be fraught with difficulties, especially those of a robust nature or dealing with consumer issues. Care should be taken to say on air that no names should be mentioned, and that warning must be reiterated to individual callers before they go to air. Producers may also want to take the name and phone number of contributors, and to put the station into 'delay' to guard against the risk of a libel being transmitted. If a potentially defamatory comment is made, then the presenter should distance themselves and the station from it immediately and take the caller off air. Care should be taken not to repeat the statement. Technically, the station could be in trouble for broadcasting (or 'publishing') the statement, but this is unlikely to happen. It is called the 'Live Defence' and works when you have no effective control over the speaker, have taken all reasonable precautions, and you had no reason to believe a defamatory statement would be made.

It is not enough to use the word 'allegedly' if you make a potentially defamatory statement. Lack of knowledge of the law is no defence anyway, but by using 'allegedly' it gives the impression that you realize there may be something untrue in the statement.

Repeating a libel made by someone else is no defence. If allegations are made about a television celebrity in a tabloid newspaper, which turn out to be untrue, the presenter could sue the paper and you if you had repeated the allegations.

Libel laws also apply to anything published on the Internet or on your radio station website.

CONTEMPT

The word contempt in the legal sense might suggest to you something like throwing tomatoes at a judge. While a judge would undoubtedly take a dim view of such conduct and probably impose a severe punishment, the meaning of contempt is rather wider than mere insulting behaviour. Indeed, as well as a Magistrates' or Crown Court, industrial tribunals and mental health tribunals (although not hearings by the General Medical Council) are also included.

Contempt of court includes any act which is likely to prejudice a forthcoming or current court hearing. In the UK, nobody is allowed to prejudge a case (or even speculate about its outcome), or to interfere with a trial or influence a jury or witness. There are considerable restrictions on what can be reported while a matter is being considered by a court or *sub judice*. To exceed these defined limits is to risk being in contempt.

To publish the evidence of someone involved in a case *after* they express it in court is lawful and proper. But to publish the same evidence *in advance* – for example, a suspect's previous convictions – would be contempt. If the witness actively helped with the advance publication, or was paid, the court would take a very serious view and quite possibly jail the witness and those who published the words. Someone who also disobeys an order of the court can also be in contempt. This may occur when a judge has decided that some proceedings or names be kept confidential. This usually happens if there are two separate trials of two people, whose alleged crimes are linked in some way. To report legally on the outcome of one before the other has finished may influence the jury in the second trial.

The penalty for contempt is not laid down by law. The theoretical maximum punishment is therefore an unlimited fine and a life sentence. In reality, it is not unknown for a contemptuous person to be jailed for an indefinite period. Lawyers say that the jail sentence ends when the guilty person has 'purged his contempt'. This means convincing a judge that they are truly sorry and will not repeat the offence. A formal apology in court is often required. There is also a cost to the state for abandoning the trial and the possibility that a guilty person walks free.

Both criminal and civil cases are covered by contempt law, but the criminal case is more carefully protected. There are special rules which apply to the reporting of juvenile and matrimonial courts.

In criminal cases, complications can arise if the police are too enthusiastic in saying that they have caught 'the person responsible' for a crime. This is for the court to decide and you should not collude with the police in prejudging a case. As mentioned elsewhere, the fact that the police told you something does not mean that it is legal for you to broadcast it. Police forces have been known to have to pay out hundreds of thousands of pounds after, for example, libelling members of the public.

The key question concerning contempt is whether or not what is broadcast is likely to help or hinder the police in their investigation or undermine the authority of the judicial process.

A step-by-step guide to contempt

Contempt is only possible at certain stages in a criminal case. To illustrate this, let us look at the foul and brutal murder of Bill Smith, found battered to death one wet Saturday night outside a pub. This is only intended as a guide. It is your responsibility to make sure you know as much detail as possible about what you can and cannot say.

Stage 1: Smith found by police. They appeal for witnesses. Nobody is in custody.

You can say what you like – as long as it is true, of course. A detective may give an interview describing the 'savage murder' and say he is launching a county-wide hunt for a 'dangerous killer who may strike again'. You can broadcast an appeal for witnesses, the details of the victim and what's believed to have happened ('thought to have been stabbed...'). Although you can speak to locals to get their reaction to the death, and whether they saw or heard anything, they should not attempt to describe the identity of anyone they saw, or say why they think the attack took place. It is very easy to call any suspicious death a 'murder': only do so if that is what the police are calling it. If you do not have much information there are certain procedures police will always carry out in such circumstances. Check that they have sealed off the area, doing fingertip searches, carrying out door-to-door enquiries and so on. All this information, which the police may not think to give you but will confirm if asked, can help fill out a voice report.

If the police ask your help in finding someone they want 'to help with their enquiries' then there's unlikely to be any prosecution for contempt. Such appeals are often seen on television's *Crimewatch* programme.

Stage 2: Man arrested. It is the pub landlord. No charge yet.

You are immediately constrained. Bill Smith has now *not* been murdered. He has 'died'. It is *not* brutal. No adjectives are allowed at all. It is not *the* man who police were seeking who has been arrested but *a* man. It is up to a jury to decide the circumstances surrounding Smith's death (a post-mortem may say he died from stab wounds, a jury may decide on hearing further evidence that he stabbed himself, or fell on his knife during a struggle with someone else). You should not identify the pub landlord, even if an incautious police officer tells you who has been arrested – it may be that he is released without charge and to link his name with the offence could result in allegations of defamation. You could write:

> Detectives in Blanktown have spent the night questioning a man in connection with the death of Bill Smith, whose body was found outside the Red Lion pub in West Street two days ago. Mr Smith, who was 42, lived in Cross Street, Blankstown. Police say they're likely to make a further statement later today.

The reason you can say very little is that it could be contempt of court if there's a 'substantial risk of prejudice' in the trial.

Contempt laws take effect when proceedings become 'active'. That is: when an arrest has been made; when a warrant or summons for their arrest has been issued; when an indictment or other document specifying the charge has been served; or when a person has been orally charged with a crime.

You may hear of any arrest on a police voicebank tape, although the press office *may* contact you direct. It is up to you to take 'reasonable care' that your information is as up to date as possible: contact the police station before the bulletin and ensure no arrest is imminent or someone's been charged. Make a note of the time you called and who you asked.

At this stage be careful of broadcasting a police news conference live. Some of the information given out may be in contempt.

Stage 3: Landlord due in court today, charged with murder.

The word 'murder' may now reappear because you are allowed to name the charge. However, other constraints stay. *Think carefully* before naming someone at this stage, although the practice is common. What if the charge is withdrawn before the court appearance? The pub landlord could then sue for libel. If in the rare circumstance that the charge is withdrawn, you would certainly have to broadcast that fact to reduce the chance of any action. In Stage 3 you can say:

> A man is expected to appear before Blankstown magistrates today charged with the murder of 42-year-old Bill Smith, whose body was found outside the Red Lion pub in West Street. Mr Smith lived in nearby Cross Street. His body was discovered by a police officer.

If the landlord is released without charge, then criminal proceedings cease to be active again, unless he is released on police bail. (This also applies when the defendant is acquitted or sentenced; found to be unfit to be tried or plead; a verdict, finding or other decision puts an end to the proceedings; the case is discontinued; or no arrest is made within 12 months of the issue of a warrant. On this last point, if a person is subsequently arrested, proceedings become active again.)

Stage 4: Landlord appears in magistrate's court for committal to Crown Court.

The rules change again. Generally you can now name him, although you should restrict your report to name, age, address, charge and result:

> A 53-year-old pub landlord from Blankstown has appeared before the town's magistrates charged with murder. George Jones, of the Red Lion in West Street, is accused of murdering Bill Smith of Cross Street in Blankstown. Mr Smith's body was found in West Street last Saturday night. Jones has been remanded in custody for seven days.

You must distance yourself from the previous reports. A potential juror cannot be reminded of what happened before an arrest.

Stage 5: Case goes to Crown Court.

You may now report what happens each day in court and quote the judge, witnesses, counsel and the defendant himself. The words must have been said during the trial, in front of the jury and must not be paraphrased in the report. They must be attributed and allegations clearly signposted by the use of such phrases as: 'Prosecuting counsel alleged that ...'; 'The judge warned the jury not to ...'; 'The court was told that ...'. The name of the court must be included, as well as an indication that the case is proceeding: 'The case continues.' Beware of interruptions from the public gallery. In general, these *must not* be reported in detail, as they do not form part of the court proceedings and therefore will not be protected from any libel action. In summary, the report must be fair, accurate and contemporaneous.

Stage 6: Jones found guilty of murder.

For the end of the case itself, the rules are the same as in Stage 5:

> The judge told Jones that this was a savage and unprovoked attack ... and that a life sentence was inevitable. He also recommended that Jones should serve at least 20 years.

So, you can quote the result, and sentence (indeed, you must do this if you have been reporting the case up until now) and anything that the judge says to the court.

Do not criticize the judge, the severity or leniency of the sentence, or give any hint of bias or prejudice.

You *may* broadcast your background feature on the murder and the trial between the time the jury has given its verdict and when the judge delivers his sentence – sometimes several days. This is because, even though the jury could be swayed, the judge is deemed to be above influence. All the same it would be wise to omit, at this stage, anything in your report that talks about what the sentence should be. Be aware that such a piece should not be broadcast if the defendant is facing further charges, or multiple charges in the same case, or if there's a court order in force postponing the reporting of evidence.

Stage 7: After the case.

You can almost go back to Stage 1. You can broadcast a detective's opinion that: 'Jones is a savage man who must stay behind bars for a long time.' You may interview relatives of the murderer or victim. They may say what they like, including criticism of the sentence. The usual rules of libel still apply. It must not, for example, be alleged that the judge, jury or counsel were dishonest, although a solicitor announcing an appeal can identify the grounds for appeal. Also, Jones must not be accused of other crimes, unless he is facing further charges. Once an appeal is lodged (rather than talked about being lodged), the case is *sub judice* again.

If a retrial is ordered the same rules apply as at the first hearing. It is therefore contempt to repeat anything heard in the previous trial. Indeed, even to call it a 'retrial' rather than a 'trial' is in contempt.

COURT REPORTING

Reporting legal proceedings is a skilled job and entire books have been written on the subject.

In practice, radio journalists seldom spend much time in courts. Smaller stations cannot routinely afford to let their journalists sit in a courtroom press box for maybe hours while a case proceeds. Instead, court copy will be filed by news agencies. Their time is well spent because they can send a report of a single case to a number of different outlets – radio, television and newspapers – and, of course, be paid for each one.

So radio journalists are most likely to deal with court copy written by someone else, filed by phone or fax. Such copy may be reduced to a couple of paragraphs or, if more interesting, written as a voicer.

Be aware of the increasing trend of organizations distributing news releases on court cases that they have a vested interest in. You may receive them from the police, Customs and Excise or Health and Safety Executive. They are often several days out of date (so broadcasting them would not be contemporaneous), and can sometimes be from that organization's viewpoint and not necessarily fair.

Only in really major cases will most radio journalists go to court. Even in a big case, though, there is little point in allocating a radio reporter to court throughout the hearing. Any interview with a witness or other person involved while a case is in progress would almost certainly constitute a serious contempt of court. Interviews with people involved in a case may be used after the trial is over, so long as what is said is not libellous.

You cannot record the actual proceedings for broadcast, or even take a recorder, mobile phone or microphone into the court. Leave them in your car or at the front desk. You can record outside 'the precincts' of the court, but this is different at every building. This is to keep the court a dignified place, and to keep the privacy of those about to appear.

Court staff are there to help, so if you miss details of a charge ask one of the court officers. Your colleagues on the press bench are also likely to oblige.

Basic rules

However the information is obtained, there are some basic rules of court reporting which must be followed scrupulously every time:

- Name the court and, if you wish, the examining justices.
- All court reports must identify accused people beyond reasonable doubt, if they are to be named at all. Therefore, a name is rarely sufficient and the address should be given as well. The address may be abbreviated and a house or flat number is never used. It is usual, though not compulsory, to add an age and occupation.
- It is illegal to identify certain defendants, such as children appearing in a youth court. A woman alleging rape is also entitled to anonymity (see 'Reporting restrictions' below).
- The charge or charges must be reported. In a complicated indictment, some abbreviation is customary in a radio report: 'Smith faces nine charges, including one of robbery, as well as insulting behaviour and breach of the peace.'
- The plea must be made clear. It is particularly important that any plea of not guilty is included in each report, but the actual words need not be used. A phrase such as 'Smith denies the charge ...' is sufficient.
- The names of the counsel and solicitors in the proceedings, if you wish.
- Allegations reported must have actually been made in court and that fact must be made clear: 'The court was told that Smith had drunk seven pints of lager before the assault took place ...'; 'The jury heard that Smith had visited the bank at least three times before the robbery ...'. Phrases such as 'Prosecuting counsel told the jury ...' are similarly acceptable.
- Court reports must be balanced as far as possible. If you quote the prosecution case, you must say what the main line of defence is too (although not necessarily in the same report).
- You must make it clear if your report comes midway through a case. Such reports customarily end with a phrase such as 'The case continues ...' or 'The case is proceeding ...'.

- You must obey any special instruction of the court – for example, that the name and address of a witness or defendant shall not be broadcast. It is the responsibility of the news agency to make sure that any such instructions are included in their filed copy. Sometimes special points are included in a separate paragraph headed 'memo to newsdesk'.
- Before writing your story for radio, read filed court copy *very* carefully, *all* the way through, and query anything doubtful immediately with the source. If a mistake is broadcast, it is at least a partial defence to show that you took all reasonable steps to check the accuracy of the copy. However, there is never any excuse for guessing any particulars in a court case. The old maxim applies – *if in doubt, leave it out* – even if it means dropping a doubtful story entirely for a bulletin until checks are made.
- Although the proper place to check agency copy is with the agency, some court clerks are willing to help out by confirming, for example, when a case is likely to resume. Any information you obtain from a clerk, though, is your responsibility.

At a committal or remand hearing you can also state whether legal aid has been granted; whether reporting restrictions were lifted; whether the accused is committed for trial; the charges and the name of the court where they are committed to; the date and place to which the committal is adjourned; and if any bail arrangements have been made, what they are.

If bail is refused, you cannot say why: a future jury may be prejudiced by knowing there was a fear that the defendant may offend again. For the same reasons, social workers' reports are not reported on at a committal or remand hearing.

In summary, court reporting for radio usually means converting the copy of someone else who has been writing primarily for print. If you abridge a court report, make sure you omit nothing which affects the balance by, say, leaving out the defence case. Above all, ensure that your report is accurate, does not libel anyone and does not prejudice a case which is proceeding.

Reporting restrictions

An order not to publish or broadcast is known as a 'reporting restriction'. The restriction may be statutory (as in the case of committal proceedings), or it may be made by a judge in a particular case.

Sexual offences

Statutory reporting restrictions, contained in Acts of Parliament, are intended to protect certain people. For example, a woman (or man) alleged to be the victim of a rape (plus attempted rape, incitement to rape etc.) cannot be named (although the accused can be). This restriction can be lifted in certain circumstances: to bring forward potential witnesses or if the victims themselves waive their right to anonymity. Anonymity is also provided for the alleged victims of a whole series of other sexual offences. This may not purely be the broadcasting of their name, but also their workplace, description or other background details. Be careful that, although it's permissible to name the defendant in a rape trial, to do so may also identify the victim – for example, in a case where a man is accused of raping his wife. (See 'Jigsaw identification)'. Note again, there are particular differences regarding the law governing rape in Scotland and Northern Ireland.

Children and young people

In England and Wales, 'children' are those under 14 and 'young people' are those between 14 and 18. None of them can be named from *the moment the police start a criminal investigation*, rather than from the time proceedings start. In England and Wales, those under 18 are dealt with by 'youth courts' – closed to the public but open to journalists. (There are different restrictions in Scotland and Northern Ireland.) The name, address, school or any other details which identify a child or young person cannot be reported – that includes whether they are witnesses or defendants. In some circumstances, if found guilty, a child or young person may have their anonymity removed by the judge – for example, the child killers of Jamie Bulger.

A child appearing on a joint charge with an adult before a Crown Court can be named *in some circumstances*. This is an unusual event, and the wise journalist checks the exact position with the court before going ahead with the broadcast.

Judges and magistrates have the power to order special reporting restrictions in appropriate cases. For example, a judge may order that the name and address of a witness should be withheld if broadcast would place them at risk. It is also possible for an order to be made withholding a defendant's name where publication could reasonably help to identify a child in the case.

If you are involved in rewriting court copy, you must be aware if reporting restrictions apply. If they do, it is good practice to include in your story that 'reporting restrictions were not lifted'.

Jigsaw identification

As discussed above, the law says that you are only allowed to broadcast certain facts about a rape victim or a child, so even if they are pieced together the person cannot be identified. So, in the case of a man who's accused of raping his daughter, you could either say 'Lee Jones, accused of raping an eight-year-old girl ...' (which will not lead to identification of the 'rape victim' or the 'child' in the case). Or you could say 'A Blankstown man is accused of raping his daughter ...' and not name the accused, as you are telling the relationship, but not identifying whose relationship is on trial.

But there is a potential problem if you use one of the above sentences and the radio station down the road uses another – listeners could put the different pieces of information together (like a jigsaw) and come up with identification of the child (possibly the wrong one).

It is therefore convention to use the name of the accused in reports and only identify the victim of abuse within the family as 'a child' or a 'young woman' – that is, without any reference to their relationship. You should certainly not use the word 'incest' (indeed, the phrase 'serious sexual offence' is to be used instead). You should in these situations be extremely careful with ages, addresses and schools – as by giving too much other information it could then be worked out that the child is Jones'. Additionally, to mention that the alleged assault happened 'in the child's bedroom' may link the child to their attacker.

Occasionally, details of the *offence* are published (by newspapers or by broadcasters) and, in these circumstances, the agreement changes and the name of the *offender* is omitted from the reports. In all circumstances, the jigsaw must not be completed even if it means not covering the trial.

OTHER CASES

Civil law

Civil law cases include any action between two or more parties which results from a conflict of some kind over rights, money or property. The border between civil and criminal cases is very carefully drawn, but it can be fairly narrow.

For example, to refuse to pay for food in a restaurant is not, in itself, a criminal act, in spite of anything the proprietor may say. If the refusal is caused by the low standards of food and if the complainant willingly identifies himself before leaving, it is up to the restaurant owner to sue for his money through the court. If, however, someone tries to leave surreptitiously without paying the bill, or orders food without the means to pay, that is a crime.

Common examples of civil cases include attempts to recover unpaid bills, the allocation of children's custody rights in divorce, and actions for defamation.

Civil cases are heard in the County Court or High Court, whereas criminal proceedings begin in a Magistrates' Court (in England and Wales) and proceed to Crown Court if the charge is serious enough. Criminal charges are generally brought by the Crown Prosecution Service following police action, but many civil cases involve arguments between two members of the public only.

A judge in a civil case may make an order in favour of the plaintiff or the defendant at the end of the hearing, and perhaps grant an injunction. This frequently prevents someone acting in a certain way and can be granted temporarily until a case can be fully aired in court. For example, a noisy family might be the subject of an injunction granted to neighbours, forbidding them to have parties late at night. If the parties continue, those responsible are in contempt of court and may be punished.

Reporting a civil case involves much the same responsibility as a criminal trial. Reports of what is said in court must be accurate. It is more difficult to be in contempt of a civil case by discussing it in advance, but take care. Before a civil case, you may outline the cause of the argument, but avoid a lot of detail and make sure that a summary of the disagreement is fairly presented. Steer clear of interviews with potential witnesses.

Such cases are active when arrangements are made for the case to be heard, and cease when they are disposed of, discontinued or withdrawn.

Inquests

An inquest is run by a coroner, who is frequently medically qualified. Proceedings are active from the time when the inquest is opened. His or her job is to discover the cause of death where it may have been caused by accident or violence. Some serious cases – usually industrial accidents – may include a jury. A coroner sitting alone *records* a verdict. A coroner's jury *returns* a verdict. There are several verdicts which may be reached. They include death by accident, misadventure, justifiable homicide, unlawful killing and suicide. If the cause cannot be established, the result is an 'open' verdict.

Inquests cannot be prejudiced and there is no contempt in this sense. This is because an inquest is not trying to attach any blame to an individual, but there to determine who the victim was, and the circumstances of their death. Beware, though, when reporting suspected suicides. If a woman is found dead in her car with the engine running and a hosepipe from the exhaust fed through a window, you *must not* say it is suicide. That is for the coroner to decide. You can describe the circumstances in which the body was found and use phrases like: 'Police do not suspect foul play ...'; 'Detectives say there are no suspicious circumstances ...'; 'Police aren't looking for anyone in connection with the incident ...'. If it appears some- one has shot himself, all you can say is that the body was found '... with a shotgun lying nearby'.

Official secrets

The issue of official secrets is very complex, but few radio journalists will come into conflict with it often. Journalists do not sign the Official Secrets Act, but can be prosecuted for publishing information which might be useful to an enemy of the state.

The most usual contact between journalists and state secrets is the 'D-Notice' (with D standing for Defence – see previously). This is a vol- untary system which identifies sensitive subjects. It is set up by editors and government officials and overseen by a committee. The publication of a D-Notice itself is restricted because they are confidential. Examples of the kind of subjects which could be covered are the locations of military sites, details of equipment on them, details of factories or products involved in defence, and the identities of certain Crown servants. Contravention of a D-Notice is not an offence in itself, but might well lead to further action.

Injunctions

This is when someone seeks a court order stopping a broadcast, as they believe their interests or reputation are about to be damaged. Additionally, they may be made to stop children being identified in childcare proceedings. They can be granted or enforced at any time, and to break them is a serious offence. The information will usually be passed on via a telephone call and backed up with the necessary paperwork. Ensure all reporters and senior staff know the company name or family name that must not be broadcast, in case something is transmitted by mistake.

12 Newsroom management

RESOURCES

The problem of running any newsroom is that it is expensive. As far as many senior managers in commercial radio are concerned, it is seen as an expensive necessity. They have to balance the need to provide a news service to their listeners (and also that their radio station's officially agreed format may require it) with the fact that news spends money but rarely brings it in. It is a very labour-intensive department. For the BBC, though, news on local radio is seen as the station's lifeblood and better resources are provided because the news and speech output is greater than that of commercial radio.

Rotas

In a simple news operation, working rotas are easy to put together. The bigger the news operation, the harder rotas become. Do not forget to allow everyone the opportunity for variety within their jobs. Also allow for holidays and days off in lieu when people work weekends. Try to keep people on the same shift throughout the week. It is dispiriting to have to work an 'early' for two days to be followed by the rest of the week on a 'late'. Be aware of individual preferences, but in the end you have the final say and make the decisions.

Budgets

As a News Editor, you will be given a working budget. You are responsible for estimating your own costs. If you agree the budget, it is vital to work within it. The budget you negotiate with your station's senior management will probably be an annual figure. Break this down into a monthly sum and divide it among all the key areas of expenditure. Keep a careful record of all expenditure, especially invoices for freelance contributions. These are much easier to follow on a month-by-month basis with the use of a spreadsheet. Suitable headings for budget expenditure include: salaries, freelance cover, agency copy, staff expenses, travel, entertainment, telephones and stationery (Figure 12.1).

Estimating costs

Always try to work out your estimated budget for the year ahead based upon your actual expenditure last year. Study the figures carefully to see where you have overspent and underspent and adjust your estimates accordingly. Be realistic. In a situation where you have to barter for your budget (almost always) with other departments, make sure you are fully prepared to justify your planned expenditure. Allow for inflation and give yourself the flexibility to act within budget. If anything, overestimate. Think ahead and plan a contingency budget for coverage of unexpected events which may be costly, such as elections.

Cutting costs

You may be required to cut costs for a variety of reasons. For example, it may be because you have overspent your originally agreed budget or that the commercial environment means that cuts are required by all departments of the radio station.

Do not panic. First, try to limit any damage by making sure there is no unnecessary expenditure on copy from agencies or that reporters are incurring unnecessary mileage. If the situation becomes really bad, you will have to consider cutting costs drastically. However, your primary concern must be to protect the output of your newsroom as far as possible. Your aim must be to see through the crisis while creating the *cosmetic* impression on the air that the service is normal. This means that bulletins should continue unchanged as far as possible.

Here are some suggestions for gradual cost cutting:

- Cut freelance agency copy, especially the coverage of those court cases which are less important.

Radio Local News – 2002/3 Budget Submission*

1 News Agency Copy (monthly)

Miles News Agency	30 stories @ £6.36	£190.80
Wheeler's Press Agency	15 stories @ £6.36	£95.40
Ward News Agency	20 stories @ £6.36	£127.20
Abbott's Agency (court copy)	Fixed fee	£180.00
	Monthly Agency Total	£593.40

2 Freelance Journalist Cover (monthly)

Weekend Cover: 8 weekend (Sat/Sun) shifts (or
replacement for staffer) @ £60 per day   £480.00
Holiday cover: 12 staff × 4 weeks' annual leave = 48
weeks to cover. 4 weeks per month @ £300 per week
(£60 per day)   £1200
                                                    Monthly Freelance Total   £1680.00

3 Expenses (monthly)

4 reporters out on road 5 days a week. Average
10 miles a day @ 30p per mile = £15 a week each.
Therefore £60 × 4 weeks   £240.00
Parking and miscellaneous   £50.00
                                                    Monthly Expenses Total   £290.00

4 Sundries (monthly)

Public Relations/Entertainment	£30.00
Training	£50.00
Contingency (Elections, Major Incidents)	£250.00
Monthly Sundries Total	£330.00

TOTAL MONTHLY NEWSROOM BUDGET (excluding salaries)

News Agency Cover	£593.40
Freelance Cover	£1680.00
Expenses	£290.00
Sundries	£330.00
Total Monthly	£2893.40

ANNUAL NEWSROOM RUNNING COSTS

£2893.40 × 12 = £34,720.80

*This budget excludes salaries and assumes that allowances for telephones, tapes,
newspapers, National Insurance, stationery, depreciation, etc. are allocated to central
departments.

Figure 12.1
A typical budget submission

- Cut all mileage for face-to-face interviews. Only go out on stories when there is the chance of good audio and background sound. Do not just go to do an interview 'in a quiet corner somewhere'. Do phone interviews, or better still, persuade more interviewees to visit the studio. If you do go out, can you do several interviews on one trip?
- Do not use freelance journalists at all. Cover the shifts with staff. Or share bulletins with a neighbouring station (see 'news hubs' and 'shared bulletins' earlier).
- Reduce the use of unnecessary stationery. Do not buy extravagant items like high quality pens. Get news releases e-mailed to you rather than faxed, to cut down on paper costs.
- Reduce the use of the phone. Obviously, important check calls need to be done but it is surprising how many unnecessary calls are made. This can be changed with just a little thought before picking up the phone. Have a comprehensive contacts book to save you calling Directory Enquiries. If you do need to search out a number, use a website to get it for free.
- You may be able to help the station *make* money. Could your commercial radio news department produce features for the music shows? A weekly package on the latest film releases or lifestyle features, for example, are eminently sponsorable.

If more cuts are needed, you will need to agree with your Programme Director or Managing Editor a restructuring of the day's news bulletins to ensure that the most effort goes into the bulletins with the biggest audiences – that is (usually), the ones broadcast at breakfast time. Even some BBC local stations drop news bulletins on a Sunday afternoon, because the number of people listening does not warrant the expenditure – staff are then moved to other shifts where they can be more productive. Above all, try and make all the cuts without having to make the biggest cut of all – that of making one or more of your staff redundant. People are your greatest resource of all and, as a manager, you should do everything to protect them.

COMPLAINTS

No matter how careful you are, mistakes sometimes get through on the air. Most of us do not like saying we are wrong, let alone admitting it publicly by broadcasting a correction. Complaints need to be dealt with and treated seriously.

Phoned complaints

People who phone the newsroom to complain about a story can either be polite or abusive. Whatever their attitude, you should remain calm and courteous. First ask for a name, address and telephone number. If they have a genuine complaint, they will not object. If the complaint is unjustified or on a minor matter, this will discourage them. Then let the person explain fully why they are upset. Try not to interrupt, go on the defensive, or apologize at this stage. Take notes. Sometimes the very act of being able to talk to someone about the complaint will enable them to 'get it off their chest' and they will not want to take matters further. Whatever happens, act rather than react. The best advice is to say you will look into the matter and call them back. Most stations require a log to be kept of all complaints and some provide a form to be filled in.

Correcting errors

Check that a mistake really has been made. There is a surprising number of complaints made to broadcasters on the basis of something which has been misheard or heard on another radio station. Some complainants have even been told about something by a third party who has relayed an incorrect account of what was actually broadcast. Check the computer archive file of text or audio, or the logger (a recording – usually on a long play VHS or on a computer hard drive – of the station's output which is kept for a period of time).

Do check all complaints. Many are the times a journalist has taken a phoned-in correction at face value and changed their copy, only to find after the next broadcast a flurry of phone calls, resulting in the cue being changed back to its original form!

If you are at fault, ring back. This will have given you time to gather your thoughts, check the copy, speak to the reporter, chase a mistake in the news release and so on. Try to smooth ruffled feelings by apologizing. Never put the blame somewhere else. If the inaccurate report came from a freelance agency, you simply say the report came from an experienced journalist and was broadcast in good faith. Do not on any account lie. Say it was an honest mistake, you are very sorry and steps have been taken to ensure it doesn't happen again ('The reporter concerned has been spoken to'). Thank the listener for bringing it to your attention and for giving you the opportunity to discuss it. They will have respect for you and your station.

If that is not enough, a listener may demand an on-air apology. If you are wrong, you should say so, but on-air apologies will be rare and sanctioned only by a senior member of staff. They should be broadcast in a time-slot corresponding to when the story was first aired. Be careful, in such an instance, not to repeat the initial inaccuracy! But do not let the listener dictate editorial policy. On-air or written apologies are very rare indeed.

If *that* is not enough, ask them to write in (they may not get round to it; this gives you time to consider and consult, and it reduces heat on both sides). A complainant can also write in good time to the regulatory body concerned (regulators require such letters to be received within 42 days of the original transmission).

Remember that listeners will, in general, have greater respect for you if you admit your mistakes and do not try to hide them.

Solicitors

A solicitor's letter can be daunting when received in a newsroom. Do not panic if you receive one. However, never ignore it (Figure 12.2).

Usually, it will request a transcript of the broadcast. It is up to you whether or not you supply this transcript. In the end you can be forced to do so. The best advice when dealing with solicitors is to use your own legal advisers. Although this is expensive, it is nevertheless important to make sure your legal dealings are correct and everything is done properly. Your solicitor will advise you on what to admit, if anything, and also draft any reply.

Never read a transcript or play a recording down the phone to someone without receiving a letter from him or her. You are not obliged to and it may be a solicitor trying to save time and money, a member of the public trying to catch you off guard, or even a rival reporter trying to get a story 'for free'!

In the unlikely event of you having to reply to a solicitor's letter on your own, be sure to include the words 'without prejudice'. This means your letter is legally off-the-record. Make sure your company is covered by specific insurance which is available to broadcasters in case you are taken to court for libel.

CHANTLER, STEWART & CO.
SOLICITORS AND COMMISSIONERS FOR OATHS

BANK CHAMBERS, 14 TAVISTOCK STREET
CANNING, SOMERSET CG1 4ER
TELEPHONE CANNING 23908 (5 LINES)
FACSIMILE CANNING 33618

The News Editor
Newtoon Radio Limited
Tolworth Cross
Canning
CG2 4RR

31st January 2003
Our ref.   MBW/AG

Dear Sir

re Newtoon Radio News, 3rd January 2003

We are instructed by Mr. John Doe, Managing Director of AB Engineering Limited, Priorswood, Canning, concerning an interview broadcast on the above programme with Mr. Richard Roe, Chief Shop Steward of the Associated Operators Union.
You are of course aware that there is currently a dispute between our client's Employer Company and the Associated Operators Union. We are instructed that the following words of Mr Roe, quoted verbatim, were broadcast by yourselves: "The real problem is that the management of ABE are incompetent. I don't think the Managing Director could measure a piece of string and get the right answer. They can't manage anything, and they don't know much about engineering either, for what I can see."
Your legal advisors must surely have informed you that the dissemination of such a statement by Newtoon Radio is defamatory of our client and we are instructed to seek damages in libel from yourself for its broadcast.
Since it took place our client has found difficulty in the business community in handling the affairs of the company due to the wholly unjustified attack of Mr. Roe broadcast by yourselves.
We enclose a form of apology which we require to be broadcast on the same programme within seven days of today at a point in the programme commensurately prominent to the original broadcast. Please advise us by return when the broadcast will take place.
Furthermore, unless we receive written confirmation within seven days of your preparedness to pay a reasonable sum in damages for your libel against our client, a writ seeking damages, together with a claim for interest and costs, will be issued without further reference to yourselves.
We look forward to hearing from you within the time limit specified.

Yours faithfully

A

for Chantler, Stewart & Co.

THIS FIRM IS REGULATED BY THE LAW SOCIETY FOR INVESTMENT BUSINESS

Figure 12.2
A (fictitious) solicitor's letter alleging libel. Make sure you always use your solicitors to reply

At the BBC, you have access to 24-hours-a-day legal advice through the corporation's lawyers. A check with the duty solicitor is, of course, free to BBC journalists.

Regulatory authorities

The two main regulatory authorities you may have dealings with are the BBC itself and OFCOM, which gradually took over from the Radio Authority for commercial radio from late 2002.

BBC radio is 'regulated' through its handbook *Producers' Guidelines*, which details extensively what is expected with regard to the Corporation's values and standards. The Board of Governors has the ultimate sanction of stopping a programme being broadcast. The BBC also has to be aware that it broadcasts through its renewable Charter, granted by Parliament and currently due to expire in 2006. The BBC's Programme Complaints Unit deals with serious complaints, although in the first instance listeners are likely to contact the radio station concerned.

OFCOM is the Office of Communications, the regulator to oversee radio, TV and telecommunications. It replaced the Radio Authority (for commercial radio regulation), The Broadcasting Standards Commission (and also Oftel and the Independent Television Commission).

At the time of writing, OFCOM's precise remit, powers and practices are yet to be confirmed, but as far as commercial radio is concerned it will, like the Radio Authority before it, be responsible for the regulation of its commercial licensees' programming, advertising and transmissions.

The BBC requires (and the Radio Authority required) stations to keep recordings of all their broadcasts for 42 days, longer if a case is already active! Outside this time, there may be no recordings to which to refer and complaints may not be pursued. Commercial stations have also been required to keep a record of all written complaints for 12 months from date of receipt.

Twenty-five announcements publicizing the Radio Authority's regulatory duties had to be broadcast between 7 a.m. and 7 p.m. in a three-week period once a year. At the time of writing, there is no consideration that OFCOM is likely to change this requirement.

Regulators investigate complaints of inaccuracy, bias and offensiveness, taking action if necessary. Stations can be 'named and shamed' in Quarterly Reports of complaints and findings, and broadcast apologies or corrections can be demanded. Commercial stations may also stand the risk of having a penalty imposed, which can include a fine and the shortening or revocation of a licence. The Reports are available to the public and make interesting reading, as they give examples of what listeners may find offensive and what radio regulators can do about it.

Privacy

Many complaints to newsrooms centre around an alleged invasion of privacy. You should remember the following:

- *Phone interviews* are potentially dangerous. Anyone who is recorded in a phone interview or put live on air must be told that he or she is talking to a radio station and must give his or her consent to the interview being broadcast. In the case of pre-recorded 'wind-up' calls, where to tell someone in advance would destroy the joke, the 'victim' must be told at the end of the call and still give their permission for it to be used on air.
- *Hidden microphones* should only be used as a last resort. Before broadcasting anything recorded with a hidden microphone, advice needs to be sought from senior management in the BBC or OFCOM. You would usually have to prove that you were investigating criminal or antisocial behaviour – that is, something in the public interest.
- *Intercepted radio.* It is illegal to rebroadcast any material recorded off air from the emergency services or aircraft.
- *Children.* Any interviewing of children without parental permission requires great care. They should not be interviewed about private family matters (see Chapter 11).

WINNING AUDIENCES

News has to be seen in the context of the programming of the radio station as a whole. There is no point in broadcasting news if nobody is listening. With most radio sets now equipped with push-button pre-set tuning, it is all too easy for a listener to switch to another station if something is broadcast which bores, irritates or is irrelevant. It is therefore the job of the newsroom as well as other programmers to contribute to the overall aims of the radio station of keeping as many people listening for as long as possible.

Audience figures

The success of a station is usually judged on audience figures. These are the key to earning revenue for commercial stations and for justifying the licence fee within the BBC.

Audience figures for both the BBC and commercial radio are produced by RAJAR (Radio Audience Joint Research), which is the company set up to manage the UK's agreed system of audience measurement. Diaries are placed in a demographically selected and representative number of households in a specific area and people are asked to keep a record of their radio listening, not only to which station but also for how long. This data is then analysed and audience figures are produced. The inherent problem with this method is that respondents are obliged to remember the stations that they heard during the day and sometimes listeners do not complete their diaries until several days later. This can lead to inaccurate reporting – for example, by those who put a tick alongside well-known station names and not next to those they were exposed to when in a shop or taxi (Figure 12.3).

At the time of writing, there are some moves within the radio industry to adopt the use of an electronic measurement, such as a special kind of wristwatch or pager-style device, which it is claimed would be more accurate. The watch or pager 'listens' to the output of the radio and records what it hears. When the stored information is downloaded and analysed, the device's recording is automatically matched with recordings of each radio station. When the two match, it can be determined to which station the wearer was listening (Figure 12.4).

The current RAJAR surveys – or 'sweeps' – take place continuously. However, most local stations have results only once or twice a year, depending on the size of the potential audience. Some smaller stations choose not to be surveyed at all for reasons of cost. The sweep is for a period of three months and the figures are then analysed and published six weeks or so later. The audience figures are vital for commercial stations, as many advertisers make decisions on how much money to spend based on them. For BBC stations they are less important due to the corporation's public service agenda.

Figure 12.3
A RAJAR diary ready for completion (*Source*: RAJAR)

Figure 12.4
The Radiocontrol watch (*Source*: RAJAR)

The figures show the weekly 'reach' of a station – that is, the number of listeners who tune in for a set minimum period over a week – expressed in thousands of listeners or a percentage of the total population. They also show 'average hours' – that is, the average number of hours a listener tunes in each week – and also the 'market share' or percentage of total radio listening enjoyed by a station compared to others in the area. It is possible to see the total number of people listening every half hour to the radio station throughout the day and analyse their demographic make-up. For example, you can tell whether a station particularly appeals to females aged 25–34 or males aged 55+.

However, if the electronic watch described above was taken up, it could have great significance for radio stations' news departments. Station managers would be able to determine much more accurately and much faster what programme segments were working – for example, whether audience figures dropped when a certain song was played. They would also therefore have access to figures which may show that at the top of the hour people tuned in or out as the news came on. And that may make an argument to cut newsroom resources, staff or even to replace news completely by playing another song.

It is therefore in the interests of each journalist to ensure that their bulletins contain well-targeted stories, told in compelling language and in an accessible way. It is important to remember that the methodology for the current RAJAR research measures what people *remember* they listen to rather than what they *actually* hear. This is why it is vital to ensure stations are adaquately identified on air to ensure the station gets proper credit for the listening it enjoys.

Targeting audiences

As mentioned previously, a growing number of News Editors believe that they not only have to consider radio's traditional advantages over other media as a source of news, but take this a step further by targeting stories to specific groups of listeners.

They consider the format of the station when making decisions about the editorial agenda and what stories to cover. For example, a 'hotter hits' pop station needs to have stories about pop personalities in its news to make it relevant and a black music station needs stories about the black community. It is your job to tell your listener what is going on with specific reference to his or her interests. One way their interest can be identified is the fact they are tuned to your station and therefore enjoy the music it plays. Use this as a cue to target stories about that music and related affairs. If your audience is in the 25–44 age group, it is important to highlight stories about home-buying and bringing up children. If your audience is 55+, you might need to be talking more about retirement issues.

Take careful note of the audience figures and the demographic breakdown of the listenership. This will give you a clue as to your editorial agenda. The key advice when targeting audiences is to make your stories *relevant*.

Many stations are now including news and an audience's news values in specially commissioned audience research projects such as focus group discussions, where listeners describe their likes and dislikes in news. Beware, though, that listeners speaking in groups often say what they think *you* want to hear rather than what they actually think.

It is human nature for a listener to claim in front of others that stories about crime do not interest them and that they would prefer instead to hear more about environmental issues. However, viewing figures for police and detective shows show no signs of decreasing, while Britain's record on recycling has been one of the worst in Europe.

Such research then should be used simply as a tool and just one of the things a News Editor or Programme Director makes use of to improve output. You should never be led blindly by research alone.

Presentation formats

There are a variety of different ways of presenting news on the radio. The most traditional is the top-of-the-hour news bulletins. Some stations, though, prefer news at five minutes to the hour, or even 20 past, and throughout its history, BBC Radio One has carried its main news bulletins at half past the hour. The reasoning is often that their rivals in a crowded marketplace carry news at the top of the hour. If they are playing music, they believe they have a chance to attract listeners who may try another station looking for music when the news is on.

Rolling news is another format. This means there are constant news updates throughout the clock hour, either read by the presenter or newsreader. BBC local radio is now required to be mostly speech in output and many stations are totally speech at peak times, such as breakfast. This speech will include not only extended news bulletins, but also live interviews and topical features. Because of the success and resources of BBC radio, both national and local, talk formats on commercial radio are less common. Three obvious examples are the national station TalkSPORT (once known as Talk Radio), which as its name implies, broadcasts sports comment, debate and commentaries; and the two London stations LBC and LBC News.

Other formats which have become more popular include the 'double header', with a DJ and a newsreader co-presenting a show which takes in music as well as an informal, chatty look at the news. Live interviews can also be incorporated into this format. Another sort of double header has become popular on commercial stations, where the news presenter is part of a breakfast show 'crew' or 'posse' consisting of the DJ, travel reporter and other studio personnel. As we saw earlier, this is often called a 'zoo'. It is important where this happens to ensure that, among all the fun and frivolity, the news presenter does not become too embroiled in the entertainment so that he or she loses the credibility with which to present serious, often tragic, news stories.

Make the style and sound of your news bulletins or programmes match the radio station style as a whole. It is no use having BBC World Service-style presentation on a Top 40 music station or vice versa. Think of the listener and what is relevant. Whatever style of presentation you choose, the important thing is to make sure your bulletins are authoritative and believable.

Promos

Remember the value of good promotion of news. This includes everything from mic flags with your station logo on, to telling listeners how good your news bulletins are. Other aspects of the radio station are 'sold' on the air, why not your news? If something is worth doing well, it is worth promoting well.

You can initially remind people that your bulletins are there, and give them a reason for listening (see 'Teasers' earlier). Listeners inevitably think 'the news' is boring and has no relevance to them, but they *are* interested in subjects that affect them directly. That affects not only the stories you choose, and how they are written and presented, but you may also consider dropping the word 'news' from your bulletins. Some stations call their top-of-the-hour broadcasts 'The Update', others 'The Source' or 'The Way It Is'.

If you have had particularly good coverage of a story, usually a dramatic breaking story, include clips in a montage to run on subsequent days. But don't fall into the trap of being too introspective and crowing about your success. Remember to see your coverage from your listener's point of view. A promo will have more impact if you talk about your coverage during, for example, the storms with inclusive angles. So, 'we know how important it is to know if your children's school is open, or if the trains are running, because we live and work here too ... XYZ FM' will have more impact than 'with a list of 200 school closures and travel news every ten minutes, XYZ FM had the best storm coverage'.

Sponsorship

Sponsorship of news bulletins is not allowed in UK commercial radio. This is because of fears that editorial independence could be compromised. For example, if your sponsor was a chemicals company, it could be difficult to do a story criticizing that firm.

However, news is an expensive business and there are arguments to say that it would help if news was sponsored just like other parts of the station's output, such as the travel and weather news. There is no shortage of companies willing to have their name associated with a news bulletin because of the authority it conveys. Many commercial stations carry special advertisements called Newslink at peak times. These are commercials juxtaposed to the news bulletin and therefore command a premium price. IRN finances the cost of its operation by the sale of these commercials and even gives a proportion of the revenue back to the stations which have 'bartered' their airtime. In this way, stations do not pay a fee for the IRN service and indeed earn money from it.

Perhaps in the future more direct sponsorship of news bulletins will be allowed, easing the burden of financing news gathering for small stations.

However, if this happens, it will be vitally important to maintain the editorial integrity of the news and ensure there are guarantees of editorial independence. Existing advertisers are unable to influence a story which criticizes them or brings them bad publicity, and future sponsors must agree to similar controls.

13 Small newsrooms

Many smaller local radio stations are coming on the air. Although these stations have small budgets, it is still possible to set up an effective newsroom with just one or two journalists. However, the skills and organization needed are different from the way in which larger newsrooms operate. The key thing to remember is that you cannot do everything, certainly not at once. Do not try. Learn to create priorities and deal with them in order.

SETTING UP

First tasks

When you are given the job of setting up a small newsroom for a new local station, you will usually find that the radio station itself is far from ready. Building work will be going on all around you and you will be lucky if you even have access to a phone.

You first need to create your own space – one room preferably – with a phone, desk, chair, word processor and printer, a supply of headed note-paper, an A–Z book for contacts, a desk diary and a filing cabinet. Of course, this needs to be complemented eventually by the necessary broadcast equipment to get on the air. Once you have these basic requirements, you can start the main job of talking to people and getting a flow of news coming into the radio station. Ideally you need at least three weeks for this, although it has been done in less time.

Making contacts

Your main task, after setting up your basic newsroom, must be to let people know who you are, when you will be broadcasting and how to get in touch with you.

In the first instance, you should target the emergency services (police, fire, ambulance and, if appropriate, coastguard), the councils and local MPs. Your next priority after that is to contact as many voluntary organizations and large local employers as possible. You will also need to acquaint your-self with local freelance journalists and news agencies.

It is usually worth phoning the emergency services' press officers to arrange to visit them. You should have a list of all your phone numbers (newsroom and studio ex-directory) and take some radio station publicity material with you. Try and make friends with them. Bear in mind they will have other priorities as far as the press and broadcasters are concerned and you will be an unknown quantity. Tell them about your station, its target audience, on-air date, its news output and what you need from them. It is important to agree a set of times you can do check calls with them.

You also need to visit the press offices of the local district and county councils. Arrange for your address to be added to their mailing lists so you can receive council papers, agenda, minutes and news releases. Ask if you could write a letter to all their members. Do this, photocopy it and ask if the council could include it in their next mailout. It needs to tell people you exist and how to get in contact with you.

Also write to the MPs with the same information. Make contact with the local voluntary organizations. Usually, there is an 'umbrella' organization to which all voluntary groups in an area belong. Ask them if you can write a circular letter to their member groups which they can distribute in their next mailshot. Go through the same process with organizations such as the local Chamber of Trade.

All the time you need to be selling your station, its potential audience and yourself. You need to be promoting the ways in which radio in general, and your station in particular, can help them. Very soon you will have an impressive flow of news material coming into your new newsroom.

Technical requirements

The minimum you need is a portable recorder and microphone, facilities for dubbing onto computer hard disk, facilities for recording phone interviews, editing facilities, and a studio where you can record face-to-face interviews.

Filing systems

With the amount of press releases and council papers flowing into the newsroom, you will need to set up a proper filing system to cope with it all. Even though computers are useful in organizing things electronically, you still need to cope with the inevitable paper news releases coming in. You need to create the following files:

- *Diary file*. Two sets of files labelled 1 to 31, corresponding to the days of the month. Use one set for this month, the other for next month. Set aside a special file for beyond that. As events come into the newsroom, enter them under the appropriate date in the desk diary and file the relevant paperwork under the date in your file.
- *Contacts file*. Some newsrooms prefer to list the names of contacts in a book with an A–Z index. You can also set up an on-screen contacts file on your computer system.
- *Background file*. File background information, newspaper cuttings, news releases and so on under the appropriate heading. Have a file for each council and emergency service, as well as files on such subjects as schools, buses, trains and specific running stories such as crimes and court cases.
- *Archive file*. Once you are on the air, you need to file all your bulletin and voicer scripts for reference purposes. There are a number of ways of doing this. In a computerized newsroom, you can set up such files on your system. One of the easiest systems in a newsroom working off paper is to have a ring binder file for each month and file the copy there after each day's broadcasting. However, this can also be done electronically on your station's computer system.
- *Letters file*. Keep a copy of each letter you receive, as well as any you send. Subject headings help.
- *Futures file*. Maintain a general file of potential or forthcoming stories, culled from newspaper clippings or news releases. Mark on them the newspapers they come from and the date.

There is also one more file – arguably the most important of all. It is the 'circular' file – the dustbin. In the early days of a newsroom, it is important to keep as much as possible because you never know what may be useful, but you will start to receive unsolicited commercial junk releases which have no relevance to your audience at all. Throw them away. But be careful to look at *everything* you receive. You never know where a good story may be lurking!

Calls list

Your list of calls to the emergency services either needs to be written down on paper, displayed on a large easy-to-read board or, preferably, stored in the memory buttons of your phone system. It needs to have all the phone numbers you use regularly and, if the list is written, the rank of officer you need to ask for when you get through. Direct lines should be used where possible, especially for the voicebank-recorded information.

When setting up the list and going to see the emergency services, try to agree a set of regular times when you can include them in a 'round of calls'. For example, a station broadcasting news bulletins from 6 a.m. to 3 p.m. daily needs to make the calls at 5 a.m., 9 a.m., 12 noon and 5 p.m. The important thing is to make sure the frequency of your calls is sufficient to satisfy your editorial needs without making yourself too much of a nuisance.

GOING ON AIR

Preparing for the first day

There are innumerable jobs to be done simultaneously in readiness for the first day the station goes on the air (Figure 13.1).

Apart from making contacts and creating files, you should start looking for potential stories and getting interviews 'in the can'. Try to assemble a list of potential stories as you make contacts. Ask each contact what he or she sees as the biggest local issue. Read the local newspapers thoroughly. Use the run-up to going on air as the opportunity to gather as much material as possible. Remember, this is a comparative luxury. After the station goes on the air, you will be responsible for putting out daily news bulletins and will just not have the time to rush around everywhere recording

1. Create your own space
2. Acquire personal computer, chair, desk, telephone, headed notepaper, and A–Z book for contacts, large size diary, filing cabinet
3. Acquire portable tape recorder, microphone, dubbing facilities from cassette, digital recorder, facilities for recording telephone calls
4. Contact emergency services
5. Contact MPs and councils
6. Contact voluntary organizations
7. Contact freelance journalists
8. Create filing system to cope with flow of information
9. Create a calls list
10. Agree times of news bulletins with Programme Director
11. Recruit staff if budget allows
12. Start making a list of potential stories
13. Start getting interviews 'in the can' for the first few days of broadcasting
14. Look for an exclusive or two for the first day's broadcasting
15. Start dummy-running news bulletins using your calls list and writing from press releases and conducting follow-up interviews

Figure 13.1
Checklist for setting up a small newsroom

interviews and talking to people in depth. Then you will be relying on the quality of the contacts you have built up during this period.

You will also need to be discussing with the Programme Director the quantity and scheduling of news to be broadcast each day. Should there be a bulletin each hour when the station is staffed by a journalist? Or is that journalist better used in gathering material for the following morning? It is obviously important for the main news bulletins to be scheduled hourly during breakfast time, when the biggest potential audience is available. But should you have half-hour headlines or updates every 20 minutes? These are questions which need to be answered in talks with the programme controller and balanced against the resources and staff you have available. Try not to do too much too soon. It is easier to build up something than to start with a superb service which you then have to cut because there are insufficient resources.

Getting exclusives

During the run-up to going on air, aim to get a number of 'exclusives' ready for the first few days of broadcasting. Bear in mind that many listeners will be sampling the station on its first few days, so it is important to make as big an impact as possible. Look for new angles on long-running local sagas; persuade a local VIP to comment on something he or she feels strongly about; find out about new developments or plans for the area. The criteria for these exclusives should be to find a story which affects your listeners directly or something about which they will have strong feelings. Remember to keep one exclusive for launch day and two others for subsequent use during the first week.

RECRUITING STAFF

Your station may only have the budget to employ you in the newsroom or you may be lucky enough to have the money to recruit other people. If the latter is the case, it is likely that you will have come to the area experienced in broadcasting but without detailed local knowledge. It is therefore important to recruit someone with that essential local awareness.

The best place to try is the local newspaper. You will probably have contact with these journalists in any case, as they will be writing stories about the new radio station for their own papers. Always be on the lookout for the newspaper journalist who has an interest in radio and is looking for a break.

If the budget allows, try advertising in the trade press. Depending on where the station is located, you may be able to take on someone from a training course. Care is needed in wording the advertisement. You need to be specific about duties, responsibilities, opportunites and salary.

Try to compile a shortlist of candidates and invite them for an interview. You should be present, as should the Programme Director. You should look for the following qualities:

- a good voice;
- an easygoing and adaptable personality;
- evidence of professional skills;
- evidence of an interest in radio;
- evidence of dependability;
- an eye for detail;
- training in the basics of law;
- knowledge of public administration;
- experience of (or at least an interest in) the technicalities of radio;
- local knowledge and contacts.

Overall, it is important to recruit the person with whom you feel you can best work. You are going to have to work together as a tight team. You need someone who is dependable and will work hard and whose skills complement your own. They need to have a good deal of common sense and a healthy attitude.

Training and coaching

If they have no experience of radio but you feel they have the right potential, they need to be trained in the rudiments quickly. Ideally, send them for experience at a working station or get them booked on one of the basic skills radio training courses. You could even give them a copy of this book!

Remember that training staff on the job is vital for their career development and so you can delegate more tasks to them. As a News Editor, whether in a small or large newsroom, the value of individual coaching is immense; always take the trouble to listen to a tape of a package or news bulletin and let your team member know what you do not like (and, of course, equally important is to let them know what you do like!).

One good idea is a 'copy clinic', where you analyse the good and bad points of a sample of a journalist's cues and scripts. If you do not have the time to conduct such sessions or feel that criticism is better coming from an outsider, consider bringing in a trainer. It can be quite cost-effective.

14 Programme production

Radio journalists are increasingly called upon to act as producers for speech programmes. Many of the basic qualities are the same, but the role of a programme producer is a demanding one and requires additional skills to those of reporter, broadcast journalist or news presenter.

THE PRODUCER

Responsibilities

The Producer is the person who is ultimately responsible for the content and style of a particular programme. He or she is the person to whom the Programme Director delegates authority over the output for the duration of a programme. It is he or she who has the final decision over what goes in and what gets left out.

Producers make everything come together, from the reporter's live Q-and-A to an expert guest. They decide which stories to cover, how to cover them, the emphasis they get within the programme and the time allocated to each item.

The running order is the Producer's responsibility. During transmission, they make decisions about what items get dropped. In some stations where there are fewer staff, the Producer will fix guests, write linking scripts, meet and greet interviewees – and even make the presenter's tea.

One important part of the Producer's job is to look after the presenter. Often, Producers are called upon to be 'nursemaid' and help them. Good Producers fulfil this task without complaint, as they know a happy presenter does a better job and produces a better programme, which in turn also makes their life easier.

Qualities

One of the biggest assets of a Producer is the ability to think of lots of ideas. For inspiration, Producers look to newspapers, magazines, the Internet, TV, other radio stations – and their own lives.

Producers need to be good at spotting connections. This means that, in addition to developing a curiosity even more well honed than their journalistic colleagues, Producers are well informed enough to make connections between topical events which could produce a good programme item.

Ideas themselves are not good enough. The ideas have to be tailored to suit the audience. And a good Producer knows the station's audience and what they will find relevant and interesting.

PREPARATION

Programme items

As with many things in radio journalism, preparation is the key to success. In a live programme, some guests will let you down and suddenly be unavailable. There may also be unexpected technical glitches. For this reason you should prepare more items than you can use in the programme. Remember the old radio adage that your programme is only as good as what has been left out.

Another good tip in preparing for a programme is to do as much as possible as early as possible. As transmission time gets closer, more and more pressure will accumulate, so you will be grateful for the scripts, links and items which have already been prepared.

Treatments

As a Producer, remember that you have the whole range of radio treatments from which to choose to make your items listenable and ear-catching.

You can choose from a straightforward Q-and-A with a reporter to a live guest. You can choose to set up an OB or you can use pre-recorded actuality or music. You have access to phone lines, ISDN lines and radio cars.

You can select guests from those directly involved in a story to a pundit or expert such as an academic who can take more of a dispassionate overview.

Running orders

The running order is a detailed list of items and the times at which they will appear in a programme. Everything the listener will hear is listed. It is the programme's most essential tool, which will be used by everyone involved, from researchers to engineers to presenters.

Many regular programmes have a running order template on computer. This makes it easier to construct every day. Start by putting in the times and durations of fixed items such as news bulletins and, on commercial stations, ad breaks. Then fill the gaps with programme items. Include full details of guests, together with contact phone numbers. Indicate where audio, voicers or pre-recorded interviews will be played. It is particularly important to be consistent in using the same catchlines for a particular piece of audio, both on the playout computer and on the running order.

Pot points

In radio, a 'pot' is not a jam jar. It is a place in a piece of audio where transmission can be stopped before it has finished. Pots got their name from the old days of radio, where the volume was controlled by potentiometers or pots. An item could be ended early by quickly turning the knob to zero during a pause or breath or preferably at the end of a sentence. You need to find pot points in your pre-recorded audio before they go on air. The pot points should be carefully noted on the running order.

FIXING GUESTS

Fixing guests to appear on programmes is almost a specialist skill in itself. Indeed, in television, many researchers are employed especially for this purpose (Figure 14.1).

Many BBC local radio programmes are speech intensive, notably the breakfast show, but also very often the lunchtime and drive programmes.

Figure 14.1
Producer Jamie Edwards fixing guests at TalkSPORT

There is a lot of work involved in arranging guests for these shows – it is not as easy as one telephone call leading to one guest. You may have to find a story to begin with, call around contacts to find the most appropriate person to be interviewed, then call that person and confirm their appearance on the show. At the end of any or all of these calls may be an answerphone, someone being unhelpful, someone who is obviously not a good speaker for the radio or someone who just does not want to appear.

Choosing guests

An event may be scheduled in the newsroom diary, about which you can quite easily find a guest to speak. Alternatively, you may have to think a bit more laterally: does a national event or story have a local angle or impact? Could you get a local representative, perhaps an expert from the local university, or of a union, to speak about a national issue? What is certain is that you must build up contacts to speak about various subjects, so you do not always use the same ones, even if they are good talkers and offer themselves for interview.

When making an initial enquiry to an individual with a view to them being a guest, you will be able to work out within moments whether they have a good voice and style to speak on air. If not, you may be able to ask if there is someone else they can suggest instead – maybe you are looking for a woman instead, or someone directly involved in the story rather than a 'talking head' expert or official.

Indeed, 'real people' are often better than trained media professionals, as they bring a reality to the interview that press officers don't. To that end, try and arrange a diversity of guests, not just in the subjects that they are booked to talk about, but also in ages, sex, background and voices. Try and change preconceptions about a subject: if you want an expert on space science from the local university, a young female professor may surprise your audience, who will listen more than if they heard an older man.

Whatever you do, do not fall into the trap of being elitist with your choice of guests: those who may be considered to be talking down to the audience. Radio is a great medium for getting a message *across*, so often your choice of interviewee will be representative of your listening public. See whether you can turn an interview on its head: if there's a story about fewer students going into the building trade, avoid speaking to the person who compiled the report, or a representative from a firm of housebuilders. What about some builders-to-be on a local course, or some young people saying why they do not want to enter the trade?

Approaching potential guests

When you have found your interviewee, it is easy to sit back and breathe a sigh of relief. But the hard work is not over. Ensure you tell the interviewee what is expected of them, what they are to be interviewed about, when, by whom, whether it is live or recorded and how long the interview will last. (Then they can pace their answers.) You will also want to give them an idea of the kind of questions likely to be asked – although you should avoid giving them a list of the exact questions, as this will encourage 'answers by rote'.

You should also tell the guest if they are to be interviewed alone, or as a round-table discussion, and whether they will be expected to react to a recorded package, or to another guest in the studio or on the telephone.

In some cases, it may be necessary to do a 'pre-interview', where you ask the questions likely to be asked on air by the presenter in order to discover fresh information or a person's opinion. If the interviewee is taking part via a phone interview, it is particularly important to ensure you have the right number where they will be when the item is aired.

If they are coming in, do they have directions to the station? If it is a remote studio, talk them through how to get in and use the equipment. If on the phone, you must take and check which number they will be on. Either way, a mobile phone number for backup is a necessity.

The main qualities needed are persistence and persuasiveness. Some potential guests will be reluctant to be interviewed and will come up with all sorts of excuses. It is your job to coax and persuade them to appear. One tip is never to rely on anyone to call you back on the phone. If a PA tells you that your potential guest is speaking on another line and will return your call, politely insist on holding until they finish the conversation.

One of the most important things to do is to make it easy for an interviewee to take part, especially those who have busy lives. This means realistically explaining the amount of time it would take and, if they are to appear in the studio, possibly arranging transport. Some big radio stations have a policy of paying a small contributor's fee, especially for expert guests. If this is the case, this should be offered.

Before going into the studio, remind the guest of studio etiquette and to turn off their mobile phone!

Often, a guest will ask for a recording just as they go into the studio – or worse, just as they come out! A good Producer may have a box of cassettes to hand for just a situation and offer a recording in advance – most interviewees will be pleased to make a small contribution to the station charity for the chance to hear their moment of fame again!

STUDIO PRODUCTION

Think ahead

The best advice for a Producer once in the studio is to think ahead as much as possible. Using the intimate knowledge of the programme accumulated from putting together the running order, you should be thinking ahead at least five or ten minutes. It is in this way you can see problems before they arise and prepare other contributors. It is also important to anticipate the presenter's needs.

Tech Ops

As Producer, you are likely to be working closely with an audio engineer, sometimes known as a Technical Operator or 'Tech Op'. This person will operate all the equipment, 'drive' the desk and ensure that everything going on air is slick and smooth. It is vital you communicate well with each other, as he or she needs to know what buttons to press at the right time! Of course, the running order will help, but at times when things go wrong, the correct chemistry between a Producer and a Tech Op will pay dividends (Figures 14.2 and 14.3).

Discipline

Professional discipline in the studio is important. There may be many people involved in the production of a programme – not only the researchers, reporters, presenters and tech ops, but also the studio guests. You must work as a team, keep calm in a crisis and maintain strict discipline. This is a serious business and there is no time for messing around.

Keep conversation to a minimum. Concentrate. Speak only when it is necessary. Your ear should always be listening to the output. If there are changes to the running order or script, firstly tell the presenter via the talkback, then write the changes on the visual talkback and tell everyone involved.

The presenter should have the discipline to know that the microphone is always live. Technical mistakes can mean things go to air that are not intended. This means presenters cannot chat inconsequentially or say things they would not wish to be heard saying. Many is the time when an

Figure 14.2
A tense moment in the TalkSPORT control room for Producer Jamie Edwards

unfortunate swear-word has crept onto the radio because a pre-recorded item has floundered or ended early.

Trails, teasers and promos

One of the most important things to remember about programme production is the reason why you are broadcasting in the first place – to keep listeners listening longer.

To this end, it is vital to build reminders into the running order to trail ahead to forthcoming items. This needs to be done frequently and certainly before any news bulletin or commercial break. Be specific. Do not simply say: 'We'll have more on the Northern Ireland situation in a moment.' Instead, it is far better to say: 'At ten past eight, we'll be talking to the Northern Ireland Secretary about fresh hopes for the peace process.' People need specific reasons for listening. Take time to script a good trail or teaser for your presenter.

Figure 14.3
The Technical Operator or Tech Op in charge of the output in the control room at TalkSPORT

Also, do not forget the value of a good promo to promote the programme. This needs to be made well in advance and scheduled by the station programmer.

A good Producer is always in charge, always thinking well ahead, always confident and always well informed – as well as being on top of the detail.

15 Specialized programming

THE NEWS ROUND-UP

The news round-up programme is different from a bulletin in that it may use older stories and also longer versions of stories.

Content and style

Older stories means by hours, not days. A news programme at, say, 6 p.m. may well include anything from that day's events that is worth having and is still current or can be adapted to be current. Many listeners will have heard nothing since they left for work at 8.15 a.m.

Presentation of these programmes will be different too. For example, they can be double-headed – in other words, using two presenters. The style can be less formal, even chatty, and there may well be 'guest appearances' from other people giving travel and financial reports.

A typical format

Here is a fictional, but typical, format for an evening news programme on a station, anchored in 'flip-flop' style by two presenters:

```
00:00   Opening signature tune with headlines – JANE
00:30   Teasers – JANE
01:00   News bulletin – JOHN
05:00   Travel – JUSTINE (via AA Roadwatch)
06:30   AD BREAK 1
09:00   Live interview 1 – JANE
```

11:00 Package 1 – CUED BY JOHN
13:00 AD BREAK 2
15:00 Headlines – JANE
16:00 Financial report
18:00 Live interview 2 – JOHN
21:00 Sport – MICHAEL
25:00 AD BREAK 3
27:00 Package 2 (1′30″) – CUED BY JANE
28:30 Headlines – JOHN (prefade signature tune at 29:00)
29:20 Closing sequence – JANE and JOHN
29:59 Signature tune out

This type of programme is designed for an evening audience who may well be driving home and dipping in and out every few minutes. You would not have to hear the whole programme to get a reasonable idea of the day's main news stories and you would probably hear at least one in depth.

The note to 'prefade' the one-minute signature tune at 29:00 means that the music will run from 29:00 to 29:59. It can be faded up at any time and still end neatly on schedule. This is the job of the Producer, Technical Operator or Studio Manager.

A programme like this is not always driven by the presenters because they do not have enough time to check that everything is ready, including the three 'guest' reporters, two live interviews and the commercial breaks, as well as present the programme.

Since this schedule is fairly tight, in reality the second package would probably be an expendable item. One and a half minutes can easily be absorbed by a couple of extra commercials or an overrun by the financial or sports presenter.

Jingles and 'beds'

Jingles and idents (identity music 'stabs') play an important part in keeping a programme like this moving. There will be separate versions of the signature tune for the start and finish and probably several short versions which are recognizably part of the same piece, maybe between three and ten seconds long. These can be played at intervals during the programme, such as around the headline sequence, to maintain continuity and remind the listener what the programme is all about.

Many stations like using music 'beds' over which headlines can be used. Take care to choose music which is non-intrusive and be especially careful with the volume at which the music is played as many listeners, especially those in cars, sometimes find it difficult to hear what is being said over poorly balanced music beds.

FEATURES AND DOCUMENTARIES

Feature pieces are a chance to tell a story in more depth. A package or wrap consists of at least one clip of audio, which is linked by a reporter to make a complete story. A package is, in effect, a voicer with some audio inserted into it. A news package may run 35 seconds or so with just one piece of audio; at the other end is the news documentary, which may run for an hour and have dozens of clips in it.

Using audio

In each case, the basic principles are the same. Audio should add to the story, not just repeat what the reporter has just said. Each link into each clip can be treated like a separate news cue, except that the opening line of each cue does not, of course, start the story from scratch. Each cue should move the overall story on in some way by expanding an earlier part or contradicting it.

The great advantage of a feature is that, by using appropriate audio, both sides of an argument can be aired in the same piece. Often, conflicting views have greater impact if they are heard in quick succession by the listener. Another point to note is that longer features can be far more creative, using sound effects and music as well as speech.

The essence

Here is the beginning of a fictitious documentary about railways:

FX: Bristol Temple Meads station. Atmos at 5 a.m. Down and under ...
REPORTER: Temple Meads station, Bristol, at five in the morning. Most of the city is fast asleep ... but Temple Meads never sleeps.

> Even at Christmas there are still people on duty, even though no
> trains run for the public. The Area Manager is Tim Parfitt...
> PARFITT: In: 'We can never close a station...
> OUT: '...day or night, we are here.'
> FX: Station sounds. Down and under...
> REPORTER: Every day, thousands of people use Temple Meads.
> To deal with them, there are staff like Leading Railman Chris
> Simmonds...
> SIMMONDS: In: 'My dad joined the Great Western Railway in...'

The radio documentary must have a shape and a story to tell. You, as
Producer, must know whether it will have a definite conclusion to reach, or
whether it is a series of individual pictures in sound, put together because
they are more effective in a single frame. Remember that other people's
words are often more effective than your own, and that there are many
sounds other than words. This is the essence of documentary making. Use
all these resources and your documentary will be memorable.

Setting up

The making of a documentary is hard work. On a local radio station, it
may be a single-handed job. If you need to interview perhaps 20 people,
that means 20 separate appointments to be made and kept. Try not to
get too much audio from each one. If you record half-hour interviews, that
adds up to ten hours of continuous speech to assess later! Editing on
this time-scale can be tremendously time-consuming. So rationalize your
efforts at the start. If you will want at the most one minute from each
person in the finished production, ten interview minutes recorded should
be enough unless the interviewee turns out to be particularly fascinating.

Make sure that you have access to the music and sound effects you need. Is
your documentary one of a series? If so, does the series have a distinctive
house style – a standard beginning and end with its own signature tune? Any
standard introduction will have to be accommodated in your particular piece.

Editing

Be ruthless when you edit a documentary. It is a common mistake to
include too much. A one-hour documentary on a commercial station is

actually 48 minutes; the other 12 minutes are taken up by commercial breaks and the hourly news. In those 48 minutes, you will do well to include more than about 35 minutes of audio, unless your own contributions are very brief.

Look for voices and sounds that are startling and consider one to end your documentary. Make the listener listen by the force of your material and do not let it sag. If something seems rather boring, leave it out. Keep the pace moving and use shorter rather than longer clips of audio.

Remember to use the whole range of production techniques. For example, do not simply identify an interviewee and then play an audio clip in its entirety. Vary the pattern by including a sentence or two of audio and then introduce the speaker. The sequence above could be edited slightly differently, like this:

> REPORTER: Temple Meads station, Bristol, at five in the morning. Most of the city is fast asleep ... but Temple Meads never sleeps. Even at Christmas there are still people on duty, even though no trains run for the public.
> PARFITT: 'We can never close a station. It's always busy and there's always something which needs to be done.'
> REPORTER: Area Manager Tim Parfitt.
> PARFITT: In: 'Even at four in the morning people are rushing ...
> Out: ... day or night we are here.'
> FX: Station sounds. Down and under ...
> REPORTER: Every day, thousands of people use Temple Meads. And there are scores of staff to deal with them.
> SIMMONDS: 'My dad joined the Great Western Railway in the 1920s but the job's changed enormously since then.'
> REPORTER: Leading Railman Chris Simmonds.
> SIMMONDS: 'It's a great place to work as there's ... '

Finally, a complete programme must be recorded in good time before transmission. Do not forget to book a studio and anyone needed to drive the audio inserts while you record the links between each one. Or you can self-op as you would a bulletin. If possible, allow some time between the master recording and the transmission date. Editing documentaries on the day of transmission is not unknown, but work done in a hurry may not be your best.

OUTSIDE BROADCASTS

Planning

Planning an outside broadcast – or OB for short – is like planning a battle. You must have everyone in the correct place at the correct time with the correct equipment.

Many of the difficulties encountered on outside broadcasts are technical rather than journalistic. The hospital to be visited by the Prime Minister next week will turn out to be in a low part of the area where radio links are not effective. This means either an ISDN landline or driving to nearby high ground with freshly recorded material and transmitting it from there.

Generally, outside broadcasts must be planned ahead as far as possible – preferably at least one month before. For example, deciding to cover a Royal visit the day before will be pointless – in practice, a reporter is unlikely to be allowed anywhere near without the precious 'Royal Rota' pass issued to journalists by the Central Office of Information. You must apply for these passes well in advance.

There are a number of ways of getting material back from an outside broadcast and each has its own set of advantages and problems. The main ways are:

- radio links;
- ISDN landlines;
- telephone links;
- couriers.

Radio links

The UHF radio link is one of the most common ways of doing outside broadcasts in local radio. The transmitter in the station radio car or radio van uses an ultra-high frequency that is well outside that available on domestic radio receivers, but it can be heard by anyone with the right equipment; it is not, therefore, watertight. Anything sent back to the studio in this way is therefore being broadcast. Such a link is also vulnerable to the failures of aerials or transmitters. It may well be useless in some kinds of situations, such as low ground or areas well screened by trees or tall buildings.

If radio links are to be used, a site check in advance is essential. On the day, beware that other electrical equipment could cause interference.

Before using a radio car transmitter, you must be trained. Broadcasters have been killed by erecting an aerial too close to power lines, the electricity causing fatal shocks.

ISDN landlines

One of the most popular and simplest ways of sending material back to the studio from an outside broadcast is by the use of temporary ISDN lines (ISDN stands for Integrated Services Digital Network). These are high quality phone lines capable of sending full quality stereo signals via dial-up lines throughout the world. However, you need to plan ahead as telephone companies take a few days to install the necessary facilities. Many stations are now installing permanent ISDN points at key buildings throughout their area, such as theatres and council offices, to make it easier to link to the studio on a dial-up basis when necessary.

Telephone links

The telephone provides only low quality output, adequate for a reporter's voice but not much else. Mobile phones can be used but sometimes the signal is weak and using them for live work is usually a last resort. If you have to use a phone to go on the air, try and use a landline phone.

Couriers

Using a motorcycle courier to bring recordings back to the studio means that all semblance of live outside broadcasting is lost. There is no chance of reacting to sudden events at the OB site. Coverage restricted to a courier service is not really an outside broadcast at all.

Standby presenters

Outside broadcasts are still risky in terms of being confident that everything will be working properly as planned. They need to be carefully thought out, well ahead. It is likely that at least two of the communication methods outlined here will have some role. One more element is also crucial for OBs – the availability of a standby presenter in the studio to cover emergency breakdowns.

PHONE-INS

For many years, the phone-in programme has been the staple diet of local radio. Critics say it is no more than a cheap way of filling airtime, but properly produced phone-ins can be provocative, interesting, useful – and a small slice of democracy, letting people have a say on the issue of the day. What determines the success of a phone-in is the way it is put together and planned.

Selecting subjects

The phone-in is a very flexible format. There are a number of different sorts of phone-in, which include:

- an 'open line' discussion on current affairs in general;
- an advice line with a guest such as a doctor or lawyer;
- a topical discussion on one particular subject with a guest such as an MP or celebrity.

When planning an open line programme or topical general discussion, the best source of material is undoubtedly daily newspapers. These often provide the spur to which the listener can relate. However, it is easy to forget that your own news output is likely to be more up to date. Too many Producers automatically reach for the papers instead of listening to their own output for inspiration.

Studio operations

It is possible for the presenter to take calls off air and then 'line them up' while a song is playing, if the phone-in consists of music as well as calls. However, the best way of running a phone-in is to have calls 'screened' or answered by an assistant, sometimes called a 'phone op', who is an important part of the process as it is he or she who makes the initial judgement on whether a call should be aired or not. They need to be sharp, make editorial assessments and be diplomatic.

The phone op needs to write down the caller's name, the area from where they are calling and a phone number (for reference). They also need to check whether the line is broadcastable, whether the caller is coherent, whether the point is relevant and whether the caller can hold on until the presenter is ready to talk to them. You may have a station policy of calling listeners back or ringing those back who have been on hold for some time. The signal may have been lost on a mobile phone and it is always another line of defence against someone who makes a libellous statement.

The caller is then put on hold and the details passed to the presenter, either on paper or by means of a visual talkback unit, such as a computer screen onto which words are typed in the control room and appear simultaneously in the studio.

Before the caller goes on the air, he or she needs to be told to turn their radio volume down to avoid 'howl round' or feedback, or indeed the effects of an electronic delay system. The programme assistant also needs to make sure the caller is sensible, with a legitimate question or point of view.

Another way of running a phone-in is to invite calls before the programme starts, take callers' phone numbers and call them back while on the air. This gives you much more control over the editorial direction and development of the programme.

Phone-in presenters

Phone-in presenters need to be fluent, witty, wise, provocative and occasionally rude. They need to be positive and stimulate conversation.

There are generally two sorts of phone-in presenters. Firstly, the type who takes the role of a neutral chairman, marshalling arguments from both sides and urging listeners to call to 'let us know what you think' about a particular issue. Then there is the presenter who takes an opinionated position and argues his case, inviting listeners to call if they disagree (Figure 15.1).

Figure 15.1
BBC Essex phone-in presenter Dave Monk. Note how Dave wears his headphones so that he can hear not only the station output, but also the resonance of his own voice (*Source*: Ingrid Bardua)

It goes without saying both kinds of presenters need to be quick-thinking, alert to defamatory or contemptuous comments from callers, and sufficiently broad-minded and democratic to let all callers put their points.

The delay

Almost all stations insist on an electronic delay system to regulate phone-ins. This means that the whole programme is shifted in time for about ten seconds via either a special tape machine or similar digital device. The reason is that if a caller says something defamatory or obscene, this can be deleted or 'dumped' a few seconds before transmission and the delayed recording can be replaced by a jingle to avoid the offending remark going out.

Problem phone-ins

You need enormous sensitivity to handle a problem phone-in, which have been accused of being exploitative and the aural equivalent of voyeurism. It is a great responsibility and has to be taken seriously.

Expert guests are needed, such as psychiatrists, doctors and lawyers, to handle the calls about sexual matters and emotional relationships, medical conditions and legal queries. Remember, the callers are using the radio station as a friend who can give specialist, unbiased personal advice. During this type of phone-in, you are no longer 'broadcasting' but 'narrowcasting' and talking to the individual, hoping that other listeners – who might never be courageous enough to phone – can identify with the particular problem being discussed.

THE MUSIC–SPEECH MIX

The radio programme which mixes both speech and music is probably one of the most difficult to do well. It is the ultimate test of the all-round broadcaster, combining the music skills of the DJ with the skills of a reporter and interviewer. It is hard and demanding work, but can be highly satisfying and rewarding.

Qualities of presenter

The presenter needs to be at home handling music, interviews, scripts and studio equipment. In addition, a logical, well-organized mind is required, with the ability to think quickly and react to what is happening. A good working knowledge of current affairs and the ability to ad lib rather than simply relying on scripts is an asset, as is the ability to talk 'to time'. In short, you need to be able to cope with anything and everything. In general, it is easier for a journalist to adapt to becoming a music presenter than the other way round.

The right mix

In most programmes, it is necessary to make sure there is not too much speech or too much music. The exact proportion will be defined by the station policy – for example, many BBC local radio stations have a policy of a specific percentage of speech to music at certain times of the day.

Arguably, the safest rule for mixing music and speech is to limit speech items to no more than four minutes, the average length of a song. This means listeners are likely to stay tuned through something in which they are not interested simply because they know it will not last long and something more appealing may follow. An interview with a celebrity, for example, could be spread out in three four-minute segments with music in between, rather than in one 12-minute block.

Music selection is particularly important in programmes which have a speech content. All the music must be familiar and popular in order to prevent the listener tuning out simply because they do not recognize something. Listeners are remarkably tolerant of music they do not like that has been a hit just because it is familiar to them. The idea is to keep the listener listening for as long as possible. You need constantly to tease what is coming up in the programme, including features, interviews and music.

Blending

The programme is likely to consist of audio, packages, live phone interviews, studio guests, links to the radio car, links to unattended studios, a phone-in element, traffic and travel news, sports news and, of course, music. It requires the highest standards of professionalism to blend all these things together slickly.

The key to all this preparation is being well organized in advance. Before going on air, everything needs to be sorted so you know exactly what you are going to use and when you are going to use it. Interview introductions need to have been scripted and a few questions prepared in advance in case there is a distracting panic to do with some other part of the programme just before the live interview.

When you are on the air, you need to be thinking about five or ten minutes ahead of yourself to ensure that the next item is all ready to go. It is a good idea always to have a music CD cued up for emergencies in case the audio playout system in the studio fails.

If you are creating a new programme, the best advice is not to be too ambitious at first. Start small and build up the content gradually as you become more adept at handling the technical and editorial complexity.

Try to develop the skill of voicing over the introductions of songs. It is, of course, important you do not talk over the vocals. Most DJs find they can do this after a while through instinct, although you might need to watch the CD timer at first. The effect of this is that voicing over intros helps to blur the edges between the music and speech and prevent the 'stop–start' type of presentation that sounds dated.

Avoid your voice battling with the level of the music. There is another dated technique which is still heard where the presenter talks in short bursts over a long instrumental song introduction, raising the music for a few seconds in between. This should also be avoided.

ELECTIONS

Elections make good radio. There is the buzz of the count, the excited claims of rival candidates and the dramatic moment when the result is revealed.

Increasingly, local party representatives monitor local radio stations for any hint of bias. This is even truer during election time than it is during the rest of the time. It is up to us as broadcasters not to fall foul of their stopwatches and spreadsheets, but more importantly, to accurately follow the law to represent the candidates to the democracy.

The law takes a stern view of anyone who prejudices the fairness of an election. You must be sure that your radio station does not let enthusiasm overtake prudence and that you follow the rules. One commercial station was once fined £75,000 after a presenter pledged both money and alliance to one candidate in the London Mayoral Elections. Regulations meant that fine could have been as much as a million pounds. It is therefore important that colleagues in other on-air roles at the station also know what they can say or, better still, know not to say anything at all. There is a timetable which lays down what may and may not be done. As soon as an election is announced, this timetable takes shape. We will deal here with General Elections, although the rules for media coverage of local elections are similar. This chapter is current at the time of writing and refers to the broadcasters' codes which replaced the repealed section 93 of the Representation of the People Act of 1983 (the RPA).

The changes mean that broadcasters are freed from many of the problems they had previously when booking guests for a round-table discussion – one party candidate declining the offer may have scuppered the entire programme. There is now no legal difference between the time *before* the close of nominations and that *after* it.

General guidelines

At a BBC station, with a high speech–music ratio, *each* news-based programme should achieve balance between the main parties within *each*
week of the campaign. (The 'main parties' are Labour, Conservative and
Liberal Democrats in England, with the addition of the SNP in Scotland
and Plaid Cymru in Wales. In Northern Ireland it is solely the Ulster
Unionists, the SDLP, the DUP and Sinn Fein.) Care must obviously be
taken during the campaign that single programmes are not covering one
party more than another, as problems adjusting the coverage will occur as
election day approaches.

Commercial stations, with less speech coverage, can record their balance
over the full length of the campaign. At both station types, produce 'timing
sheets' to note, for each day, the coverage given to each party, the duration,
in what form (copy line, interview), and the time of day it was broadcast.
This should be timed to the second. It is also a good idea to keep copies of
all scripts and audio until 42 days after the election in case of any query.

Possible problems are with the launch of each party's manifesto – which
is certain to give them more coverage on that particular day. That is fine,
as long as equal coverage is given to other manifesto launches. (Local stations should cover manifesto launches of all parties which are standing in
more than one-sixth of their area's constituencies.) Some issues are not
necessarily party political, so you may have to decide how to log their
coverage on a case-by-case basis. For example, the subject of Europe is
strongly debated not only *between* but also *within* the parties.

Be aware that, if working for a national station, some issues (education,
health and home affairs, for example) are dealt with by the regional
assemblies – the Scottish Parliament, the Northern Ireland Assembly and
the Welsh National Assembly. Therefore, not all the topics you broadcast
will have an influence on some of your listeners. In addition, those
regional assemblies may still be sitting during a UK General Election
campaign, and careful coverage should continue to be given to their debates.

Closing of nominations

This is the first important stage when all would-be candidates must make
sure they have been validly nominated. At this stage, all 'prospective

parliamentary candidates' cease to be prospective. From now on, you must observe the specific rules of balanced political coverage.

For a working example, we will assume there are four candidates for the fictional constituency of Blanktown West. From the close of nominations, each candidate for Blanktown West *must* have equal airtime. 'Equal' can, of course, include none. But if you interview the Conservative candidate Michael Blue, you must give the same time to the other three – though, as we have seen, not necessarily on the same occasion.

If 25 seconds of Mr Blue is broadcast after the close of nominations, even if it is recorded beforehand, you must provide 25 seconds, as near as possible, with the other three. If you do not, they could report you and you could face prosecution (although a warning and a request to restore the balance is more likely).

Programme packages

Local stations have their main problems when compiling reports from each constituency, and the issues that are particular to those voters. In putting these together, representatives of each of the three main parties must be interviewed and included, but so should others who are also standing and carry some weight. This may include parties which have gained a few seats recently, local (serious) personalities who may have previously stood for another party (and become an 'independent', for example) or those with a current groundswell of backing. (This latter category you will have to judge for yourself with your own local knowledge.) In addition to this, you should mention the name and party of every single other candidate in that area – and you could also direct people to your website where the full list could also be found.

Those whom you interview should, where possible, be the candidates themselves. There may be times when they are unavailable and in which case they can nominate a representative (party official or agent – these should be from the same region, although not necessarily from that constituency). However, it should be mentioned on air that that particular candidate was invited and why they could not take part. Alternatively, your package could be made up solely of party representatives. As mentioned above, and in a change to previous regulations, if one party declines to put up anyone to speak, the feature or programme can now go ahead without them. (In the past those sitting MPs in safe seats may have stopped debate about local issues simply by refusing to be interviewed themselves.)

Discussion programmes

You may have the idea that instead of a recorded package as described above, you will get all four candidates round a studio table for a live discussion in this period. On the face of it, this is fine. But take care. If all four turn up, they must get equal time during the programme as far as possible. The law is reasonable on this point, and the presenter or journalist chairing the live discussion is not expected to use a stopwatch. But there must be no glaring discrepancy. (Guidelines on who must be invited, and the circumstances in which those other than candidates can speak in their place, are the same as described above.)

Practice during recent elections, if not the letter of the law, suggests that candidates from minor parties, if not present, should be mentioned by name and party during the programme. Although the person chairing the discussion should be impartial, that does not prevent the policies of absent candidates being put forward for discussion around the table.

Other news items

The Prime Minister can still, of course, be interviewed about national issues and the clips played on your station during this period. They must not, though, speak about issues in their own constituencies. It is unlikely that you would want to hear them – unless of course your station covers their constituency. The same is true of the Home Secretary, Leader of the Opposition and so on. In such circumstances ensure that if they are speaking in their national role, local policies are not mentioned.

It is similar, of course, if the local Liberal Democrat candidate saves a child from a burning house. The rescue is obviously a news story and you may want to interview the 'hero of the hour', but no mention should be made of their part in the current election process. It would also be wise not to use a clip of him saying, 'The fire would have been put out sooner if the local fire station wasn't closed down' – although someone else could make this point.

Election phone-ins

In another change to the previous guidelines, candidates can now be encouraged to call radio phone-ins (previously they were barred). However, you must know at the station whether or not they are a candidate, so listeners can be made aware from what position they are talking. You should obviously take care that over time the same single candidate isn't allowed to get through to the programme, to the detriment of others.

Opinion polls

Opinion polls represent what people think about certain subjects. Many of them reported as 'news' during the year question just a handful of people about a trivial subject. However, election opinion polls are much more scientific, although they can also be wrong.

Polls are news themselves and should be reported during a campaign, as long as the reporting is done carefully and the terminology used is correct.

The guidelines are to use a reputable polling organization; not to look at a single result but a series or a trend (a 'poll of polls' is often used for this); remember polls 'suggest' they don't 'show' and never 'prove' a particular trend; report the margin of possible error and the company which carried out the survey.

Polling day

The poll opens in a General Election at 7 a.m. and ends at 10 p.m. Local elections start an hour later and finish an hour earlier. During that time, you must not broadcast any political propaganda at all, even if balanced between all candidates in a constituency.

News reports from 7 a.m. must keep to the basic facts that the polls have opened, that it is a sunny day (or otherwise), that the turnout is predicted to be heavy, and other non-political issues. From 10 p.m. that night, all special restrictions end. But watch that no candidate (in an excess of enthusiasm) says anything about one of the others which could be libellous. The law of libel is *not* suspended in an election!

THE CHANCELLOR'S BUDGET SPEECH

Many basic skills of radio journalism are the same for all broadcasting organizations – for example, the writing, reading and interview techniques. However, as we have seen before, the production of programmes such as Election coverage is different on the BBC's speech-rich stations than on the commercial stations. Coverage of the Chancellor's Budget speech in the House of Commons also fits into this category.

Experts

At a commercial station, the likelihood is that the basic information on 'booze and fags, petrol and tax' will be given in extra headlines through the afternoon, possibly with cuts of the Chancellor's speech.

At a BBC station, the lunchtime show is likely to be given over to coverage of the event and can become quite complicated. You should draw up a list of local experts or representatives of businesses and charities who you can contact if the need arises. You will usually only contact them if the budget has a newsworthy line on their particular area. There is usually no need to bother interviewing them if the tax affecting them remains unchanged.

Other experts include local representatives of the employers' group the CBI, a trades union, a garage owner or operator, maybe a local brewer, representatives from Age Concern and so on. You will, of course, be able to gauge what are likely to be the hot topics as Budget Day approaches. It is imperative that, as a local station, you quiz your guests about the effects the changes will have on your area – you can tell them this in advance so they can be prepared. Does your area have a high proportion of elderly people who will be affected by pensions? Are any major businesses or industries likely to be affected? Remember that it is very easy to get bogged down in the minute detail of the speech, which is not what the majority of your listeners will want. Your strong point at a local station is to put the speech into a local context, so speak with local experts who can do just that. You may want to have reporters at various places to gauge reaction – for example, a pub, petrol station or shopping centre.

Some of the leads for expert speakers may, at a commercial station, come from your sales department. It is a great opportunity for news and sales to work together to benefit everyone. Indeed, the extra budget bulletins can be sponsored, but only if they are separate from the usual news bulletins.

The presenter may like to have in the studio with them a 'personal finance' expert who is able to translate the various facts and figures quickly for your audience. Make sure you have access to a TV monitor in the studio, tuned to your parent TV company, to see the flashes as the news comes up: it is inevitable that you will be talking at a crucial moment and could otherwise miss that beer duty is going up 20 pence a pint!

The speech itself

It is crucial on Budget Day for the whole of the newsroom to work together. Information has to be provided to the presenter on air, interviews – whether live or recorded – need to be turned around for the afternoon bulletins, and possibly for the next morning's bulletins too.

The start of the Chancellor's speech sets out the financial state of the nation; the 'meat' of it comes midway through – then all the relatable information is dealt with within just a few minutes. It means you have to work hard and fast to get the information to air.

Remember that this information is important and will affect everyone over the coming year. But a steady stream of facts and figures is intrinsically boring. Think with your colleagues before the day how you can bring the information to life. Can you adapt ideas that television or newspapers use? Perhaps another voice of the station can be the 'summarizer', giving 'fact file' information on the most noticeable changes. The use of language, music beds and even sound effects may enhance the presentation and aid understanding of the stories as they unfold, so it is the 'budget bulletins without the boring bits'.

COMMENTARIES

The commentary is the broadcaster's chance to paint pictures for the listener. In most cases, the event itself will be a 'diary' one, which will be known about in advance, and we will discuss that here. There is another type of commentary, though – the completely unexpected moment when a news story breaks before your eyes and you have a microphone. As the rioters advance up the street, or as you watch an aircraft dive into the ground, you must literally make up what you say as you go along. There are very few pieces of advice which will come in useful then, except *keep talking* and paint a word picture.

Planning

If you are to commentate at a major event, read all you can in advance. If the Queen is scheduled to meet the Sea Scouts, know the name of their commanding officer. If she will be greeted by the Lord Lieutenant of the county, make sure you know not merely his name but also why he received the DSO in 1944. It may come in handy. It is no accident that, during great national events, the commentators always have something to say. It is rare for a hold-up to occur with Coronations and other ceremonial occasions, but when one does happen, you discover just how much research the commentator has done. Much of your research will never be heard, but you will be comforted, on the day, that you have a reservoir of material which you will have reduced, naturally, into easily read notes in front of you.

Also make sure, by a visit in advance, that *you* will see what is going on! It will be very embarrassing to admit that your view has been blocked by a new bandstand which was put up overnight. Speak at length with the organizers. Make sure they know you will be there on the day and what you need.

Mood

Great occasions can be happy or sad, and it is up to the radio commentator to convey the general emotion by tone or voice. Describing the Lord Mayor's Show is not the same as describing a Remembrance Day ceremony. Be sensitive about the type of event you are covering. Nobody wants you to be a ham actor, but there are shades of emotion which you should properly use.

Style and content

What you say will depend on the opportunities you are given. It may be that you are called on to provide several two-minute pieces into another programme. There is no time, then, for long reminiscences details. On the other hand, you could be carrying the progra longer. Then more detail is essential.

Whatever else you leave out, do not forget to describe the clothing of female Royalty in as much detail as you reasonably can. Many listeners, particularly older ones, are fascinated by what colours the princess has chosen for her spring collection. If male Royalty wears anything other than the usual lounge suit (maybe a kilt?), then of course that should be mentioned too.

Using silence

When you are facing a microphone which is callously live for a long period, you may feel a temptation to fill every second. Resist it. However golden your tone, the listener would like a rest from it now and then. Remember that the sounds of the day itself are also available to tell their own story. Pause for a few seconds as the Prince gets out of the car; let the sound of the platoon coming smartly to attention speak for itself. Your words are no substitute for the unmistakable 'thwack' of dozens of army boots all hitting the ground at precisely the same moment. If you provide the frame, the listener will be able to see the picture.

SPORT

The essence of a successful sports programme is simple – supplying a fast, accurate and instant service of information. A whole book could be written about sports reporting and presenting, but here are a few hints and tips.

Match reports

Match reports are a bonus, and coverage of major events such as league soccer is governed by national contracts. Your radio station may or may not be allowed access to the match depending on these contracts, which also stipulate how many reports can be filed in a match and for how long. It is obviously important you know the extent of these agreements so that you do not breach them.

They've sprung the offside trap	He buried the cross from six
The goalkeeper hasn't been	yards
getting his knees dirty	He hit the ball well wide of the
A classic match of two halves	post
The strikers have been firing	His telescopic sight needs urgent
blanks all day	repair
The visitors' defence pressed the	He headed it nowhere in
self-destruct button	particular
The goalkeeper has so little to do,	The manager must have wished
he is in danger of frostbite	he'd stayed in bed
He slammed the ball into the	He's going to take an early bath
back of the net	

Figure 15.2
Well-worn sporting clichés to be avoided

The listener wants to know instantly that a goal has been scored and by whom. This is the crucial news. A reporter can add more details a few minutes later.

The main difference between TV and radio sports reporting is that on radio you are the link, whereas on TV you are the missing link. In other words, the audience can turn the voice off on TV and still follow what is going on. On radio, you are the only link with the action. The general rule for match reports and previews is to keep your pieces simple and factual. Over elaboration confuses the listener. Avoid the overused sporting clichés which have grown over the years (Figure 15.2).

The sports diary

The effective use of a diary is one of the most important factors in running a successful sports desk. All the match fixtures should be entered of course, but more importantly, notes should be made of follow-up stories. For example, on the first of the month you ran a story with a local team manager saying Smith is out of action for three weeks with a hamstring injury. Then, immediately, you enter the story for the 21st and check with the manager again. Not only will that show the manager that you are on top of matters, but it will also create a similar impression with the listener.

Daily sports bulletins

A successful radio sports operation's credibility is also dependent on the quality of the daily sports bulletins, as well as match reports on a Saturday afternoon. These reports should be authoritative and informative. The guidelines to writing sports copy are exactly the same as for news. The key to success is to establish good relations with your contacts, such as football managers or rugby coaches. To fill a sports bulletin, you have to begin from nothing. Unlike the newsdesk, you cannot rely on check calls to the emergency services, although you can establish a 'round' of calls to your club contacts.

There are three important things to remember when dealing with sports people. Firstly, be courteous. Secondly, be certain of your facts (football managers have been known to walk away from interviewers who have asked: 'So who are you playing tomorrow?). Thirdly, avoid too much speculation, however tempting.

OBITUARIES

With many deaths that you will report on your news bulletins – for example, sports people or entertainers – try and dispense with the clichéd topline: 'Tributes are pouring in for the popular … '. Not only is it an over-worked phrase that adds nothing to the story, it always suggests that, for someone less popular, tributes would only 'trickle' in!

This section, however, deals in the main with deaths of national importance, a major Royal or major politician. It is difficult to predict the mood of the nation for each individual death, although evidence of the deaths of Diana Princess of Wales and The Queen Mother suggests that the nation's love of the Royal family shows little sign of diminishing. It is up to you, your station managers and indeed their seniors to suggest how to proceed with any coverage. It is likely though that consideration will be given to the following:

- the person whose death has been announced and their previous 'popularity';
- their age;
- whether it was a sudden or unexpected death or whether it came at the end of a long illness;

- whether it was violent;
- whether it was in public;
- the lead given by the population at large and other media.

You will realize from this list that the death of Princess Diana was 'newsworthy' in almost every regard.

The obit alarm

Each network will have their own way of alerting stations to an obituary or obit for short – check with the GNS, IRN or SNR as appropriate, and do it well before any announcement is thought even remotely possible. They will provide you with a list of major Royals who are considered to be worthy of a newsflash in the event of a death. This list also includes members of the Cabinet and the Prime Minister. It would also include a major international event like the September 11th attacks. It is obvious that not every eventuality can be planned for in advance.

In the main, a light will flash on the presenter's studio desk and a message will flash on the terminal screens. The obvious problem is what happens if a story breaks overnight, when programmes are being networked from another station many miles away? Station groups must obviously organize their own call-out procedure.

The first rule is to check, check and triple-check. Nothing must go to air unless verified. It does not matter too much if you are a few minutes late with the announcement of the Prime Minister being shot dead, for example, if when you do put it out you know it to have been verified. The obvious sources are other media and television news (check and see what your non-affiliate TV station is broadcasting). Do not trust the Web or phone calls from the public.

Senior managers and the News Editor must be informed immediately. Depending on the severity of the situation, it is likely that adverts on commercial stations will be dropped as a mark of respect and to stop any jarring programme segues. Even before an announcement has been made on air, presenters should adopt a middle-of-the-road style. If that means that the wacky breakfast DJ says nothing at all, so be it. The next few tracks to be played should be checked for double or unsuitable meanings in their titles or group names and dropped as necessary.

Breaking the news

After confirmation, the newsroom will take over. A formal story will be read, preferably by your main news anchor – the voice of authority rather than the youngest sounding newsreader who is new to the station. It is an obviously dramatic time for everyone and the story cannot be fluffed on air or, worse still, nerves getting the better of a reader, resulting in a fit of giggles.

All music should be examined for the rest of the day's output at least (this process being updated as the mourning continues). Jingles too should be played off air before being broadcast, in case of sensitive liners or inappropriately bouncy music beds.

Extra news bulletins, and in some cases a rolling news service, will be put into operation. In some cases it will be unnecessary to get a local angle or reaction to the events unfolding (September 11th), but on others you will be able to (the death of Diana). Did the person concerned have a link with the area (you probably have used this line while they were alive)? Then speak to the local church leaders and MPs – both of whom represent 'the general public'. Vox pops are easy to come by in such circumstances and a phone-in is also very popular. It can make dramatic radio to hear people pass on their thoughts, their horror, their memories – although this would not happen while events were still unfolding.

Back to normal

In some circumstances, Diana's death again, the national mourning goes on for more than a week. It is difficult to get back to normality in the news in this time, and many of your bulletins may consist entirely of news of the death. Local angles will be memorial services that are being held, events in schools, minutes' silences, flags being lowered and so on. You will have to use your judgement when things can return to normal – it can be a difficult judgement to make and, with Diana's death, some stations reverted to format too soon and then had to return to their 'mourning' coverage.

An added problem can be when to include other stories in your news bulletins and how to do it. A reader should be able to pause slightly between the two sets of stories, change their tone and use the phrase 'in other news … '. All the same, ensure the juxtaposition of stories is not too jarring. Obviously, kicker stories should not be used for the duration of this mourning.

Glossary

Actuality   Usually used in the BBC to denote a recording of someone speaking, or of an event.

Ad   Advertisement or commercial.

Add   Word added to slug indicating an additional piece of audio that follows the main audio – for example, response to a critic, e.g. 'Hospital Add Smith'.

Ad lib   Speaking without a script.

Aircheck   A recording of a broadcaster or programme. Sometimes used for demonstration purposes.

ALC   Automatic Level Control, often found on portable recorders.

AM   Amplitude Modulation. The abbreviation for broadcasts on Medium Wave.

Ambience   Low-level background noise.

Anchor   Person acting as main presenter of a programme.

Angle   The varying way in which a news story can be told from different points of view.

Archive   A file of old stories for reference, either in copy form, audio form or both.

Atmos   Atmosphere. Impression of location created by evocative background sounds. See also *Wildtrack*.

Audio   Literally any sound, but frequently used in radio, especially commercial radio, to mean the same as actuality.

Audio feed   Transmission of audio to other stations or studios.

Back anno   Back announcement after audio to give extra information.

Balance   Control for changing the relative volume of left and right stereo channels.

Balancing unit   See *TBU*.

Barter   A way for paying for a programme or feature in commercial radio by exchanging a fee for airtime. IRN Newslink is organized on a barter basis. See also *Contra*.

Bed   A short piece of music over which information, news or headlines are read.

Bi-media   Used in the BBC to indicate working both for television and radio.

Booth   A small studio usually designed for one or two people (BBC).

Break   Pause in programme for commercials or news.

Bulletin   A short news programme, usually at the top of the hour. Also known as a 'bullie'.

Cans   Slang for headphones.

Catchline   A one-word name used to identify a story. See also *Slug*.

Ceefax   BBC television news and information text service.

Check calls   Routine phone calls from a newsroom to the emergency services, often called 'the checks' as in 'a round of checks'.

Clean feed   The programme output in which a remote contributor hears all the elements apart from their own.

Clip   Usually used in the BBC to denote a piece of news audio.

Clock   Schedule of broadcast hour with precise time in minutes and seconds.

Contra   Trade exchange in commercial radio where goods and services are traded for advertising airtime. See also *Barter*.

Copy   Written material ready for broadcasting.

Copy story   A news story without audio.

Courier   Brand name for a portable digital recorder made by Sonifex.

CRCA   Commercial Radio Companies Association. The trade body to which most commercial radio stations belong.

Cross-fade   Fading one source out while fading in another.

Cue (1)   The start point on a recording.

Cue (2)   The start signal to a live speaker.

Cue (3)   The written introduction to a piece of audio.

Cut   Usually used in commercial radio to denote a piece of news audio.

DAB   Digital Audio Broadcasting. New technology enabling large numbers of stations to broadcast to a certain area in CD quality without interference.

DAT   Digital Audio Tape. High quality recording on digital tape enclosed in a small plastic box smaller than a cassette.

DAVE   Digital Audio Visual Editing. A portable digital recorder and editing device.

D-cart   Trade name. A popular hard disk newsroom system.

Delay   A device which inserts a time delay between studio and transmitter, usually used to censor profanities and other undesirable material during live phone-in programmes.

Demographics   The categorization of audience by age, sex and social group used in audience research.

Demo tape   A recording of a broadcaster or would-be broadcaster, usually on cassette, sent with a job application.

Disco   BBC abbreviation for a discussion.

DJ   Disc Jockey, sometimes also called a 'jock'.

Dolby   System for reducing audio noise and improving high-frequency response, used especially on recording equipment.

Double ender   Short length of audio cable with a jackplug on each end used to connect pieces of equipment or jacks on a jackfield.

Double header   Item or programme presented by two people.

Drive time   Usually afternoon commuting time with high numbers of in-car listeners.

Dubbing   Copying a recording, either onto another tape or onto computer disk.

Dur   Abbreviation for duration.

Editing   Changing a recording after it has been made, usually by removing part of it either physically on tape or digitally on computer.

Enco DAD   Trade name for a computer playout system.

ENPS   Electronic News Production System. Computerized newsroom system for managing stories and editing text, used by the BBC.

EPK   Electronic Press Kit or Audio News Release. Audio sent to radio stations produced by commercial companies or civic organizations.

Equalization (EQ)   Changing the frequency response of a device, usually a microphone. A voice may be made deeper or crisper by equalization, but EQ controls should only be adjusted by the experienced.

Fader   Slider on broadcast desk to increase or decrease volume.

Feed   Supply of audio.

Feedback   See *Howl round*.

Fire   To start a piece of audio.

Flag (1)   A computer setting to alert the user to prearranged search criteria.

Flag (2)   To mark temporarily a possible edit point on a recording.

Fluff   Mistake.

FM   Frequency Modulation. The abbreviation for broadcasts on VHF.

FX   Abbreviation for sound effects.

Gain control   Volume control.

Gate   A self-imposed deadline beyond which no material can be accepted for broadcast, often five minutes before a bulletin, to allow for preparation.

GNS   General News Service, the BBC's internal news agency, supplying news material to local radio and other sources.

GTS   Greenwich Time Signal, or the 'pips'.

Hard disk   The area of a computer permanently storing material for instant recall and editing.

Heads   Abbreviation for headlines.

Head-to-head   Interview.

Hot   A piece of audio that has been recorded and could be used for transmission.

Hourly   Network newscast beginning at the top of the hour.

Howl round   High-pitched tone created by high-level sound feeding back through a live microphone.

ID   Station identification or ident.

ILR   Independent Local Radio, now usually known as commercial radio.

Insert   A piece of audio in the middle of a report.

Intro   The introduction to a recorded report.

IQ   In cue. The first words on a piece of audio or actuality.

IR   Independent Radio, now usually known as commercial radio.

IRN   Independent Radio News, commercial radio's biggest national news agency.

ISDN   Integrated Services Digital Network. High quality dial-up telephone landlines which can be used for broadcast purposes, usually on a temporary basis.

Jackplug   A connecting plug used to route sources or destinations.

Jingle   Short piece of recorded music played to identify a station.

Key   Switch.

Kicker   Light-hearted story at the end of a news bulletin. See also *Zinger*.

Landline   A special cable link which can carry sound at full bandwidth for broadcast purposes, usually used for linking permanent sites.

Lead (1)   The first story of a news bulletin.

Lead (2)   The first sentence of a news story.

Lead (3)   Cable.

Levels   The measurement of volume recorded or a pre-recording check on an interviewee's voice level.

Link   A cue between items, sometimes on the same subject.

Live   Happening now.

Live shot   Live report from a journalist at the scene introduced by a news anchor.

Lockout   See *SOC*.

Logger (1)   A slow-speed recording of a radio station's output made for regulatory and reference purposes.

Logger (2)   A master recording made of the satellite or landline feed from a national news supplier for newsroom reference use.

Marantz   Trade name of a popular cassette recorder.

MCPS   Mechanical Copyright Protection Society, which licenses the reproduction of recorded sound.

MCR   Master Control Room.

Menu   Short teasers to indicate items to be covered in a programme.

Mic flag   A circular or square attachment to a microphone which identifies the radio station from where it comes, usually with a logo, and used for PR purposes.

Minidisc   Portable recording device half the size of a CD.

Mix   The merging and balancing of several sound sources.

Mixer   Studio equipment which allows different sounds to be mixed.

Mono   Single sound source, as opposed to stereo.

Myriad   Trade name for a computer playout system.

NAB   National Association of Broadcasters (US).

NCA   Network Contribution Area (BBC).

Newsbooth   Small studio where news bulletins are presented on air.

Newslink   The advertisement played on commercial radio next to peak time news bulletins, by which local stations pay for the national news agency IRN.

NPA   News Production Area (BBC).

OB   Outside Broadcast.

OFCOM   Office of Communications. The government body which oversees the development and regulation of radio, television and telecommunications.

Optimod   Trade name for a popular transmitter processing device.

Opting   The practice of leaving or joining a network for programmes.

OQ   Out cue. Last words of a piece of audio or actuality.

Out   The last few words of an audio insert, written as a warning it is about to end.

PA (1)   Press Association.

PA (2)   Public address system.

Package   A broadcast report consisting of a journalist's voice plus at least one insert of audio.

Par   Abbreviation for paragraph.

P as B   Usually used in the BBC to mean Programme as Broadcast.

P as R   Usually used in the BBC to mean Programme as Recorded.

Patching   Using jackplugs and cords to redirect sound sources on a jackfield.

Phone op   The person in charge of answering phones in a studio.

Plosive   The popping sound heard when a 'p' or a 'b' is spoken too close to a microphone.

Popping   The break-up of signal from a microphone caused by explosive consonants when speaking too close.

Pop-shield   See *Windshield*.

Pot point   A suitable moment, such as the end of a sentence, in which a piece of audio can be stopped early if required.

PPL   Phonographic Performance Ltd, which licenses the broadcast of music and other recordings.

PPM   Peak Programme Meter. A device with a scale used to measure sound levels (more technically, the measurement of peak values of broadcast output).

Prefade   Listening to an item before playing it on air, usually used to check levels.

Presser   Slang for press conference, referred to on air as a 'news conference'.

PRO   Public Relations Officer.

Promo   An on-air (and usually pre-recorded) promotion for a forthcoming programme, item or event.

Prospects   A list of the day's stories to be covered.

PRS   Performing Rights Society, which collects royalties and redistributes the money to composers, publishers and performers.

Q-and-A   Question-and-answer, where a reporter is quizzed by a presenter. See also *Two-way*.

RAB   The Radio Advertising Bureau, the organization which publicizes the benefits of commercial radio in general to advertisers.

Racks   The room in a radio station containing engineering equipment.

RadioMan   Trade name for a computer playout system.

RAJAR   Radio Audience Joint Research. The agreed method of audience measurement between commercial radio and the BBC.

RCS   Radio Computing Systems. Trade name for a computer playout and editing system.

Remote studio   A small studio, usually unstaffed, connected to a main studio centre by landline, ISDN or radio link.

Rip'n'read   News bulletin copy sent from the central newsroom intended for instant reading on air without rewriting.

ROT   Record Off Transmission. Literally, a recording of the broadcast via a radio set. Sometimes used, less accurately, to mean any recording of studio output.

RPA   The Representation of the Peoples Act, which governs elections and the reporting of them.

RSL   Restricted Service Licence. The Radio Authority grants RSLs to groups for one month to broadcast over a small area of a few miles for a special event or as a trial service for a new permanent licence.

Running order   List of items within a programme, giving titles and durations.

RX   Recording.

Sadie   Trade name for a popular studio on-screen digital editor, mainly used for production purposes more than news.

Script   Written out version of a news story, the text of which is read on air.

Segue   Pronounced 'seg-way'. The following of one item immediately after the other without interruption or pause.

Self-op   The process of self-operation of a studio control desk by a journalist or presenter.

Slug   Short identifying name given to a news story on a computer or a script.

Snap   A newsflash.

SOC   Standard Out Cue, sometimes known as a lockout. Final words of report including name of reporter, station and location.

Soundbite   Used in both BBC and commercial stations to describe an audio or actuality cut with a short (less than 30-second) excerpt of an interview.

Sounder   Short jingle used to introduce segments of the broadcast, e.g. the travel news.

Spot (1)   A recorded commercial.

Spot (2)   An item regularly appearing in a programme.

Stab   A short, emphatic jingle or ident.

Sting   A short, emphatic jingle or ident.

Strapline   A short slogan used to promote the radio station in general or a particular part of its output.

Stringer   A freelance reporter covering an area where there is no staff reporter available.

Sweep   A period of time when audience research is being carried out.

Talkback   Intercom device for talking to people in other studios or other parts of the radio station. See also *Visual talkback*.

TBU   Telephone Balancing Unit. A piece of equipment used to match the studio output with an incoming telephone line for recording or live transmission.

Teasers   Short and intriguing headlines to promote a forthcoming programme or item.

Tech Op   Technical Operator. The person operating all the equipment in a studio.

Teletext   ITV's on-screen text-based information service.

TO   Technical Operator. The person operating all the equipment in a studio.

Topline   The first line in a copy story or cue.

Traffic (1)   Used in commercial radio to denote the department of the station which schedules commercials for transmission.

Traffic (2)   Reports on road traffic and travel.

Trails   A short promotion for a forthcoming programme or item.

Two-way   A reporter interviewed on air about a story.

TX   Transmission.

UHF   Ultra-High Frequency.

Umbrella   A single story incorporating a number of similar items under one banner.

Update   A revised report with new information on a running story.

Visual talkback   Screen-based system used for communication between control room and studio.

Voicebank   The telephone system used by emergency services to distribute information on incidents to the media.

Voicer   A news story explained by a reporter within a bulletin.

Vox pop *Vox populi*, Latin meaning 'voice of the people'. A series of comments on a single issue gathered at random from members of the public and edited into a sequence.

VU meter Volume Unit meter. A device to measure sound levels. It is less common in professional use than the PPM meter, being more inaccurate at some frequencies.

Waveform The system used by a computer to display a recorded sound for editing purposes on screen.

Wildtrack Background noise recorded on location for later use in wraps and packages.

Windshield A foam cover for a microphone which helps reduce noise and popping.

Wire services News agencies.

Wrap Usually used in commercial radio to denote a broadcast report consisting of a journalist's voice plus at least one insert of audio.

XD Ex-directory phone number, usually in a studio.

Zinger Unusual and sometimes funny 'and finally' story at the end of a bulletin.

Index

Access radio, 7
Accord and satisfaction, 175
Accuracy, 78–9
Acronyms, 69–70, 90–1
Actuality, *See* Audio/actuality
Americanisms, 60
Analogue transmissions, 1
April Fools Day jokes, 170
Attribution, 68
Audience:
    figures, 200–2
    targeting, 202–3
    See also Listeners
Audio/actuality, 117–24, 147–8
    choosing the cut, 147–8
    dubbing, 118
    features/documentaries, 225
    labelling, 151–2
    levels and equalization, 118
    location interviews, 118–21
    receiving audio, 153
    sound edits, 117
    sound quality, 117
    studio discipline, 123
    studio interviews, 121
    talkback, 123–4
    telephone interviews, 121–2
    telephone versus quality audio,
        122–3
Audio cut, 64
Audio editing, 106–9
    digital editing, 107–9
Audio news releases, 37
Audio recording, 103–6

Balance, 79–80
BBC, 1, 198
    Corporate Recruitment department, 20
    digital transmissions, 5–6
    General News Service (GNS), 13, 29
    local radio, 2, 3–4, 73, 204
    Radio One, 1, 76
    Radio Two, 1
    Radio Three, 1
    Radio Four, 1–2
    Radio 5 Live, 2
    training schemes, 17–18
    World Service, 2
Beds, 224–5
Body language, 23, 129
Bomb threats, 168
Breaking news stories, 97–100
    open-ended coverage, 99–100
Briefing, 140–1
Broadcast Journalism Trainee Scheme, 17
Broadcast Journalism Training Council (BJTC), 17
Broadcast journalist/reporter, 26–8
Broadcasters, *See* Radio journalists
Budget speech, 240–1
    experts, 240–1
Budgets, 191–2
Bulletin Editor, 26, 162
Bulletins, *See* News bulletins

Cable services, 6
Capital, 1
Car park voicers, 147
Casualty figures, 69
Cause and effect, 69
Chancellor's budget speech, 240–1
    experts, 240–1
Children:
    interviewing, 137
    reporting restrictions, 186

Index

Civil law, 187–8
Classic FM, 2
Cliché questions, 132
Clichés, 58–60
Clips, 48
Clock end bulletins, 95
Colleagues, as sources of news, 39–40
College courses, 16–17
Comment, 80
Commentaries, 241–3
  mood, 242
  planning, 242
  style and content, 242–3
  using silence, 243
Commercial radio stations, 1, 72
  local radio, 2–3, 4–5
Commercial interests, 46
Comparisons, 62
Complaints, *See* Newsroom
  management
Computer hard disk, 106
Computerized newsrooms, 109
Contacts, 45
  making contacts, 208
Contempt, 171, 178–83
Contractions, 56
Copy, 47
Corrections, 89–90
Costs:
  cutting, 192–4
  estimation of, 192
Councillors, 38
Couriers, 229
Court reporting, 183–7
  basic rules, 184–5
  children and young people,
    186–7
  jigsaw identification, 187
  reporting restrictions, 185
  sexual offences, 186
Criminal libel, 176
  See also Libel
Criminals, interviewing, 137–8
Crisis management, 162–3
Cues, 62–6, 149
  audio cut, 64
  detail, 63
  into the audio, 64
  layout, 64–6
  topline, 62–3
Cuts, 48
CV, 20, 21

Data feeds, 32
Dates, 61
Deadlines, 142, 153
Defamation, 172
Defence advisory notices, 169,
  189
Demo, 20
Digital Audio Tape (DAT), 106
Digital cartridges, 105–6
Digital editing, 107–9
Digital News Network (DNN), 31
Digital radio (DAB), 1, 5–6
Digital recording, 103–6
Digital television, 6
Documentaries, *See* Features/Documentaries
Double header, 204
Dubbing, 118

Editing, 106–9
  digital, 107–9
  features/documentaries, 226–7
  sound edits, 117
Elections, 235–9
  closing of nominations, 236–7
  discussion programmes, 238
  election phone-ins, 239
  general guidelines, 236
  opinion polls, 239
  other news items, 238
  polling day, 239
  programme packages, 237–8
EMAP, 1, 76
Embargoes, 46–7
Emergency services, 34–5, 208
  check calls, 160–1, 210
ENPS (Electronic News Production System), 31,
  109, 151
Equalization, 118
Errors, correction of, 195–6
Exaggeration, 68–9
Experts, 80–1
  budget speech, 240–1

Fair comment, 174–5
Fairness, 79–80
Features/documentaries, 225–7
  editing, 226–7
  essence, 225–6

setting up, 226
using audio, 225
Filing systems, 209–10
Foreign names, 91
Freelance journalists, 19, 40

General elections, *See* Elections
General News Service (GNS), BBC, 13, 29
Global Radio News, 31
Grammar, 54–5
Guests, 216–19
approaching potential guests, 218–19
choosing guests, 218
GWR, 1

Hard disk, 106
portable, 103
Head of News, 25–6
Headlines, 161
Headphones, 112–13
Hoaxes, 170
Hospital Broadcasting Association, 15
Hospital radio, 15–16
Hub system, 77–8
Human Rights Act, 171

Idents, 224
Independent Radio News (IRN), 13, 29–30, 32, 205
Independent Television News (ITN), 30
Indirect libel, 176
Infotainment, 75–6
Injunctions, 190
Inquests, 188–9
Internet, as source of news, 41–2
Internet radio, 7
Interviews, 47, 125–39
children, 137
criminals, 137–8
emotional, 126
informational, 125–6
interpretive, 126
interviewing other reporters, 137
live interviews, 134
location interviews, 118–21, 127–8
news conferences and 'scrums', 135–6
politicians, 138–9

preparation, 127–9
location, 127–8
question technique, 129–34
after the interview, 134
asking one thing at a time, 131–2
cliché questions, 132
coaching interviewees, 133
eye contact, 130–1
leading questions, 132
listening to answers, 131
one-word answers, 133–4
thanks, 134
refused interviews, 139
studio, 121
telephone, 121–2
unattended studios, 136–7
victims or relatives, 138
vox pops, 134–5
witnesses, 138
See also Job interview
ISDN landlines, 229

Jargon, 57–8
Jigsaw identification, 187
Jingles, 224
Job advertisements, 19–20
Job interview, 22–4
awkward questions, 23–4
body language, 23
journalistic tests, 23
nerves, 22–3
preparation, 22
thank you note, 24
Journalese, 58
Justification, 173

Kickers, 81
Kiss, 76

Language, 54–5
body language, 23, 129
Leading questions, 132
Legal issues, 171
civil law, 187–8
elections, 235
injunctions, 190

Index

Legal issues (*continued*)
  inquests, 188–9
  official secrets, 189
  See also Contempt; Court reporting;
    Libel
Levels, 118
Libel, 171, 172
  defences, 172–5
    accord and satisfaction, 175
    consent, 173
    death, 173–4
    fair comment, 174–5
    no identification, 173
    one year, 174
    privilege, 175
    truth, 173
  kinds of, 176–7
    criminal libel, 176
    indirect libel, 176
    nameless libel, 176
    problem areas, 177
    unintentional libel, 176
'Life' of a story, 75
Listeners:
  as sources of news, 39
  as sources of pressure, 46
  target listeners, 71–2
  See also Audience
Live defence, 177
Live interviews, 134
Live news bulletins, 32–3
Live reports, 146–7
Local elections, *See* Elections
Local news sources, 33–42
  colleagues, 39–40
  emergency services, 34–5
  freelance journalists and agencies, 40
  Internet, 41–2
  listeners, 39
  news releases, 36–7
    audio news releases, 37
  politicians and councillors, 38
  pressure groups, 40
  public utilities, 37–8
  rivals, 40–1
  your own station, 41
Local radio, 2–5, 73–4
  BBC, 2, 3–4, 73, 204
  commercial, 2–3, 4–5, 72
Location interviews, 118–21
  preparation, 127–8
Location reporting, *See* News reporting

Match reports, 243–4
Microphone technique, 87
Microphones, 113–14
Minidiscs, 105
MPs, 38, 208
  See also Politicians
Multi-version bulletins, 78
Music–speech mix, 233–5
  blending, 234–5
  presenter qualities, 233
  right mix, 233–4

Nameless libel, 176
Names, 60–1
National news, 28–33
  data feeds, 32
  live bulletins, 32–3
  local intake, 31–2
  radio news agencies, 29–31
  television audio, 33
  wire services, 33
National radio, 1–2
Network Contribution Area (NCA),
  28
News agencies, 40
News blackouts, 168–9
News bulletins, 71–81
  accuracy, 78–9
  agenda, 71–5
    'life' of a story, 75
    place names, 74
    quality versus quantity, 74
    relevance, 73–4
    socio-economic groups, 72–3
    target listeners, 71–2
  balance and fairness, 79–80
  comment, 80
  construction of, 153–9
    avoiding repetition, 156
    breaking the rules, 158–9
    developing stories, 158
    finding the lead, 153–4
    following stories, 157–8
    judging editorial priorities,
      156–7
    snaps/newsflashes, 159
  daily sports bulletins, 245
  experts, 80–1
  kickers, 81
  self-op bulletins, 92–7

clock end bulletins, 95
mistakes and failures, 96–7
preparation, 92
presentation, 94–5
studio checks, 92–4
signposting, 80
styles, 75–8
hub, 77–8
infotainment, 75–6
multi-versions, 78
pre-recorded bulletins, 78
regional bulletins, 77
versioned bulletins, 76–7
youth stations, 76
taste, 79
tone, 80
See also News presentation; News reporting;
News writing
News conferences, 135–6
News Editor, 25–6
News hub system, 77–8
News presentation, 82–92
breaking news stories, 97–100
open-ended coverage, 99–100
breathing and relaxing, 85–6
checking and rehearsal, 84
corrections, 89–90
formats, 203–4
keeping the voice level, 86
listening to, 91
microphone technique, 87
microphone voice, 82–3
personality news presenters, 100
pronunciation, 90–1
quotations, 89
sounding interested, 83
speed, 87
stress, 88–9
technical mistakes, 85
tone, 86–7
understanding the story, 83–4
'zoo' format, 101–2, 204
See also News bulletins; News reporting
News Producer, 26
News Production Area (NPA), 26
News releases, 36–7
audio news releases, 37
News reporting, 140–2
audio production, 147–9
choosing the cut, 147–8
wrapping or packaging, 148–9
writing cues, 149

briefing, 140–1
filing material, 144–7
car park voicers, 147
getting on the air, 144–5
live reports, 146–7
on-the-spot voicers, 145
Q-and-As, 146
fixing ahead, 141–2
on location, 142–4
dealing with officials, 143–4
dealing with other reporters, 144
eyewitness accounts, 143
on arrival, 142–3
radio reporters, 140
working to deadlines, 142
See also News bulletins; News presentation;
News stories
News round-up, 223–5
content and style, 223
jingles and beds, 224–5
typical format, 223–4
News stories:
breaking news stories, 97–100
open-ended coverage, 99–100
context, 67–70
attribution, 68
casualty figures, 69
cause and effect, 69
descriptions, 70
exaggeration, 68–9
organizations, 69–70
titles, 70
truth, 70
follow-up, 157–8
planning and development, 42–7, 158
developing stories, 44
embargoes, 46–7
newsdesk resource management,
43–4
newsroom contacts, 45
newsroom diary, 42–3
resisting pressure, 45–6
treatment, 47–9
copy, 47
cuts, clips and soundbites, 48
interviews, 47
newsroom style guide, 49
voicers or voice pieces, 47–8
wraps and packages, 48–9
See also Local news sources; National news;
News bulletins; News presentation;
News reporting; News writing

Index

News writing, 50–4
  language and grammar, 54–5
  telling the story, 50–4
    for the ear not the eye, 51
    keeping adjectives to a minimum, 53–4
    keeping it happening now, 53
    keeping it short, 51–2
    keeping it simple, 52–3
    talking to yourself, 54
  writing devices, 55–62
    Americanisms, 60
    clichés, 58–60
    comparisons, 62
    contractions, 56
    dates, 61
    jargon, 57–8
    journalese, 58
    names, 60–1
    numbers, 61–2
    punctuation, 56–7
  See also News bulletins
Newsdesk management, 150–70
  allocation of reporters, 161–2
  bomb threats, 168
  bulletin construction, *See* News bulletins
  check calls, 160–1, 210
  crisis management, 162–3
  deadlines, 153
  defence advisory notices, 169
  giving orders, 162
  headlines and teasers, 161
  labelling audio and scripts, 151–2
  network contributions, 159–60
  news blackouts, 168–9
  organization, 150–1
    computerized newsdesks, 152–3
  practical jokes, 170
  priorities, 162
  resource management, 43–4
  stormlines and snowlines, 165–8
  suicide reporting, 169–70
  taking audio, 153
  travel news, 164–5
  weather news, 163–4
Newsflashes, 159
Newspapers, 9
  work experience, 15
Newsroom diary, 42–3
Newsroom management, 191–206
  complaints, 194–9
    correcting errors, 195–6
    phoned complaints, 195

    privacy, 199
    regulatory authorities, 198–9
    solicitors, 196–8
  resources, 191–4
    budgets, 191–2
    cost cutting, 192–4
    costs estimation, 192
    rotas, 191
  winning audiences, 199–206
    audience figures, 200–2
    presentation formats, 203–4
    promos, 204–5
    sponsorship, 205–6
    targeting audiences, 202–3
  See also Small newsrooms
Newsroom structure, 25–8
  broadcast journalist/reporter, 26–8
  Bulletin Editor, 26
  Head of News/News Editor, 25–6
  one-journalist newsrooms, 28
  Senior Broadcast Journalist/News Producer, 26
  television journalists, 28
Newsroom style guide, 49
Numbers, 61–2

Obituaries, 245–7
  back to normal, 247
  breaking the news, 247
  obit alarm, 246
OFCOM (Office of Communications), 5, 198
Offence, avoidance of, 66–7
Official secrets, 189
On-the-spot voicers, 145
Open-ended coverage, 99–100
Opinion polls, 239
Organizations, 69–70, 90–1
Outside broadcasts, 228–30
  couriers, 229
  ISDN landlines, 229
  planning, 228
  radio links, 228–9
  standby presenters, 229–30
  telephone links, 229

Packages, 48–9, 148–9
Paper-free environment, 109
Peak programme meter (PPM), 118
Phone-ins, 230–3

delay, 232
election phone-ins, 239
presenters, 231–2
problem phone-ins, 232–3
selecting subjects, 230
studio operations, 230–1
Pirate radio, 8
Place names, 74
pronunciation, 91
Playout systems, 114–17
Political correctness, 66–7
Politicians, 38, 45
interviewing, 138–9
Portable hard disk, 103
Pot points, 216
Practical jokes, 170
Pre-recorded bulletins, 78
Presenters, 12
music–speech mix, 233
personality news presenters, 100
phone-ins, 231–2
standby presenters, 229–30
Press Association (PA), 33
Pressure groups, 40
Pressures, 45–6
commercial interests, 46
listeners, 45
political parties, 45
Privacy, 199
Privilege, 175
Producer, 214–15
News Producer, 26
qualities, 215
responsibilities, 214
Programme production:
fixing guests, 216–19
approaching potential guests, 218–19
choosing guests, 218
preparation, 215–16
pot points, 216
programme items, 215
running orders, 216
treatments, 215–16
studio production, 220–2
discipline, 220–1
Tech Ops, 220
thinking ahead, 220
trails, teasers and promos, 221–2
Promises of Performance, 3, 5
Promos, 161, 204–5, 222
Pronunciation, 90–1
Public relations (PR) companies, 36–7, 46

Public utilities, 37–8
Punctuation, 56–7

Question technique, *See* Interviews
Question-and-answer pieces, 146
Quotations, 89

Radio Academy, 14
Radio journalists:
getting the job, 14–19
BBC training schemes, 17–18
college courses, 16–17
CV, 20, 21
demo, 20
freelancing, 19
hospital radio, 15–16
local newspapers, 15
persistence, 20
restricted service stations, 18
student radio, 16
traffic and travel broadcasting, 18
work experience, 14–15
See also Job interview
qualities of good journalists, 11–12
starting out, 12–13
Radio links, 228–9
Radio news agencies, 29–31
BBC's General News Service (GNS), 29
Digital News Network (DNN), 31
Global Radio News, 31
Independent Radio News (IRN), 29–30
Sky News Radio (SNR), 30
UBC, 31
Radio reporters, 140
See also News reporting; Radio journalists
Radio strengths, 9–11
localness, 11
making pictures, 10
person-to-person, 10–11
speed and simplicity, 10
versus newspapers and television, 9–10
RadioMan, 114–17
RAJAR (Radio Audience Joint Research), 200–2
Recruitment, 212–13
Regional bulletins, 77
Regulatory authorities, 198–9
Relatives of victims, interviewing, 138
Relevance, 73–4

Index

Reporters, 161–2
Reporting restrictions, 185
    children and young people, 186–7
    jigsaw identification, 187
    sexual offences, 186
Reporting, *See* News reporting
Representation of the People Act (1983), 235
Restricted Service Licences (RSLs), 7, 18
Restricted service stations, 18
Reuters, 33
Rivals, as sources of news, 40–1
Road traffic accidents (RTAs), 57–8
Rolling news format, 204
Rotas, 191
Running order, 216

Satellite services, 6–7
Senior Broadcast Journalist, 26
Sexual offences, reporting restrictions, 186
Signposting, 80
Skillset, 14
Sky News Radio (SNR), 30, 33
Slander, 172
Small newsrooms, 207–13
    going on air, 210–12
        getting exclusives, 211–12
        preparation for first day, 210–11
    recruiting staff, 212–13
        training and coaching, 213
    setting up, 207–10
        calls list, 210
        filing systems, 209–10
        first tasks, 207
        making contacts, 208
        technical requirements, 209
    See also Newsroom management
Snaps, 159
Snowlines, 165–8
Socio-economic groups, 72–3
Solicitors letters, 196–8
Sound quality, audio, 117
Soundbites, 48
Speed for news reading, 87
Sponsorship, 205–6
Sport, 243–5
    daily sports bulletins, 245
    match reports, 243–4
    sports diary, 244
Stormlines, 165–8
Stressing important words, 88–9

Student radio, 16
Student Radio Association, 16
Studios, 109–17, 220–2
    discipline, 123, 220–1
    headphones, 112–13
    microphones, 113–14
    phone-in management, 230–1
    playout systems, 114–17
Style guide, 49
Suicide reporting, 169–70
Sweeps, 200

Talkback, 123–4
TalkSPORT, 2, 204
Tape-free environment, 109
Target listeners, 71–2
Targeting audiences, 202–3
Taste, 79
Teasers, 161, 221
Technical Operator (Tech Op), 220
Telephone interviews, 121–2
    telephone versus quality audio, 122–3
Television, 9
    digital television, 6
    television audio, 33
Television journalists, 28
Titles, 70
Tone, 80, 86–7
Topline, 62–3
Traffic news, 18
Trails, 221
Training, 213
    BBC training schemes, 17–18
    college courses, 16–17
Travel news, 18, 164–5
Truth, 70
    as libel defence, 173

UBC Media Group, 31
Unattended studios, 136–7
Unintentional libel, 176

Versioned bulletins, 76–7
Victims, interviewing, 138
Virgin, 2
Voice test, 23

Voicers/voice pieces, 47–8
Vox pops, 134–5

Weather news, 163–4
    stormlines and snowlines, 165–8
Wire services, 33
Witnesses, interviewing, 138
Work experience, 14–15
    local newspapers, 15
World Wide Web, 41–2

Wraps, 48–9, 148–9
Writing, *See* News writing
Written test, 23

Youth stations, 76

'Zoo' format, 101–2, 204

Focal Press

www.focalpress.com

Join Focal Press on-line
As a member you will enjoy the following benefits:

an email bulletin with **information on new books**

a regular **Focal Press Newsletter**:

- featuring a selection of new titles

  keeps you informed of **special offers, discounts and freebies**

  alerts you to **Focal Press news and events** such as author signings and seminars

complete access to **free content** and reference material on the focalpress site, such as the focalXtra articles and commentary from our authors

a **Sneak Preview** of selected titles (sample chapters) *before* they publish

a chance to have your say on our **discussion boards** and **review books** for other Focal readers

Focal Club Members are invited to give us feedback on our products and services.
Email: worldmarketing@focalpress.com – we want to hear your views!

Membership is **FREE**. To join, visit our website and register. If you require any further information regarding the on-line club please contact:

Lucy Lomas-Walker
Email: l.lomas@elsevier.com
Tel: +44 (0) 1865 314438
Fax: +44 (0)1865 314572
Address: Focal Press, Linacre House,
Jordan Hill, Oxford, UK, OX2 8DP

Catalogue

For information on all Focal Press titles, our full catalogue is available online at www.focalpress.com and all titles can be purchased here via secure online ordering, or contact us for a free printed version:

USA
Email: christine.degon@bhusa.com
Tel: +1 781 904 2607 T

Europe and rest of world
Email: j.blackford@elsevier.com
Tel: +44 (0)1865 314220

Potential authors

If you have an idea for a book, please get in touch:

USA
editors@focalpress.com

Europe and rest of world
focal.press@elsevier.com